Scottish Philosophy

Selected Readings 1690–1960

Edited and Introduced
by Gordon Graham

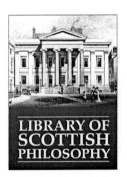

LIBRARY OF SCOTTISH PHILOSOPHY

ia

IMPRINT ACADEMIC

Published in the UK by Imprint Academic
PO Box 200, Exeter EX5 5YX, UK

Published in the USA by Imprint Academic
Philosophy Documentation Center
PO Box 7147, Charlottesville, VA 22906-7147, USA

ISBN 0 907845 746

A CIP catalogue record for this book is available from the
British Library and US Library of Congress

Full series details:

www.imprint-academic.com/losp

Contents

Series Editor's Note

The principal purpose of volumes in this series is not to provide scholars with accurate editions, but to make the writings of Scottish philosophers accessible to a new generation of modern readers. In accordance with this purpose, certain changes have been made to the original texts:

- Spelling and punctuation have been modernized.
- In some cases, the selected passages have been given new titles.
- Some original footnotes and references have not been included.
- Some extracts have been shortened from their original length.
- Quotations from Greek have been transliterated, and passages in foreign languages translated, or omitted altogether.

Care has been taken to ensure that in no instance do these amendments truncate the argument or alter the meaning intended by the original author. For readers who want to consult the original texts, full bibliographical details are provided for each extract.

The Library of Scottish Philosophy was launched at the Third International Reid Symposium on Scottish Philosophy in July 2004 with an initial six volumes. Attractively produced and competitively priced, these appeared just fifteen months after the original suggestion of such a series. This remarkable achievement owes a great deal to the work and commitment of the editors of the individual volumes, but it was only possible because of the energy and enthusiasm of the publisher, Keith Sutherland and the outstanding work of Jon M.H Cameron, Editorial and Administrative Assistant to the Centre for the Study of Scottish Philosophy.

Acknowledgements

Grateful acknowledgement is made to the Carnegie Trust for the Universities of Scotland for generous financial support for the Library of Scottish Philosophy, and to the University of Aberdeen Special Libraries and Collections for permission to reproduce the engraving of the Edinburgh Faculty of Advocates from *Modern Athens* (1829).

Gordon Graham,
Aberdeen, July 2004

Introduction

I
Philosophy in Scotland

Scotland's contribution to commerce and engineering is well known, and striking; the Bank of Scotland, founded in 1695, was the first joint stock bank in the world; in the nineteenth century ships built in Scotland carried the world's trade. But in most other respects, as is only to be expected of a small poor country on the fringes of Europe, Scotland's role in the formation of Western culture was relatively minor. There are some good Scottish composers, but none to be ranked alongside those of Germany and Austria. There are a few noted painters, but nothing on the scale of Italy or the Low Countries. There is a recognizable and valued body of Scottish literature, but most of it came relatively late in the nation's history, and very little of it compares with Shakespeare, Donne or Dickens, with the great Russian poets and novelists, or even (arguably) with the literature of Ireland.

The outstanding exception to this generalization is philosophy, where Scotland's contribution is almost unrivalled. Only Germany, a very much larger and richer country at the heart of Europe, has produced such a long list of identifiably influential philosophers. When in the late nineteenth century, the Princeton academic James McCosh compiled his substantial volume *The Scottish Philosophy* (1875), he was able to identity the names of forty seven individuals who through teaching, or publication, or both, had been significant contributors to the intellectual debates of their day and later. If he had revised the book thirty years later, there would have been at least half a dozen further names to add because Scottish philosophers continued to make major contributions to philosophy and cognate subjects into the first decades of the twentieth century.

The influence of the Scottish philosophers was far flung. It is possible to find their ideas being enthusiastically explored in England, France, Germany, Ireland, Italy and Spain, even Chile and Venezuela. Most importantly, perhaps, they laid the foundations of higher education in the United States and Canada and established the special place of philosophy within it. The expression 'the Scottish Enlightenment' only came to be used in the twentieth century, but it gave a name to something long recognized — that extraordinary explosion in the European world of

ideas that emanated from Scotland in the eighteenth century and continued to influence long into the nineteenth. And at the heart of this enlightenment was a conception of philosophy and how it ought to be studied
and taught.

II
The Scottish Philosophical Tradition

The contention that educated Scots made a major contribution to the
development of European philosophy, though true, does not in itself
license the expression 'Scottish philosophy'. For a variety of reasons,
Scots also made a striking contribution to the emergence of botany in the
early decades of the nineteenth century, the most famous of them being
David Douglas who gave his name to the mighty Douglas Fir, which he
introduced to Europe. Douglas's mentor was William Hooker, Professor
of Botany in Glasgow, and one of the founding fathers of the subject. But
it would be seriously misleading to suggest that there is more to this
remarkable phenomenon than the fact that some of the best students of
botany happened to be Scots. There is no special branch of the subject
called 'Scottish botany'.

   Why should the position of philosophy be different? What more is
there than a collection of talented philosophers who happened to be
Scots? The answer is that we can identify over a protracted period of
time a Scottish philosophical community and a distinctive tradition of
inquiry.

   The Scottish philosophers formed a community because, unlike their
counterparts in England or France, they were almost all university
based, and were frequently related as teachers and students. It is not
always realized that in the eighteenth and early nineteenth centuries
Scotland had more universities than England and Ireland combined —
five as opposed to three. Indeed, the city of Aberdeen alone had two —
Marischal and Kings — the same number as the whole of England. Of
course they were very much smaller, as was St Andrews, and only Glasgow and Edinburgh could claim substantial international connections.
But all five had persisted with the basic mediaeval curriculum in which
moral philosophy and logic play an important, and compulsory part.
Moreover, the content of the philosophy courses was more or less the
same, and developed more or less in tandem, as the universities under-
went important reforms both with respect to curriculum and methods of
teaching. Accordingly, for the philosophers of Scotland, common intellectual interests and educational concerns came as part of the job.

   This aspect of community was emphasized and strengthened by the
fact that it was not unusual for individuals to move from one university
to another; Gershom Carmichael, for example, studied at Edinburgh,
and taught at St Andrews before he moved to Glasgow, eventually occu-
pying its first official Chair of Moral Philosophy. Over 50 years later,

Thomas Reid left King's Aberdeen to take up the same Glasgow Chair. Two generations on, J F Ferrier deputized for Sir William Hamilton in the Chair of Logic and Metaphysics at Edinburgh before being appointed to the Chair of Moral Philosophy at St Andrews. And so on.

This national focus might suggest a certain insularity, and so indeed it could have proved. But from their earliest days, the universities of Scotland sent students to Paris from whence they returned to teach in Scotland, and, as their writings make clear, the philosophers of 17th century and 18th century Scotland were acutely aware of the major trends and biggest names in philosophy in England and the continent of Europe. A distinctive community of Scottish philosophers was forged in large part by the fact that they discussed each other's work in print and in the lecture room. But it is a marked feature of Scottish philosophers up until the late nineteenth century that they also had extensive European connections, some of them being better known and more highly regarded in Europe than they were in England.

Yet there was more to unite them than this; there was also a tradition of inquiry. Whilst the Scottish philosophers read and thought about their English and European counterparts, they shared certain preoccupations. These had five identifiable elements — a methodology (the so-called 'science of mind') — a subject matter (human nature) — an overriding concern (the need to answer Humean scepticism) — a distinctive approach (the appeal to common sense) — and an educational context (the role of philosophy in the curriculum of the universities). Together these set the agenda for Scottish philosophy for over two hundred years, until a variety of factors both internal and external, caused Scottish philosophy to decline.

III
The Study of Human Nature and the 'Science Of Man'

There is some uncertainty about how far back in time the tradition of Scottish philosophy can be identified. Most commentators identify it with the great figures of the 18th century, but there is an argument to be made that the basic elements of the philosophy that was to become identified with Scotland had their origins in the philosophically sophisticated mediaeval Scottish universities of thinkers such as Lawrence of Lindores, an important figure in the early years of St Andrews, John Mair (1476?–1550) who held posts at Glasgow and St Andrews, George Lockert (1485–1547), who moved in the other direction (St Andrews, then Glasgow), and Hector Boece who returned from Paris to be come first Principal of King's College Aberdeen.

All these people taught under the system in which a 'Regent' taught all the subjects of the curriculum to the students in a given year. The first person in Scotland to be expressly designated a 'Professor' of philosophy, was Gershom Carmichael, who in 1727 was appointed to the new

Chair of Moral Philosophy at the University of Glasgow, where he had
served as Regent since 1694. Arguably, it is with the establishment of the
professorate that a distinctive Scottish philosophical tradition can first
be discerned.

Carmichael's *Philosophical Theses* of 1699 (Reading I) encapsulate
much of the spirit and content of this emergent tradition. They neatly
combine the double concerns of philosophical study and university education since their purpose was to test the ability of students to expound
and explore philosophical ideas. However, it was Carmichael's student
and successor Francis Hutcheson (an Irishman educated at the University of Glasgow) who came to greater prominence and posthumous
fame as the 'father' of the Scottish Enlightenment. Hutcheson, in common with others of his time, believed the traditional topics of philosophy (the nature of beauty and the basis of morality are the two with
which he was specially concerned) would be better illuminated by a
careful study of how human beings actually form beliefs and judgements. Instead of the logical deduction of theorems from axioms, in the
manner of geometry (a method rationalist philosophers such as the
Dutch philosopher Spinoza and the English philosopher Hobbes
employed) the proper method was, broadly speaking, empirical, one
that looked at the actual working of thought, imagination and emotion,
and even laughter (see Reading II). Appointed to the Chair of Moral Philosophy in Glasgow in 1729, Hutcheson taught generations of students
to great effect (being the first to lecture in English rather than Latin) and
by the time of his relatively early death in 1746 had become a figure
greatly revered in the intellectual life of Scotland. His major writings
were largely complete at the time of his appointment, but he revised
them extensively for later editions, and set an example that both his contemporaries and his successors followed.

Within a few decades this study of human nature had matured into
two distinct strands. The first was the close examination of the workings
of the mind with respect to perception and the formation of belief. Chief
among those who contributed to this study were Hume (in his early
writings), Thomas Reid, Dugald Stewart and Thomas Brown, and it was
on this subject that the Scottish philosophers finally went in different
directions in the late nineteenth century, some to Idealism, some to phenomenology, and others to the beginnings of empirical psychology as
we know it today. The second form in which the study of human nature
was undertaken was more social than psychological — the observation
of human beings as members of economic and political societies rather
than individual minds, and the discovery of the 'market', as a powerful
mechanism, and hence explanatory principle, in social formation. The
most prominent and influential among those who contributed to this
strand was Adam Smith, whose inquiries in *The Wealth of Nations* gave
rise to another new subject — economics. Though Smith's name is now
chiefly associated with economics he was a philosopher of considerable

substance also (see Readings VII and VIII). Not much less important than Smith were Hume in his later writings, Adam Ferguson, Professor of Moral Philosophy at Edinburgh, and Thomas Chalmers, who held a similar Chair at St Andrews.

Both strands of inquiry were conducted in what is sometimes called the 'Newtonian' spirit — a determination to apply to the study of social and moral subjects, and to the mind itself, the methods of Isaac Newton and Francis Bacon that had proved so successful in the natural sciences, and thus develop a 'science of man', a parallel set out most explicitly by one of Hutcheson's slightly younger contemporaries — George Turnbull of Aberdeen (see Reading III).

IV
The Challenge of David Hume

This ambition is expressly endorsed by David Hume in the opening pages of his appropriately entitled *Treatise of Human Nature*, with which he aims to continue the good work of Bacon in putting 'the science of man on a new footing' by providing 'the only solid foundation we can give to this science' — namely 'experience and observation'. It is an ambition that most of his contemporaries, south as well as north of the border, shared. The problem was that, in Hume's hands, the result appeared to be deep scepticism, not just about metaphysical topics like the existence of the external world and the necessity of causal connection (see Readings IV and V), but about the existence of God, the possibility of miracles (see Reading VI), and the objective reality of moral values. Hume's scepticism was perceived as threatening both the very possibility of philosophical and scientific inquiry, and the social and moral order built upon the Christian religion. Though the world in which he moved was a relatively tolerant one, so that he could include a good many of the Scottish clergy among his friends, Hume's scepticism probably cost him the Chair of Moral Philosophy at Edinburgh, his application for which was refused by the Town Council. More importantly though, Hume's sceptical conclusions, arising as they did from the application of a method in which nearly everyone believed, set the philosophical agenda for decades to come.

The contention that Scottish philosophy's identity arose partly from opposition to Hume, might be thought to carry the absurd implication that Hume himself, the most famous of all, was not in fact a Scottish philosopher. Yet there is some truth in the suggestion that in several respects Hume was deeply at odds with his contemporaries, chiefly because he rejected the background assumption of providential design. As a result there is a kind of ambivalence in his relation to the other Scottish philosophers. On the one hand, as the extracts from Reid, Brown and Taylor confirm (Readings IX, XIV, and XVII), they regarded him as an extremely able and astute philosopher. On the other, they found him lacking in any positive solutions to the problems he so ably diagnosed. Perhaps it would be most accurate to say that Hume's writings are part of the tradition of Scottish philosophy in just the way that the grit of sand in the oyster forms an essential part of the pearl — the cause of its existence more than an integral part of its distinctiveness.

The responses Hume provoked varied greatly. James Beattie (1735–1803), the Professor of Moral Philosophy and Logic at Marischal published an *Essay on Truth,* so highly regarded at the time that it earned him, among other things, memorialization in a famous portrait by Joshua Reynolds. Reprinted a vast number of times, it now seems rarely to rise above the level of rhetoric, and sometimes approaches hysteria. While Beattie appears almost to have hated Hume, his friend and colleague at Marischal, George Campbell (1719–96), even though he published a lengthy refutation of Hume on miracles, clearly admired Hume's intellectual gifts and philosophical ingenuity. Also in contrast to Beattie's belligerent rhetoric, is Thomas Reid's *Inquiry into the Human Mind upon the Principles of Common Sense,* a response to Hume of extraordinary subtlety, and a work that became the founding document of the 'School of Common Sense' for which Scotland was celebrated in the world of philosophy over the succeeding four or five decades.

V
The School of Common Sense

In founding his inquiry into the human mind on the 'Principles of Common Sense' Reid sought to pursue the study of the mind along Newtonian lines in the way that Hume aimed to do, while avoiding the sceptical impasse that Hume's investigations had led him to (see Reading IX). Reid was not proposing something wholly novel or unknown, since the appeal to fundamental principles that seem ineliminable from everyday life had been in the intellectual air for some time. But Reid conducted his inquiry with a degree of clarity and care that is as impressive as it is unusual. He also articulated an idea of 'common sense' (as opposed to the technical conception of 'sense' invented by philosophers) much more fully than had hitherto been the case (see Reading X). So impressive was his achievement in the *Inquiry* and in his later two sets of *Essays,* that admiration for his work, and subscription to its basic tenets became almost *de rigeur* for philosophers in Scotland. For some time, indeed, criticism of Reid tended to be muted, and Scottish philosophy ran the danger of degeneration from a tradition of inquiry into a mere 'school' that subscribed to a particular doctrine.

But brilliant though his achievement was, it soon became apparent that there were difficulties in the approach that Reid had advocated. First, there was the danger that his appeal to common sense on philosophical questions would result not so much in the resolution of philosophical problems as in the rejection of philosophy, the sort of rejection that Dr Johnson famously espoused when he claimed to 'refute' Bishop Berkeley's philosophical doubts about the existence of matter by the commonsensical method of kicking a stone. But by 'common sense' Reid did not mean commonly accepted beliefs about mind and the world so much as the universal principles of operation that can be found at work in human belief and judgement and that are embodied in a variety of natural languages (see Reading XI). Even so, some of his admirers, more so abroad than at home perhaps, understood him on the former interpretation, and enthusiastically adopted a 'commonsensical' approach which resulted in a jejune and sometimes philistine rejection of philosophical reflection. In this they were certainly mistaken, but even as fervent an admirer as Sir William Hamilton, the editor of Reid's *Collected Works*, noted that Reid did not sufficiently distinguish his conception of common sense from the cruder version of Beattie and Oswald.

A second difficulty lay in the fact that Reid's appeal to the fundamental principles of mental operation beyond which we cannot go, seemed to answer scepticism with agnosticism, and these two positions can appear remarkably close. Whereas Hume's scepticism (about the existence of an external world say) arose from his supposition that the human mind, being wholly dependent upon 'impressions' or mental images of objects, cannot reach beyond those impressions to the objects themselves, Reid seemed to say that, whereas we can indeed perceive the world itself, we cannot in the end know how we do this. How does this position leave us any further forward in the philosophy of mind?

Several of Reid's admirers and defenders — notably Dugald Stewart — were as alive to these deficiencies as were his critics, and set themselves to elaborate the elements of his approach more effectively. This aim — to improve and advance the philosophy of mind — led to the dominance of one strand in the 'science of man' over the more socially based inquiries of Smith and Ferguson. It also led to difficulties of a pedagogical sort. Reid gave up teaching at Glasgow, eventually, in order to devote himself to his philosophical inquiries, and this fact alone reveals a tension between the duties of the philosopher as teacher, and the study of the subject itself, a tension somewhat similar to a conflict in the modern university between teaching and research.

VI
The Practical/Speculative Division; Teaching and 'Research'

Among the better known Scottish philosophers, James Beattie was perhaps the most prominent to weigh in on the side of teaching. Beattie thought that the principal duty of the universities was to give their students a moral education that would make them good members of society and effective contributors to its well being and prosperity. Beattie was as much a man of letters as he was a philosopher, a hugely successful poet who perhaps impressed a non-philosophical public more than he impressed his fellow philosophers; Hume thought him 'silly and bigotted' for example. But in placing the emphasis on the pedagogical role of philosophy he was not alone. His predecessor at Marischal, David Fordyce (1711–1751) was best known for his *Elements of Moral Philosophy*, a student text that was widely adopted for several decades at colleges in North America. But neither Beattie's nor Fordyce's books can be found to contain much of continuing philosophical interest today, written as they were for an educational audience which has long since disappeared.

Yet it was possible for the role of teacher and researcher to be combined most effectively. Lord Cockburn, the eminent Scottish lawyer, recounts in his memoirs, the inspiring lectures that he and countless others received at the hands of Dugald Stewart, the Professor of Moral Philosophy in Edinburgh, while Stewart's *Elements of the Philosophy of the Human Mind* was widely regarded as a major contribution to the subject and led to his election as a Fellow in the learned societies of Berlin, Philadelphia and St Petersburg. Stewart himself was convinced that serious inquiry into the nature of mind had great educational value (see Reading XII).

Still, as Adam Smith expressly acknowledged in his *Theory of Moral Sentiments*, 'in treating of the principles of morals there are two questions to be considered'. The first concerns what it is that 'constitutes the excellent and praiseworthy character'. The second concerns 'what power or faculty in the mind' it is that enables us to make evaluative judgements, and, says Smith, the determination of this second question, though of the greatest importance in speculation, is of none in practice.

At the same time, neither issue could be entirely abandoned, since both the pursuit and the teaching of philosophy fell within the duties of the traditional Scottish Professor. This explains why throughout the nineteenth century, professors of philosophy from Hamilton to Caird played a major part in public debates about social and educational reform.

VII
The Decline of Scottish Philosophy

By mid nineteenth century, these tensions within the Scottish philosophical tradition were apparent. Could the philosophy of mind continue to be based upon the principles of common sense? Was the teaching of 'virtue' (to use the old expression) plausibly a duty of the professional philosopher? Some interesting results emerged as Scottish philosophers grappled with these questions. Some, like John Veitch of Glasgow, took their teaching more in the direction of what we might call 'cultural' or literary studies. Some, and especially Alexander Bain, pushed the research side of the subject ahead in a vigorously empirical way, and thereby laid the foundations of modern psychology. Others like Thomas Chalmers in

St Andrews thought to inculcate a broader sense of social responsibility and awareness, and (following the lead of Dugald Stewart) introduced classes in 'political economy' from which, eventually, modern economics emerged.

One of the most interesting Scottish philosophers of this period was JF Ferrier of St Andrews, who strove to return the study of mind from the psychological direction in which Reid had taken it to a properly 'metaphysical' basis. This meant expressly rejecting the Reidian common sense programme, which Ferrier did in the most vehement manner (seen Reading XV). Interestingly, though, Ferrier develops his alternative in a way that construes philosophy proper, not as a 'science' of some sort, but a form of moral consciousness, and this in effect made its study a continuation of the educational purpose traditionally attributed to it in the Scottish universities.

Alongside the dynamic induced by these internal divisions, philosophy in Scotland gradually became aware of the powerful continental school of German Idealism, and for some, most notably Edward Caird, Professor of Moral Philosophy at Glasgow, it was in this Idealist alternative that the 'one sidedness' of Scottish philosophy, from which its limitations arose, could be overcome (see Reading XVI).

In 1885 Andrew Seth, himself a Scottish philosopher of note, observed that 'the thread of national tradition . . . has been but loosely held of late by many of our best Scottish students of philosophy . . . [T]he philosophical productions of the younger generation of our University men are more strongly impressed with a German than with a native stamp'. This was certainly true, though 1885 did not mark the end of the Scottish philosophical tradition. Nevertheless, during Seth's tenure of the Chair of Logic and Metaphysics at Edinburgh (1891–1919), there were a series of educational, intellectual and cultural changes that eventually resulted in a dissolution of the educational tradition famously named by George Davie 'the democratic intellect'.

The process of its decline was protracted, however. Even if the unity of Scottish philosophy ended with late nineteenth century enthusiasm for Idealism (an enthusiasm shared by Seth), other aspects ensured a continuation well into the twentieth. First, although Professors of Philosophy began to be recruited from rather farther afield, among some of them a sense of continuity and community persisted, as for instance in the case of AE Taylor, Professor of Moral Philosophy first at St Andrews and then at Edinburgh, though he himself was educated entirely in England (see Reading XVII). Second, the practice of requiring all students in arts at the ancient Scottish universities to take a philosophy class, together with the tradition by which this 'general class' was taught by the Professor rather than one of his assistants, ensured for some considerable time that the most distinguished philosophers saw it as part of their task to continue a dialogue between 'professional' philosophy and 'common sense', sometimes amounting to a defence of 'vulgar' opinion on metaphysical and moral issues. A fine example of this is to be found in CA Campbell's inaugural lecture as Professor of Logic and Rhetoric at the University of Glasgow (see Reading XVIII). Third, the institution of the Gifford Lectures, which in the early decades were delivered largely by Scottish Professors at each others' universities, gave a renewed stimulus to the obligation on the part of Professors of philosophy to make their most 'professional' reflections accessible to the intellectual public at large, since this was an express condition of Lord Gifford's bequest.

All three of these (albeit attenuated) elements of continuity are to be found in the Gifford Lectures delivered in Glasgow in 1953 by John Macmurray, Taylor's successor as Professor of Moral Philosophy at Edinburgh (see Reading XIX). In *The Self as Agent*, Macmurray contends that philosophy 'must start from common experience at its most universal and its most ordinary' and that at some level or other, philosophy's 'theoretical result, if it is meaningful at all, is the solution to a practical problem'. He thereby expressly endorsed two central elements in the tradition of Scottish philosophy across the centuries, and the widespread attention given to his lectures beyond the confines of the classroom testifies to his success in sustaining the connection between professors of philosophy and the wider world of ideas.

Macmurray's Gifford lectures, remarkably, have never been out of print, but received little attention from his professional colleagues. By the late twentieth century, while the number of philosophers working in Scotland had grown enormously, as a consequence of becoming part of a hugely expanded British 'university system' very few of these looked to the Scottish tradition of philosophy. At the same time, the foundational place of philosophy in the arts curriculum was eventually abandoned. The result was twofold; philosophy played no special part in the universities of Scotland, and philosophers played no special part in the wider community of letters, becoming as elsewhere, academic specialists.

Arguably, this loss of institutional integrity, by dissolving the community of philosophers in Scotland finally brought the intellectual tradition of Scottish philosophy to a close. Yet the central elements within it — the study of human nature, the belief in a connection between philosophical reflection and ordinary life, and the intellectual marriage of the speculative and the practical — are all salutary counters to the isolated specialization that more 'professional' conceptions of philosophy reduce it to. Moreover, the evident need for such counters at the present time may do something to prompt its revival.

Acknowledgements

It has proved difficult to make a selection from the huge amount of literature properly falling under the title 'Scottish philosophy' that will both reflect its range and richness, and at the same time add up to a manageably sized paperback book. The task of doing so has been greatly assisted by advice and suggestions from many people, but especially Professor Alexander Broadie, Professor Robin Downie, Professor John Haldane, Professor James Moore and Professor the Lord Sutherland, all of whom have also commented helpfully on the introduction. Restrictions on space prevented me from including all the extracts they suggested, and I am conscious that responsibility for the final choice rests entirely with me.

I gratefully acknowledge the permission of James Moore and Michael Silverthorne to reprint their translation of Gersholm Carmichael's *Philosophical Theses*, and the permission of Aberdeen University Special Libraries and Collections to reproduce the engraving of the Edinburgh Advocates Library as the icon of the **Library of Scottish Philosophy**. The cover photograph for this volume was specially taken by Mr Mike Craig of the Reprographics Unit of Aberdeen University.

The Centre for the Study of Scottish Philosophy successfully made application to the Carnegie Trust for the Universities of Scotland for financial support that would enable the series to be launched, and wishes to record its grateful thanks. Special thanks are also due to Mr George S Stevenson for additional financial support for specific volumes. Without his initial assistance it is unlikely that a **Library of Scottish Philosophy** would ever have materialized.

One

Gershom Carmichael

1672–1729

Gershom Carmichael was born in London — the son of Alexander Carmichael, a Scottish Presbyterian clergyman, who died in 1677. His mother, Christian Inglis, later married the Scottish theologian and mystic James Fraser of Brae. Gershom Carmichael was educated at the University of Edinburgh (1687–91). He taught briefly at the University of St. Andrews (1693–4) and in 1694 was appointed Regent at the University of Glasgow through the influence, partly of the family of the Duke and Duchess of Hamilton and their son (to whom he dedicated the first of his *Philosophical Theses*), and partly that of his relative, John Carmichael, Earl of Hyndford (to whom he dedicated the second set of *Philosophical Theses*, 1707). In 1727, when the old regenting system was abandoned at the University of Glasgow in favour of the creation of a professoriate, Carmichael was appointed Professor of Moral Philosophy, the first person in Scotland to hold a professorial position in philosophy.

Carmichael was reputed to be a demanding teacher. As a regent he was responsible for teaching all parts of the philosophy curriculum — logic, metaphysics, moral philosophy, and natural philosophy (or physics). However, as can be inferred from his eventual appointment to a Professorship dedicated to just one subject, his particular speciality was moral philosophy. Much of his work in this area was dominated by considerations of natural rights. The lectures delivered at the University of Glasgow in 1702–3 outlining his views on natural rights were derived from Samuel Pufendorf's *On The Duty of Man and Citizen*, views later developed into his *Supplements and Observations upon Samuel Pufendorf's On the Duty of Man and Citizen according to the Law of Nature, composed for the use of students in Universities.*

The conclusions presented in this work were the result of many years of reflection, but also of extensive discussion. Carmichael inhabited an academic world that included moral philosophers and natural jurists well beyond the boundaries of Scotland and Great Britain, with many of whom he communicated. In particular he corresponded with Jean Barbeyrac (1672–1744) the outstanding authority on natural jurisprudence in the early 18th century. The two exchanged their commentaries on Pufendorff, and Barbeyrac expressly acknowledged Carmichael's help in coming to a clearer understanding of certain points of interpretation in Pufendorff.

Carmichael died of cancer in 1729. He was succeeded as Professor of Moral Philosophy at the University of Glasgow by Francis Hutcheson, one of his own students. Hutcheson generously acknowledged his debt to Carmichael in the work he prepared for the instruction of students, *A Short Introduction to Moral Philosophy*. In general it is true that Carmichael's work contributed, very fundamentally, to shaping the agenda of instruction in moral philosophy in eighteenth-century Scotland.

The *Philosophical Theses* reprinted here display very clearly the interplay between education and original philosophical thought characteristic of Scottish philosophy. These theses set out the views of the teacher in a form suitable for the examination of students, who were required to expound and defend the philosophical views they had been taught. Carmichael starts out from the point of view that 'one aspires to happiness by aspiring to knowledge', and thereby intertwines the pursuit of the true and the valuable. A large part of the these first *Theses* is concerned with the correct method of inquiry which at the same time is assumed to be the correct method of learning, and he rejects the rationalist attempt 'to deduce all knowable truths from one principle' characteristic of Cartesian philosophy, and warns against expecting too much from definition. By favouring careful observation and self-critical argument, Carmichael sets the tone, not just for his students, but of the succeeding practice of Scottish philosophy.

Biographical Information: *Natural Rights on the Threshold of the Scottish Enlightenment: The Writings of Gershom Carmichael*, ed. J. Moore and M. Silverthorne, Indiana: Liberty Fund, 2002.

READING I
Philosophical Theses:
On Directing the Mind to Lasting Happiness[1]

Jt is universally acknowledged that reason is the highest prerogative of human nature above any other part of the visible world. Accordingly, it has been repeated *ad nauseam* in the schools of philosophy that man is a *rational animal*. Nothing more is meant here by the term *reason* than the power or faculty of thinking (*cogitandi*), i.e., of understanding, willing, and initiating actions with self-awareness (*conscientia*) and self-approval (*complacientia*). But it is clear from the

---

[1]   Extracted from *Natural Rights on the Threshold of the Scottish Enlightenment: The Writings of Gershom Carmichael*, ed. J Moore and M Silverthorne, Indiana: Liberty Fund, 2002, pp. 21–9.

very notion of reason that man should not simply rest in this essential characteristic of his worth, but on the contrary, since every power is intended to be realized in act, he should put all his effort into the single aim of making right use of his rational faculty by aspiring to happiness. One aspires to happiness by aspiring to knowledge and love of the true and the good, however manifested, and such happiness is the proper perfection of thinking things.

. . . [T]here are certain natural means which in conjunction with the rational nature of the mind can give considerable help toward uncovering a good many truths both speculative and practical. Of these means some are in our power, others not. But the vulgar so confound these two kinds that they seem to attribute much more to the former and much less to the latter than they should. The aids to the right use of reason which are beyond our power are either internal, for example, intelligence, retentiveness of memory, etc., or external, such as a liberal education, the company of good and learned men, books, experience, and the like.

Internal factors have less importance in either intellectual or moral activity than is commonly thought, whether they are taken to be based on some natural difference between souls or (as is far more probable) on the actual arrangement of the brain and of the organs subordinate to it (which the goodness of God has made more naturally able in some men than in others). This is partly because those who consider themselves superior in the endowments of nature too often do too little work, but mostly because a natural ineptitude to carry out one function of reason is usually compensated by a greater aptitude for another, and vice versa. Consequently one may say with confidence that only a very small proportion of the errors into which men fall have their origin in any natural dullness or defect of intelligence.

As for external aids to cultivating reason, help from other people may be very useful in suggesting appropriate ideas and guiding the mind by an appropriate method; and many subjects that deserve to be investigated can only be known by external and elaborate experiments. Yet one must agree that the knowledge of what each man must know to secure his own safety and carry out the duties of social life is not dependent on the authority of precepts or books (with the exception of the divine pronouncements) or on difficult and elaborate experiments. On the contrary such knowledge (insofar as it is natural) is derivable by each man from the observation of himself and of the things he sees all round him and by the accurate comparison with each other of the ideas he gathers from his environment.

II.   Thus the natural assistance which is most valuable for making a right use of reason, and whose lack is the source of most errors, is within our own power. It is clear that it consists in just one thing: in weighing all our thoughts with unfailing attention, and at the same time in striving to direct our minds along the most suitable and direct road to the knowledge of truth.

III.   The attention required for successfully discerning truth and thus for duly controlling our inclinations and passions (so far as they depend on the knowledge of practical truths) has to be exercised both in the formation of ideas and in their comparison with each other. There is certainly a need for attention in forming ideas. Admittedly we cannot be deceived in the bare perception, whether simple or complex, of an object viewed in itself. But in abstracting ideas, in combining them together and in storing them in the mind stamped with definite names (all of which pertains to their formation in the wider sense), we often go wrong in various ways which commonly obscure our path in the pursuit of truth. First then we must be careful that each and every idea which is to be compared in our judgments and reasoning is as clear as it can be made, i.e., that it is quite vivid to the mind; this is the best way to ensure that it is distinct, i.e. that it is not confused with any other idea. This is not because the mind which is properly aware of all its thoughts ever takes one idea for two or two for one in inspecting its own ideas. It is because in thinking as well as in speaking men often lose track of their ideas, particularly if they are quite complex and have little natural affinity with the images depicted in the brain, and substitute words or other image-signs which because they have no natural connection with the ideas to which they are attached, may easily, without the closest attention, badly confuse the ideas which they are employed to distinguish. Sometimes a word is used now for one idea, now for another, without any awareness of a difference between them; sometimes two words which are supposed to express different ideas, are used for the same idea because of tiredness. Hence it is clear that we cannot really be too careful to ensure that every word we use in silent thought or talk or writing has a fixed and definite meaning for us.

IV.   This is more difficult to achieve than is commonly thought, as will be shown by considering separately the various classes of ideas which may enter our thoughts. Singular ideas are less liable to this confusion; for proper names have a closer connection with the objective or material thing signified than with any idea by which it may be represented; and their signification is grasped with sufficient precision, if the singular object to which they refer is understood, whatever the singular idea by which it is distinguished from others. But we do not need to take much notice here of singular ideas, since almost all the terms of the different branches of knowledge are universal.

Of universal ideas some are simple, others complex. And the former too are not simply one class, for some can quite easily be accurately attached to their own names, others with considerable difficulty. But however precisely all names intended to express complex ideas are supposed to be understood, yet there may still remain a serious difficulty about the names of complex ideas, whether they are ideas of modes or of substances. In the case of modes, the reason is the frequently large number of simple ideas, variously arranged, which have no definite corresponding exemplar in nature. In the case of substances the reason is ignorance of the innermost essences of the substances to which they are related and the different accounts given by different individuals of the properties which are substituted for them.

V.   To deal with this confusion of ideas, and to give to words that denote complex ideas a definite and fixed meaning for ourselves and our interlocutors, the most useful tool is *definition*. Definition is an utterance by which the simpler ideas involved in expressing a complex idea by some given name are unfolded in an individual and orderly fashion by means of several words. And since in this and no other sense definition, as it is commonly used, is rightly said to explain the *essence* of a thing, it follows that philosophers are wrong to allege some *real* definition beyond the nominal definition. Indeed in defining modes, it is not self-evident that any real essence distinct from the nominal is in view at all. And we cannot penetrate the absolute essences of substances nor enumerate all, or even perhaps the most noticeable, relative properties which proceed from them; consequently we cannot rightly be said to deliver the real definitions of them.

It is indeed true that in these ideas of substances which we fashion for ourselves, we normally assemble the most noticeable of the properties which fall under our observation. But apart from the fact that this method of making a definition does not come up to the magnificent promise of the philosophers who offer real definitions, this approach is inappropriate except in the case of substances which are designated by reference to a singular exemplar. For if the definition (as is usually the case) is attached to a specific name, either the idea to be explicated by definition is understood to this extent to underlie the name, in which case it is superfluous to offer a definition, or the meaning of the proposed name is uncertain and vague, in which case it will not be possible to get a fixed and definite sense out of the utterance which purports to give the real definition of the objects signified by that name. For the common method of distinguishing different kinds of substances is by reference to some individual objects of each kind which someone has at some time seen or come to know individually in one way or another. And while this method is valuable for everyday use, it is by no means accurate enough to satisfy the rigorous requirements of philosophy, since it only goes as far as giving standard names to a few of the most obvious properties. Hence arises the need to employ definition to explicate the names of substances no less than of modes, although we will not deny that, to designate some of their more sensible qualities, it is useful to point to the things themselves or to pictures of them.

VI.   We have restricted the use of *definition* to names signifying complex ideas, for it is quite clear from the very notion of it that simple ideas cannot be explicated by definitions, since they do not admit of resolution into a number of ideas. Hence the names by which such ideas are to be expressed should be explicated by indicating the subject to which they belong, in conjunction with certain other circumstances. Those who seek definitions here find a continually increasing obscurity rather than clarity. An excellent example of this (to pass over many others which occur often in philosophical texts) is furnished by the simplest and most general of all the ideas which our mind can form, namely the idea of *being* or of *existing* or of *something* (for we do not doubt that one and the same idea is expressed by these three terms). The metaphysicians make absurd efforts to define this idea, and in so doing destroy the universal significance clearly distinguished by these general words.

VII. Not only do we habitually attach ideas which we abstract or combine in our minds to certain names, we also assume that they more or less conform with the ideas which others have attached to the same names, and often also with actual objects existing in nature (which is particularly appropriate with ideas of substances). Hence we must be careful here to ensure that they do conform, as we assume they do, on both counts. For if they are deficient on the first count, we will not be able to understand others or be understood by them; if on the latter, the science which is meant to investigate the properties of things existing in nature will just be chasing chimaeras.

VIII. But it is not enough to have attached clear and distinct ideas, conforming to the nature of things, to definite names in accordance with common usage. For our minds would achieve no sense of completion from this unless they also made judgments, i.e., unless they gave opinions on ideas in comparison to each other, with regard to the identity or non-identity of the objects represented by them. Any other relationship that some persist in seeking among the given terms of any question may be reduced to this one relationship among the proposed ideas. In investigating this relation we must pay the most careful attention, so that it will not impose falsehood upon us in the guise of truth. The opinion which we give of the identity of the objects represented by two ideas has regard either to the identity which they are assumed to have, or not to have, on the basis of a real difference of time, past, present, or future; or to the identity which they would have, or would not have, on the basis of a possible time in which they might exist; the former may be called *absolute*, the latter *hypothetical*, judgments. And hence we infer (since every idea, which can be predicated of another idea, involves the idea of a *being* or of an *existing* thing) that nothing can be truly affirmed of things impossible; and nothing can be absolutely affirmed of things purely possible. If this had been properly noticed, the usual course of metaphysics could have been shortened by half (by cutting out the part which is occupied with what are called *nonentities*).

IX. In the case of both kinds of judgment, some are *immediate*, other *mediate*. In direct judgments the relation between the two proposed ideas becomes known by comparing the one with the other without the interposition of a third idea. In mediate judgments the relation of the two extreme ideas is inferred from the relation which connects both of them with a third idea. It is an agreement if both concur with the third in clearly designating in both cases at least one object which is the same; and a disagreement, if under the same condition one concur with the third but the other does not. But it is not required that both extreme ideas be directly compared with the same middle term, it is enough if one of the extremes is directly compared with a middle term, and this is compared with another, and so on, until one arrives at the other extreme idea, provided that each of the middle terms, as it is repeated, clearly designates on both occasions at least one object which is the same, and provided that there is not more than one negative conjunction; if there is, the conjunction of the extremes will also be negative.

Hence we may infer in passing that in every piece of reasoning, the number of principles, that is, of propositions that are assumed to be known of themselves, exceeds the number of middle terms by one. Hence the attempt to deduce all knowable truths from one or the other principle will never succeed. Furthermore that common rules of syllogisms may easily be demonstrated from our account. But as virtually no intelligent person (except those who have learned the common rules but have never penetrated to their foundations and cling to the husks of the words) would allow himself to be deceived by a viciously formulated argument, we have to admit that the majority by far of the errors into which we fall every day have their origin in false principles which we accept as true, because we are carried away by the heat of the passions or other people's authority or some other foolishness.

X. Propositions which are to be considered as principles become known in different ways depending on whether they are absolute or hypothetical. In order that the absolute existence of any thing may become known to us without proof, it must be intimately present to our mind and give a sense of itself; this is the way the mind observes its own existence and that of its thoughts. But the hypothetical connection or conflict of abstract ideas, i.e., the identity or non-identity of objects which would be represented by them if they existed, becomes known from mere comparison of such ideas despite the absence of the things themselves. On premises of the former kind depend all absolute propositions, which we also come to know by the use of reasoning. This includes propositions which are concerned with the existence of singular objects, and many also concerning the co-existence of properties which enter into specific ideas of substances and which are for the most part either singular or particular. But all propositions which are purely conditional, being concerned with the relation of abstract ideas, are free of that dependence. Countless universal propositions about the relations of modes in mathematics and the moral disciplines are like this; since they are free of all regard to this or that time and to the contingent existence in time of a created thing, and could not be distinctly conceived to be otherwise, they are rightly said to be in the most rigorous sense *necessary* . . .

XI.   In all these judgments, whether absolute or hypothetical, whether direct or indirect, due attention requires us to avoid all rashness and precipitancy and not to accept anything as certain and indubitable in which the splendour of truth does not flash out and compel the mind intent on tracking it down to give its full assent, even in spite of its own reluctance. So far as we observe this rule, so far and no further shall we assure ourselves of immunity from error. It is no objection that many people, in clinging obstinately to errors, display complete certainty and firm mental acquiescence in their opinions as true, whether by words or by anything else that one can offer as a sign of a true and certain judgment. For all that we may legitimately infer from this is that the criterion by which truth so manifests itself to our minds as to exclude all suspicion of falsity does not lie in the external profession or forms of speech which vain and dogmatic men may use, but is to be sought in the quiet recesses of the mind itself and in the innermost depths of our thought. Here everyone who refuses to cast himself headlong into hopeless scepticism must admit that some criterion of this kind is present when we assent to certain truths (or rather to any matters of which we can say that we are certainly convinced), and this cannot coexist with false assent.

XII.   To achieve the requisite attention in the formation and comparison of ideas, we must partly remove obstacles and partly use them to help us. First, there are vivid sensations and images which engage both body and mind together and are apt to divert the mind's gaze and draw its attention away from the purely intelligible. We must therefore avoid objects which strike the mind with such overly vivid sensations or images. But in our present state of union the human mind cannot avoid being strongly affected by things which affect the body, hence it should use those modes of perception in such a way that they conduce to a more distinct understanding of things. This will happen if we connect a specific sensible or imageable sign with each intellectual idea, and constantly preserve the connection; this is especially true of any sign that has a natural affinity with the intellectual idea itself. This has been the remarkable privilege of geometry, both to ensure that the truths which it demonstrates by itself were easily perceived and to throw a brilliant light on the sciences which it is employed to illustrate. But if we cannot find such suitably simple natural signs, we may profitably make use of other arbitrary signs which not only get attention, particularly if they are very simple, but also may be substituted for more complex ideas and lessen the difficulty that the mind has with these and augment its capacity . . .

XIII.   It may be further established from what has been said, that the genuine method of discovering truth turns on these two cardinal points. *First*, we must collect for ourselves ideas of the things we intend to reason about that are clear, distinct, and conforming to their originals. *Second*, in connecting a series of several truths with each other, we start from those that are simpler and easier (i.e., those which are known by themselves and those which are close to being so, or even those which, other things being equal, have simpler terms), and not only grasp their unshakeable truth but also spend some time on them before we take the step toward more composite and difficult truths (those which need a longer chain of arguments or are composed of more complex terms). However, it is not the more general truths which we should immediately regard as simpler. For just as it is far from being the case that the most general ideas are the first to take their places in our minds, so their relation is not always especially obvious to the intellect. It is true that in teaching certain abstract disciplines, especially mathematics, it proves useful to begin with some rather general axioms which dispose the mind to give assent to more particular truths, because they are few in number and contain within themselves many other propositions which have been rendered familiar by use. Yet these very sciences (which are taught in this manner today) could not have been discovered by that method. And there are certain other disciplines (such as pneumatology and physics) which cannot be rightly taught by the same method. Since they investigate the actual existence of things and the properties which experience alone teaches belong to them, they require us to proceed from the singular and less universal to the more universal.

XIV.   Among all the absolute truths, none becomes known to the mind earlier or more easily than the existence of oneself and one's thoughts; and therefore the famous phrase of the celebrated Descartes, *I thinking exist*, does nothing to demonstrate abstract truths and should certainly not be laid down as their absolutely first principle; yet it may without absurdity be assigned the first place (first in the order of our knowledge, that is) in the class of propositions which are concerned with the actual existence of things. This at least is clear, that no physical object's existence is knowable by us with such ease and certainty. For whether a physical thing which sensation leads me to believe exists, actually does exist or not, yet I cannot have doubts about the fact that there is such a sensation in me. For this purpose it does not matter whether the *thinking thing* which is in me (or rather which I myself am) is distinct from all matter (as we shall demonstrate below) or whether it is merely modified matter. For likewise the truth of our assertion is sound that the existence of our mind as *a thinking substance* becomes known to us earlier, more easily, and more certainly than the existence of any physical thing.

XV.   However the absolute essence of our mind does not become manifest to us in the same manner as its existence does. For in forming a positive idea of itself, it can scarcely itself ascend higher, since it knows about itself by primary intuition and apprehends by inner awareness that it is itself a *thinking thing*, i.e., a thing which perceives, affirms, denies, wills, refuses, etc. And since these individual modes of thinking are only accidental perfections of the mind, one succeeding the other in a continual stream, it is clear that they must in no way be confused with the essence of the mind, even though we conceive of it somehow or other in relation to them. Of general and permanent thought (in which certain celebrated authors locate the essence of mind) the mind itself has neither awareness nor idea; especially since that kind of thought is defined by its patrons as *an awareness of all things that goes on in the mind*. For awareness is either concerned with the particular thoughts of which there is awareness or presupposes particular thoughts; certainly it cannot be taken as a *subject* of thought. Thus the mind knows itself only in relation to its modes, and they are such that the mind itself only imperfectly conceives what relation they bear to their own subject. We should therefore abandon the vain hope of tracking down the absolute essence of mind and be content that the mind should look within where the way is open and reflect on the various modes of thinking in which it engages and their order and dependence; especially since each act of thought which it performs, though it does not lead to an absolute grasp of its being (*entitas*) as it is in itself, yet discloses an essential aspect of it, namely, its ability to perform such an act.

XVI.   Here *sensation* first offers itself to our consideration. Sensation is a perception in the mind excited by the occasion of something physical being present and moving the organs of our body. And we are so intimately aware within ourselves that sensation resides in the same mind as the rest of our thoughts, that it seems extraordinary that there have been philosophers who taught that the sentient mind of man is different from the rational mind; nor on the other hand do the other philosophers seem to make sense who refuse to classify sensations as thoughts (notwithstanding the manifest self-awareness which they have in themselves). Nevertheless sensations do not represent any objects (properly so called), nor is there anything like them among external objects nor anything like them among external objects nor anything which bears a greater resemblance to them than motion or figure to thought or the body itself to mind. Hence the only account which can be given of the connection between our sensations and the properties of the bodies which arouse them is the will of the creator, who has so closely united substances of such different natures and established such a correspondence between the modifications of both, that the sensations aroused in the mind in the presence of physical things serve to tell it what it should pursue or avoid for the preservation of animal life. We do not however deny that the senses are useful for the investigation of truth, provided that we derive this conception not from the sensation itself but from the intellectual idea which naturally takes it up, and provided that we attend carefully to the various cases in which that idea normally designates, faithfully or otherwise, the condition of an object.

XVII.   We experience perceptions similar to those described in the last thesis not only when an external object exists to arouse them but also in the absence of objects, except that these (which are commonly called *imaginations*) are noticeably less vigorous than the former and usually depend more on the determination of our will. When we dream we take them for sensations; for then we lack the sensations themselves, and there are no witnesses to correct the error of the imagination, nor do we have access to the greater clarity which would show up the obscurity of the imagination by comparison. In both these respects the cases of the dreamer and of the man caught in persistent error are neatly parallel to each other; nor is there a sharper distinction between the former and the waking man than between the latter and one who truly knows. But the primary use of the imagination is not only to retain what we have learned by sense, but also to implant other ideas more deeply in the memory and to save them from confusion; this has been shown in thesis 12.

XVIII.   Besides the perceptions so far mentioned (which we usually claim to share with the animals) our mind has other perceptions of a completely different kind (which are usually called pure intellections). No one can be ignorant of these who is not too much a stranger in his own home; for only intellectual ideas make contact even lightly with thinking things. Only intellectual ideas are so general that they can stretch to include objects which present themselves to the senses in different guises; on the other hand they alone are so accurate that they distinguish between objects which are offered to the senses in the same guise (for example, a circle and an ellipse, one of whose diameters is imperceptibly longer than the other's). Finally only intellectual ideas represent objects other than themselves or can be predicated of them; for when the names given for the purpose of distinguishing our sensations are applied to external objects, they import no more than an aptitude for exciting such sensations in us, and since the notion of this aptitude is relative, it is certainly represented not by the sensation itself but only by a pure intellection.

XIX.   It is abundantly clear therefore that there are pure intellections in our minds. But the question of their nature and even more of their origin, has always been considered a difficult one, and rightly so. For although we seem to be intimately aware that they are directly produced by the mind itself and do not, when viewed *materially* (as they say), contain anything in themselves which should be reckoned beyond its powers, nevertheless the further question remains as to where our minds learned that variety of forms by which they can adapt their notions to represent the almost infinite variety of external things so exactly. Experience hardly allows us to believe that the earliest exemplars of all our intellectual notions were co-created with the mind from its very origin (as one part of the learned world contends). For experience teaches us that our minds form singular notions earlier and more easily than universal notions and, even more, abstract notions (though these, if any, ought to be immediately aroused by exemplars innate to the mind). Experience also teaches that each person's mind is stocked with more notions and more perfect notions, the more they are provided by famil-

iarity with things and by a richer supply of objects, and the more apt the
structure of his organs is for perceiving them.

We can at least infer from this that the furniture of knowledge which is
actually found today in the human mind suggests an origin quite other
than that which these authors propose. In forming a conjecture on this
question, no one seems to us to come nearer the truth than those who
take the view that the exemplars of all our original notions owe their origin to the actual presence of the objects represented through them. I say
original because there is no doubt that from the singular notion which the
mind has itself formed by the occasion of a present object and which
includes several obvious features of it, the mind can abstract various
simpler notions which are contained in it, and in turn combine these
abstract notions in a new order among themselves, but in such a way
that the mind owes the material of all its natural notions (for we are not
speaking of those which are suggested supernaturally) to the actual
presence of objects.

Since therefore physical objects, though present, do not come to our
notice except by the mediation of sensations, we safely conclude that
notions of corporeal things take their origin from sensation; there are
however particular reasons for hesitation about the means by which our
minds are equipped to form notions of spiritual things. But if we observe
ourselves, if we carefully consider the objects which are most familiar to
us, by whose means the rest become more or less amenable to concep-
tualisation, they will all be seen to urge the mind to advance from contemplation of itself to form notions of the supreme deity and of other
spirits. The mind will also be seen to be aroused to reflect on itself precisely so far as it is directed to some particular thought by another object
(i.e., an external object). In thinking this thought it finds itself in action,
and in reflecting on it it acquires, by a supervening act, a more explicit
knowledge of itself and of its powers. At any rate we will not find a trace
of any other origin or process in all the notions which our minds naturally perform. And so we do not doubt that the primary furniture of all
our natural knowledge may be deduced, in all likelihood, from *sensation*
and *reflection*.

Two

Francis Hutcheson

1694–1746

Francis Hutcheson was born on 8 August 1694 in the north of Ireland. The son of a Presbyterian minister whose own father was an emigrant from Scotland, he entered the University of Glasgow in 1710, and took his MA in 1712. Hutcheson returned to Ireland in 1718 where he was licensed as a minister and accepted an invitation to start a dissenting academy in Dublin, where he remained for the next ten years. In 1725 he published his best-known work, *An Inquiry into the Original of our Ideas of Beauty and Virtue*, revised editions of which appeared in 1726, 1729 and 1738. In 1728, he completed *An Essay on the Nature and Conduct of the Passions and Affections. With Illustrations upon the Moral Sense*, which was issued in a revised form in 1742.

The widespread interest these works generated led to Hutcheson's being elected Professor of Moral Philosophy at Glasgow in 1729. He had great impact as a teacher, Adam Smith among others recording warm affection for the "never to be forgotten Dr Hutcheson". In the late 1730s and 1740s, Hutcheson met and corresponded with Hume, who presented some challenging criticism of his work. Hutcheson in turn stimulated the development of Hume's philosophical position but he did not support his bid for a professorship at Edinburgh in 1745. In 1742 his *Philosophiae moralis institutio compendiaria* appeared along with the *Metaphysicae synopsis*, later revised in 1744 *as Synopsis metaphysicae*. The *Compend*, as the Latin work on moral philosophy and natural law is commonly known, appeared in a new edition in 1744, and in a translation after his death in 1747. Hutcheson's *Logicae compendium* also appeared after his death. His last efforts were devoted to completing *A System of Moral Philosophy*, which his son published posthumously in 1755, Hutcheson having died on a visit to Dublin in 1746.

Hutcheson's *Thoughts on Laughter* originally appeared as a series of three letters. Their interest lies partly in the fact that Hutcheson is possibly the only major philosopher ever to offer a sustained philosophical analysis of humour. But his thoughts on the subject are also a fine exam-

ple of the method which marked the philosophy of the Scottish Enlightenment.

Thomas Hobbes, author of *Leviathan*, had an immense influence on
the intellectual currents of his time and subsequently. In keeping with
the egoistic basis of his political philosophy, Hobbes interprets laughter
as an element in the struggle of the individual for supremacy over others. But Hutcheson, rejecting Hobbes's quasi-geometrical deduction
from first principles in favour of a more empirical approach, argues that
Hobbes's egoism leads him, mistakenly, to take ridicule, rather than parody or burlesque, as the paradigm of humour, and hence to overlook the
important civilizing and socializing function of laughter, which unites
more than it divides.

Biographical information: Daniel Carey, *Thoemmes Dictionary of C18th
British Philosophers*.

READING II
Thoughts on Laughter[1]

I

Aristotle, in his art of Poetry, has very justly explained the nature of
one species of laughter, viz. the ridiculing of persons, the occasion
or object of which he tells us, is 'some mistake, or some turpitude,
without grievous pain, and not very pernicious or destructive'. But this
he never intended as a general account of all sorts of laughter.

But Mr. Hobbes, who very much owes his character of a philosopher
to his assuming positive solemn airs, which he uses most when he is
going to assert some palpable absurdity, or some ill-natured nonsense,
assures us, that 'laughter is nothing else but sudden glory, arising from
some sudden conception of some eminency in our selves, by comparison
with the infirmity of others, or with our own formerly: for men laugh at
the follies of themselves past, when they come suddenly to remembrance, except they bring with them a present dishonour'.

This notion the authors of the Spectator's N° 47, have adopted from
Mr. Hobbes. That bold author having carried on his inquiries, in a singular manner, without regard to authorities; and having fallen into a way
of speaking, which was much more intelligible than that of the schoolmen, soon became agreeable to many free wits of his age. His grand view
was to deduce all human actions from self-love: by some bad fortune he
has over-looked every thing which is generous or kind in mankind; and
represents men in that light in which a thorough knave or coward
beholds them, suspecting all friendship love, or social affection, or
hypocrisy, or selfish design or fear.

---

[1] Extracted from *Thoughts on Laughter and Observations on 'The Fable of Bees' in Six
Letters*, Thoemmes Press, Bristol, 1989, pp. 1–52

The learned world has often been told that Pufendorf had strongly imbibed Hobbes's first principles, although he draws much better consequences from them; and this last author, as he is certainly much preferable to the generality of the schoolmen, in distinct intelligible reasoning, has been made the grand instructor in morals to all who have of late given themselves to that study: hence it is that the old notions of natural affections, and kind instincts, the *sensus communis*, the *decorum*, and *honestum*, are almost banished out of our books of morals; we must never hear of them in any of our lectures for fear of innate ideas: all must be interest, and some selfish view; laughter itself must be a joy from the same spring.

If Mr. Hobbes's notion be just, then first, there can be no laughter on any occasion where we make no comparison of ourselves to others, or of our present state to a worse state, or where we do not observe some superiority of ourselves above some other thing: and again, it must follow, that every sudden appearance of superiority over another, must excite laughter, when we attend to it. If both these conclusions be false, the notion from whence they are drawn must be so too.

1st. Then, that laughter often arises without any imagined superiority of ourselves, may appear from one great fund of pleasantry, the parody, and burlesque allusion; [these] move laughter in those who may have the highest veneration for the writing alluded to, and also admire the wit of the person who makes the allusion. Thus many a profound admirer of the machinery in Homer and Virgil, has laughed heartily at the interposition of Pallas in Hudibras, to save the bold Talgol from the Knight's pistol, presented to the outside of his skull:

> But Pallas came in shape of rust,
> And 'twixt the spring and hammer thrust
> Her Gorgon shield, which made the cock
> Stand stiff, as 'twere transform'd to stock.

And few who read this, imagine themselves superior either to Homer or Butler; we indeed generally imagine ourselves superior in sense to the valorous knight, but not in this point, of firing rusty pistols. And pray, would any mortal have laughed, had the poet told, in a simple unadorned manner, that his knight attempted to shoot Talgol, but his pistol was so rusty that it would not give fire? and yet this would have given us the same ground of sudden glory from our own superiority over the doughty knight.

Again, to what do we compare ourselves, or imagine ourselves superior, when we laugh at this fantastical imitation of the poetical imagery, and similitudes of the morning?

> The sun, long since, had in the lap
> Of Thetis taken out his nap;
> And, like a lobster boil'd, the morn,
> From black to red began to turn.

Many an orthodox Scotch Presbyterian (which sect few accuse of disregard for the holy scriptures) has been put to it to preserve his gravity,
upon hearing the application of scripture made by his countryman Dr.
Pitcairn, as he observed a crowd in the streets about a mason, who had
fallen along with his scaffold, and was overwhelmed with the ruins of
the chimney which he had been building, and which fell immediately
after the fall of the poor mason; 'blessed are the dead which die in the
Lord, for they rest from their labours, and their works follow them'. And
yet few imagine themselves superior either to the apostle or the doctor.
Their superiority to the poor mason, I'm sure, could never have raised
such laughter, for this occurred to them before the doctor's consolation;
in this case no opinion of superiority could have occasioned the laughter, unless we say, that people imagined themselves superior to the doctor in religion: but an imagined superiority to a doctor in religion, is not a
matter so rare as to raise sudden joy; and, with people who value religion, the impiety of another is no matter of laughter.

It is said, 'that when men of wit make us laugh, it is by representing
some oddness or infirmity in themselves, or others'. Thus allusions
made on trifling occasions, to the most solemn figured speeches of great
writers, contain such an obvious impropriety, that we imagine ourselves
incapable of such mistakes as the alluder seemingly falls into; so that in
this case too, there is an imagined superiority. But in answer to this, we
may observe, that we often laugh at such allusions, when we are conscious that the person who raises the laugh, knows abundantly the
justest propriety of speaking, and knows, at present, the oddness and
impropriety of his own allusion as well as any in company; nay, laughs
at it himself: we often admire his wit in such allusion, and study to imitate him in it, as far as we can. Now, what sudden sense of glory, or joy in
our superiority, can arise from observing a quality in another, which we
study to imitate, I cannot imagine. I doubt, if men compared themselves
with the alluder, whom they study to imitate, they would rather often
grow grave or sorrowful.

Nay, farther, this is so far from the truth, that imagined superiority
moves our laughter, that one would imagine from some instance the
very contrary: for if laughter arose from our imagined superiority, then,
the more that any object appeared inferior to us, the greater would be the
jest; and the nearer any one came to an equality with us, or resemblance
of our actions, the less we should be moved with laughter. But we see, on
the contrary, that some ingenuity in dogs and monkeys, which comes
near to some of our own arts, very often makes us merry; whereas their
duller actions, in which they are much below us, are no matter of jest at
all. Whence the author in the Spectator drew his observation, 'that the
actions of beasts which move our laughter, bear a resemblance to a
human blunder', I confess I cannot guess; I fear the very contrary is true,
that their imitation of our grave wise actions would be fittest to raise
mirth in the observer.

The second part of the argument, that opinion of superiority suddenly incited in us does not move laughter, seems the most obvious thing imaginable: if we observe an object in pain while we are at ease, we are in greater danger of weeping than laughing: and yet here is occasion for Hobbes's sudden joy. It must be a very merry state in which a fine gentleman is, when well dressed, in his coach, he passes our streets, where he will see so many ragged beggars, and porters and chairmen sweating at their labour, on every side of him. It is a great pity that we had not an infirmary or lazar-house to retire to in cloudy weather, to get an afternoon of laughter at these inferior objects: strange, that none of our Hobbists banish all canary birds, and squirrels, and lap-dogs, and pugs, and cats out of their houses, and substitute in their places asses, and owls, and snails, and oysters to be merry upon. From these they might have higher joys of superiority, than from those with whom we now please ourselves. Pride, or an high opinion of ourselves, must be entirely inconsistent with gravity; emptiness must always make men solemn in their behaviour; and conscious virtue and great abilities must always be upon the sneer. An orthodox believer who is very sure that he is in the true way to salvation, must always be merry upon heretics, to whom he is so much superior in his own opinion; and no other passion but mirth should arise upon hearing of their heterodoxy. In general, all men of true sense, and reflection, and integrity, of great capacity for business, and penetration into the tempers and interests of men, must be the merriest little grigs imaginable; Democritus must be the sole leaser of all the philosophers; and perpetual laughter must succeed into the place of the long beard,

> . . . To be the grace
> Both of our wisdom and our face.

It is pretty strange, that the authors whom we mentioned above, have never distinguished between the words laughter and ridicule: this last is but one particular species of the former, when we are laughing at the follies of others; and in this species there may be some pretence to allege that some imagined superiority may occasion it; but then there are innumerable instances of laughter, where no person is ridiculed; nor does he who laughs compare himself to any thing whatsoever. Thus how often do we laugh at some out-of-the-way description of natural objects, to which we never compare our state at all. I fancy few have ever read the city shower without a strong disposition to laughter; and instead of imagining any superiority, are very sensible of a turn of wit in the author which they despair of imitating: thus what relation to our affairs has that simile in Hudibras,

> Instead of trumpet and of drum,
> Which makes the warrior's stomach come,
> And whets men's valour sharp, like beer
> By thunder turn'd to vinegar.

The laughter is not here raised against either valour or martial music, but merely by the wild resemblance of a mean event.

And then farther, even in ridicule itself there must be something else than bare opinion to raise it, as may appear from this, that if any one would relate in the simplest manner these very weaknesses of others, their extravagant passions, their absurd opinions, upon which the man of wit would rally, should we hear the best vouchers of all the facts alleged, we shall not be disposed to laughter by bare narration; or should one do a real important injury to another, by taking advantage of his weakness, or by some pernicious fraud let us see another's simplicity, this is no matter of laughter: and yet those important cheats do really discover our superiority over the person cheated, more than the trifling impostures of our humorists. The opinion of our superiority may raise a sedate joy in our minds, very different from laughter; but such a thought seldom arises in our minds in the hurry of a cheerful conversation among friends, where there is often an high mutual esteem.

II

The ingenious Mr. Addison, in his treatise of the Pleasures of the Imagination, has justly observed many sublimer sensations than those commonly mentioned among philosophers: he observes particularly, that we receive sensations of pleasure from those objects which are great, new, or beautiful; and on the contrary, that objects which are more narrow and confined, or deformed, and irregular, give us disagreeable ideas. It is unquestionable, that we have a great number of perceptions, which one can scarcely reduce to any of the five senses, as they are commonly explained; such as either the ideas of grandeur, dignity, decency, beauty, harmony; or on the other hand, of meanness, baseness, indecency, deformity; and that we apply these ideas not only to material objects, but to characters, abilities, actions.

It may be farther observed, that by some strange associations of ideas made in our infancy, we have frequently some of these ideas recurring along with a great many objects, with which they have no other connection than what custom and education, or frequent allusions give them, or at most, some very distant resemblance. The very affections of our minds are ascribed to inanimate objects; and some animals, perfect enough in their own kind, are made constant emblems of some vices or meanness; whereas other kinds are made emblems of the contrary qualities. For instance of these associations, partly from nature, partly from custom, we may take the following ones; sanctity in our churches, magnificence in public buildings, affection between the oak and ivy, the elm and vine; hospitality in a shade, a pleasant sensation of grandeur in the sky, the sea, and mountains, distinct from a bare apprehension or image of their extension; solemnity and horror in shady woods. An ass is the common emblem of stupidity and sloth, a swine of selfish luxury; an

eagle of a great genius; a lion of intrepidity; an ant or a bee of low industry, and prudent economy. Some inanimate objects have in like manner
some accessory ideas of meanness, either for some natural reason, or
oftener by mere chance and custom.

Now, the same ingenious author observes, in the Spectator Vol. I. N°
62. that what we call a great genius, such as becomes a heroic poet, gives
us pleasure by filling the mind with great conceptions; and therefore
they bring most of their similitudes and metaphors from objects of dignity and grandeur, where the resemblance is generally very obvious.
This is not usually called wit, but something nobler. What we call grave
wit, consists in bringing such resembling ideas together, as one could
scarce have imagined had so exact a relation to each other; or when the
resemblance is carried on through many more particulars than we could
have at first expected: and this therefore gives the pleasure of surprise.
In this serious wit, though we are not solicitous about the grandeur of
the images, we must still beware of bringing in ideas of baseness or
deformity, unless we are studying to represent an object as base and
deformed. Now this sort of wit is seldom apt to move laughter, more
than heroic poetry.

That then which seems generally the cause of laughter, is 'the bringing
together of images which have contrary additional ideas, as well as
some resemblance in the principal idea: this contrast between ideas of
grandeur, dignity, sanctity, perfection, and ideas of meanness, baseness,
profanity, seems to be the very spirit of burlesque; and the greatest part
of our raillery and jest are founded upon it'.

We also find ourselves moved to laughter by an overstraining of wit,
by bringing resemblances from subjects of a quite different kind from
the subject to which they are compared. 'When we see, instead of the easiness, and natural resemblance which constitutes true wit, a forced
straining of a likeness, our laughter is apt to arise; as also, when the only
resemblance is not in the idea, but in the sound of the words'. And this is
the matter of laughter in the pun.

Let us see if this thought may not be confirmed in many instances. If
any writing has obtained a high character for grandeur, sanctity, inspira-
tion, or sublimity of thoughts, and boldness of images; the application of
any known sentence of such writings to low, vulgar, or base subjects,
never fails to divert the audience, and set them a laughing. This sound of
laughter the ancients had by allusions to Homer: of this the lives of some
of the philosophers in Diogenes Laertius supply abundance of instances.
Our late burlesque writers derive a great part of their pleasantry from
their introducing, on the most trifling occasions, allusions to some of the
bold schemes, or figures, or sentences of the great poets, upon the most
solemn subjects. Hudibras and Don Quixote will supply one with
instances of this in almost every page. It were to be wished that the boldness of our age had never carried their ludicrous allusions to yet more
venerable writings. We know that allusions to the phrases of holy writ

have obtained to some gentlemen a character of wit, and often furnished laughter to their hearers, when their imaginations have been too barren to give any other entertainment. But I appeal to the religious themselves, if these allusions are not apt to move laughter, unless a more strong affection of the mind, a religious horror at the profanity of such allusions, prevents their allowing themselves the liberty of laughing at them. Now in this affair I fancy any one will acknowledge that an opinion of superiority is not at all the occasion of the laughter.

Again, any little accident to which we have joined the idea of meanness, befalling a person of great gravity, ability dignity, is a matter of laughter, for the very same reason; thus the strange contortions of the body in a fall, the dirtying of a decent dress, the natural functions which we study to conceal from sight, are matter of laughter, when they occur to observation in persons whom we have high ideas: nay, the very human form has the ideas of dignity so generally joined with it, that even in ordinary persons such mean accidents are matter of jest; but still the jest is increased by the dignity, gravity, or modesty of the person; which shows that it is this contrast, or opposition of ideas of dignity and meanness, which is the occasion of laughter.

We generally imagine in mankind some degree of wisdom above other animals, and have high ideas of them on this account. If then along with our notion of wisdom in our fellows, there occurs any instance of gross inadvertence, or great mistake; this is a great cause of laughter. Our countrymen are very subject to little trips of this kind, and furnish often some diversion to their neighbours, not only by mistakes in their speech, but in actions. Yet even this kind of laughter cannot well be said to arise from our sense of superiority. This alone may give sedate joy, but not be a matter of laughter; since we shall find the same kind of laughter arising in us, where this opinion of superiority does not attend it: for if the most ingenious person in the world, whom the whole company esteems, should thro' inadvertent hearing, or any other mistake, answer quite from the purpose, the whole audience may laugh heartily, without the least abatement of their good opinion. Thus we know some very ingenious men have not in the least suffered in their characters by an extempory pun, which raises the laugh very readily; whereas a premeditated pun, which diminishes our opinion of a writer, will seldom raise any laughter.

Again, the more violent passions, as fear, anger, sorrow, compassion, are generally looked upon as something great and solemn; the beholding of these passions in another, strikes a man with gravity: now if these passions are artfully, or accidentally raised upon a small, or a fictitious occasion, they move the laughter of those who imagine the occasions to be small and contemptible, or who are conscious of the fraud: this is the occasion of the laugh in biting, as they call such deceptions.

According to this scheme, there must necessarily arise a great diversity in men's sentiments of the ridiculous in actions or characters, according as their idea of dignity and wisdom are various. A truly wise man who places the dignity of human nature in good affections and suitable actions, may be apt to laugh at those who employ their most solemn and strong affections about what, to the wise man, appears perhaps very useless or mean. The same solemnity of behaviour and keenness of passion, about a place or ceremony, which ordinary people only employ about the absolute necessaries of life, may make them laugh at their betters. When a gentleman of pleasure, who thinks that good fellowship and gallantry are the only valuable enjoyments of life, observes men with great solemnity and earnestness, heaping up money, without using it, or encumbering themselves with purchases and mortgages, which the gay gentleman with his paternal revenues, thinks very silly affairs, he may make himself very merry upon them: and the frugal man, in his turn, makes the same jest of the man of pleasure. The successful gamester, whom no disaster forces to lay aside the trifling ideas of an amusement in his play, may laugh to see the serious looks and passions of the gravest business, arising in the loser, amidst the ideas of a recreation. There is indeed in these last cases an opinion of superiority in the laughter; but this is not the proper occasion of his laughter; otherwise I see not how we should ever meet with a composed countenance anywhere: men have their different relishes of life, most people prefer their own taste to that of others; but this moves no laughter, unless in representing the pursuits of others, they do join together some whimsical image of opposite ideas.

In the more polite nations there are certain modes of dress, behaviour, ceremony, generally received by all the better sort, as they are commonly called: to these modes, ideas of decency, grandeur, and dignity are generally joined; hence men are fond of imitating the mode: and if in any polite assembly, a contrary dress, behaviour, or ceremony appear, to which we have joined in our country the contrary of ideas of meanness, rusticity, sullenness, a laugh does ordinarily arise, or a disposition to it, in those who have not the thorough good-breeding, or reflection, to restrain themselves, or break thro' these customary associations.

And hence we may see, that what is counted ridiculous in one age or nation, may not be so in another. We are apt to laugh at Homer, when he compares Ajax unwillingly retreating, to an ass driven out of a corn-field; or when he compares him to a boar: or Ulysses tossing all night without sleep through anxiety, to a pudding frying on the coals. Those three families, have got low mean ideas joined to them with us, which it is very probable they had not in Greece in Homer's days; nay, as to one of them, the boar, it is well known, that in some countries in Europe, where they have wild boars for hunting, even in our times, they have not these low sordid ideas joined to that animal, which we have in these kingdoms, who never see them but in their dirty sties, or on dunghills. This may teach us how impertinent a great many jests are, which are made upon the style of some other ancient writings, in ages when

manners were very different from ours, though perhaps fully as rational, and every way as human and just.

III

To treat this subject of laughter gravely, may subject the author to a cen-
sure, like to that which Longinus makes upon a prior treatise of the sublime, because written in a manner very unsuitable to the subject. But yet
it may be worth our pains to consider the effects of laughter, and the
ends for which it was implanted in our nature, [so that] we may know
the proper use of it: which may be done in the following observations.

First, we may observe, that laughter, like many other dispositions of
our mind, is necessarily pleasant to us, when it begins in the natural
manner, from some perception in the mind of something ludicrous, and
does not take its rise unnaturally from external motions in the body.
Every one is conscious that a state of laughter is an easy and agreeable
state, that the recurring or suggestion of ludicrous images tends to dispel fretfulness, anxiety, or sorrow, and to reduce the mind to an easy,
happy state; as on the other hand, an easy and happy state is that in
which we are most lively and acute in perceiving the ludicrous in
objects: any thing that gives us pleasure, puts us also in a fitness for
laughter, when something ridiculous occurs; and ridiculous objects
occurring to a soured temper, will be apt to recover it to easiness. The
implanting then a sense of the ridiculous, in our nature, was giving us an
avenue to pleasure, and an easy remedy for discontent and sorrow.

Again, laughter, like other affections, is very contagious; our whole
frame is so sociable, that one merry countenance may diffuse cheerful-
ness to many; nor are they fools who are apt to laugh before they know
the jest, however curiosity in wise men may restrain it, that their attention may be kept awake.

We are disposed by laughter to a good opinion of the person who
raises it, if neither ourselves nor our friends are made the butt. Laughter
is none of the smallest bonds of common friendships, though it be of less
consequence in great heroic friendships.

If an object, action or event be truly great in every respect, it will have
no natural relation or resemblance to any thing mean or base; and consequently, no mean idea can be joined to it with any natural resemblance. If
we make some forced remote jests upon such subjects, they can never be
pleasing to a man of sense and reflection, but raise contempt of the
ridiculer, as void of just sense of those things which are truly great. As to
any great and truly sublime sentiments, we may perhaps find that, by a
playing upon words, they may be applied to a trifling or mean action, or
object; but this application will not diminish our high idea of the great
sentiment . . .

Let any of our wits try their mettle in ridiculing the opinion of a good
and wise Mind governing the whole universe; let them try to ridicule
integrity and honesty, gratitude, generosity, or the love of one's country,

accompanied with wisdom. All their art will never diminish the admiration which we must have for such dispositions, wherever we observe them pure and unmixed with any low views, or any folly in the exercise of them.

When in any object there is a mixture of what is truly great along with something weak or mean, ridicule may, with a weak mind which cannot separate the great from the mean, bring the whole into disesteem, or make the whole appear weak or contemptible: but with a person of just discernment and reflection it will have no other effect, but to separate what is great from what is not so.

When any object either good or evil is aggravated and increased by the violence of our passions, or an enthusiastic admiration, or fear, the application of ridicule is the readiest way to bring down our high imaginations to a conformity to the real moment or importance of the affair. Ridicule gives our minds as it were a bend to the contrary side; so that upon reflection they may be more capable of settling in a just conformity to nature.

Laughter is received in a different manner by the person ridiculed, according as he who uses the ridicule evidences good nature, friendship, and esteem of the person whom he laughs at; or the contrary.

The enormous crime or grievous calamity of another, is not of itself a subject which can be naturally turned into ridicule: the former raises horror in us, and hatred; and the latter pity. When laughter arises on such occasion, it is not excited by the guilt or the misery. To observe the contortions of the human body in the air, upon the blowing up of an enemy's ship, may raise laughter in those who do not reflect on the agony and distress of the sufferers; but the reflecting on this distress could never move laughter of itself. So some fantastic circumstances accompanying a crime may raise laughter; but a piece of cruel barbarity, or treacherous villainy, of itself must raise very contrary passions. A jest is not ordinary in an impeachment of a criminal, or an invective oration: it rather diminishes than increases the abhorrence in the audience, and may justly raise contempt of the orator for an unnatural affectation of wit. Jesting is still more unnatural in discourses designed to move compassion toward the distressed. A forced unnatural ridicule on either of these occasions, must be apt to raise in the guilty or the miserable hatred against the laugher; since it must be supposed to flow from hatred in him toward the object of his ridicule, or from want of all compassion. The guilty will take laughter to be a triumph over him as contemptible; the miserable will interpret it as hardness of heart, and insensibility of the calamities of another. This is the natural effect of joining either of these objects, mean ludicrous ideas.

If smaller faults, such as are not inconsistent with a character in the main amiable, be set in a ridiculous light, the guilty are apt to be made sensible of their folly, more than by a bare grave admonition. In many of our faults, occasioned by too great violence of some passion, we get such enthusiastic apprehensions of some objects, as lead us to justify our conduct: the joining of opposite ideas or images, allays this enthusiasm; and, if this be done with good nature, it may be the least offensive, and most effectual reproof.

Ridicule upon the smallest faults, when it does not appear to flow from kindness, is apt to be extremely provoking; since the applying of mean ideas to our conduct, discovers contempt of us in the ridiculer, and that he designs to make us contemptible to others.

Ridicule applied to those qualities or circumstances in one of our companions, which neither he nor the ridiculer thinks dishonourable, is agreeable to everyone; the butt himself is as well pleased as any in company.

Ridicule upon any small misfortune or injury, which we have received with sorrow or keen resentment, when it is applied by a third person, with appearance of good nature, is exceeding useful to abate our concern or resentment, and to reconcile us to the person who injured us, if he does not persist in his injury.

From this consideration of the effects of laughter, it may be easy to see for what cause, or end, a sense of the ridiculous was implanted in human nature, and how it ought to be managed.

It is plainly of considerable moment in human society. It is often a great occasion of pleasure, and enlivens our conversation exceedingly, when it is conducted by good nature. It spreads a pleasantry of temper over multitudes at once; and one merry easy mind may by this means diffuse a like disposition over all who are in company. There is nothing of which we are more communicative than of a good jest: and many a man who is incapable of obliging us otherwise, can oblige us by his mirth, and really insinuate himself into our kind affections, and good wishes.

But this is not all the use of laughter. It is well known, that our passions of every kind lead us into wild enthusiastic apprehensions of their several objects. When any object seems great in comparison of ourselves, our minds are apt to run into a perfect veneration: when an object appears formidable, a weak mind will run into a panic, an unreasonable, impotent horror. Now in both these cases, by our sense of the ridiculous, we are made capable of relief from any pleasant, ingenious well-wisher, by more effectual means, than the most solemn, sedate reasoning. Nothing is so properly applied to the false grandeur, either of good or evil, as ridicule: nothing will sooner prevent our excessive admiration of mixed grandeur, or hinder our being led by that, which is, perhaps, really great in such an object, to imitate also and approve what is really meant.

I question not but the jest of Elijah upon the false deity, whom his countrymen had set up, has been very effectual to rectify their notions of the Divine Nature; as we find that like jests have been very seasonable in other nations. Baal, no doubt, had been represented as a great personage of unconquerable power: but how ridiculous does the image appear, when the prophet sets before them, at once, the poor ideas which must arise from such a limitation of nature as could be represented by their statues, and the high ideas of omniscience, and omnipotence, with which the people declared themselves possessed by their invocation. 'Cry aloud, either he is talking, or pursuing, or he is on a journey, or he is asleep'.

This engine of ridicule, no doubt, may be abused, and have a bad effect upon a weak mind; but with men of any reflection, there is little fear that it will ever be very pernicious. An attempt of ridicule before such men, upon a subject every way great, is sure to return upon the author of it ... The only danger is in objects of a mixed nature before people of little judgement, who by jest upon the weak side, are sometimes led into neglect, or contempt, of that which is truly valuable in any character, institution, or office. And this may show us the impertinence, and pernicious tendency of general undistinguished jests upon any character, or office, which has been too much over-rated. But, that ridicule may be abused, does not prove it useless, or unnecessary, more than a like possibility of abuse would prove all our senses, and passions, impertinent, or hurtful. Ridicule, like other edged tools, may do good in a wise man's hands, though fools may cut their fingers with it, or be injurious to any unwary bystander. The rules to avoid abuse of this kind of ridicule, are first, 'either never to attempt ridicule upon what is every way great, whether it be any great being, character, or sentiments': or, if our wit must sometimes run into allusions, on low occasions, to the expressions of great sentiments, 'let it not be in weak company, who have not a just discernment of true grandeur'. And, secondly, concerning objects of a mixed nature, partly great, and partly mean, 'let us never turn the meanness into ridicule, without acknowledging what is truly great, and paying a just veneration to it' ...

Another valuable purpose of ridicule is with relation to smaller vices, which are often more effectually corrected by ridicule, than by grave admonition. Men have been laughed out of faults which a sermon could not reform; nay, there are many little indecencies which are improper to be mentioned in such solemn discourses. Now ridicule with contempt or ill-nature, is indeed always irritating and offensive; but we may, by testifying a just esteem for the good qualities of the person ridiculed, and our concern for his interests, let him see that our ridicule of his weakness flows from love to him, and then we may hope for a good effect. This then is another necessary rule, 'that along with our ridicule of smaller faults we should always join evidences of good nature and esteem'.

As to jests upon imperfections, which one cannot amend, I cannot see of what use they can be: men of sense cannot relish such jests; foolish trifling minds may by them be led to despise the truest merit, which is not exempted from the causal misfortunes of our mortal state. If these imperfections occur along with a vicious character, against which people should be alarmed and cautioned, it is below a wise man to raise aversions to bad men from their necessary infirmities, when they have a juster handle from their vicious dispositions ...

Three

George Turnbull

1698–1748

George Turnbull was born on 11 July 1698, in Alloa Scotland, where his father was minister. He began his studies at the University of Edinburgh 1711, but for a variety of reasons did not graduate until ten years later. While in Edinburgh, Turnbull was an active member of the Rankenian Club, founded in 1716 or 1717 by a group of young students dedicated to the writings of the English philosopher Shaftesbury, whose ideas were one of the sources from which the Scottish enlightenment sprang.

After graduating with a Master of Arts degree from Edinburgh in 1721, Turnbull was appointed regent at Marischal College, Aberdeen, where Thomas Reid was among his students, and in whose work the influence of Turnbull can clearly be detected. It is principally as Reid's teacher that Turnbull is known nowadays, but his writings were importantly innovative in their own right. While Regent at Marischal he introduced the study of Shaftesbury into the moral philosophy curriculum, and became the first Scottish moralist to call for the experimental method in the investigation of morals, a theme taken up much more famously, but later, by David Hume. In a similar vein he powerfully developed the analogy between moral inquiry and the natural sciences. Turnbull did not, as is often thought, owe his ideas to Hutcheson; while teaching at Aberdeen, he drew out the implications of Shaftesbury's thought at the same time as Hutcheson was doing so in Glasgow.

Despite the success with which he exercised intellectual influence on both students and academics in Aberdeen, Turnbull had an altercation with the Principal of Marischal College, and resigned his post in 1727. He found alternative employment accompanying and lecturing young aristocrats on their continental grand tours, but continued to study and write on the subjects he had taught at Marischal. His publications reflect both aspects of his career. The *Principles of Moral Philosophy* was published in 1740, the same year he published *A Treatise on Ancient Painting*. *Observations upon Liberal Education*, which was concerned with education reform, appeared in 1742. In 1739 Turnbull was ordained into the

Anglican Church. He became Rector of a small Irish parish in 1742 and died six years later on a trip to the Netherlands.

In the extract reprinted here Turnbull first sets out the principles upon which the natural world had begun to be investigated far more satisfactorily than ever before, and then explores the extension of these principles to the moral world. Although Turnbull was not the innovator of this parallel between 'natural' and 'moral' philosophy, he gives an especially lucid account of the principles underlying what was to become the standard method of philosophical inquiry across Scotland.

Biographical information: Terrence O. Moore, Jr, introduction to *Observations upon Liberal Education*, Liberty Fund, Indianapolis, 2003

READING III
The Principles of Moral Philosophy[1]

Everyone who knows what natural philosophy is, or how it proceeds in its enquiries will easily conceive what moral philosophy must mean; and how it likewise ought to be pursued: for all enquiries into fact, reality, or any part of nature must be set about, and carried on in the same way; and an enquiry into human nature is as much an enquiry into fact, as any question about the frame and texture (for instance) of any plant, or of the human body.

The objects of science are justly divided into corporeal, or sensible ones; and those which not being perceived by the outward senses, but by reflexion on the mind itself and its inward operations, are therefore called intellectual or moral objects. Hence the consideration of the former is styled Physiology, or Natural Philosophy; and that of the other is called Rational, or Moral Philosophy. But however philosophy may be divided; nothing can be more evident, than, that the study of nature, whether in the constitution and economy of the sensible world, or in the frame and government of the moral, must set out from the same first principles, and be carried on in the same method of investigation, induction, and reasoning; since both are enquiries into facts or real constitutions.

What is natural philosophy, how is it defined? or, how are its researches carried on? By it is understood an enquiry into the sensible world: that is 'into general laws, according to which its appearances are produced; and into the beauty, order, and good which these general laws produce'. And therefore in such an enquiry the following maxims are justly laid down as the foundations on which all its reasonings are built; or as the first principles from which all its conclusions are inferred; and without supposing which it cannot proceed one step.

---

[1]   Extracted from *The Principles of Moral Philosophy*, vol. I, New York: Olms, 1976 (reprinted from the original, London: J. Noon, 1740), pp. 1–23

I.   That if the corporeal world be not governed by general laws, it cannot be the object of enquiry or science; and far less of imitation by arts, since imitation necessarily presupposes knowledge of the object imitated; and science presupposes a certain determinate object; or fixed ascertainable relations and connexions of things. Upon the contrary supposition the corporeal world must be absolutely unintelligible. Nature, in order to be understood by us, must always speak the same language to us: it must therefore steadily observe the same general laws in its operations, or work uniformly and according to stated, invariable methods and rules. Those terms, order, beauty, general good, and a whole, which are too familiar to philosophers to need any definition, or explication, plainly include in their meaning, analogy and constancy; uniformity amidst variety; or in other words, the regular observance of general, settled laws in the make and economy, production and operations, or effects of any object to which they are ascribed. Wherever order, fixed connexions, or general laws and unity of design take place, there is certainty in the nature of such objects; and so far therefore knowledge may be acquired. But where these do not obtain, there can be nothing but unconnected independent parts, all must be confusion and disorder; and consequently such a loose disjointed heap of things must be an inexplicable chaos. In one word, science, prudence, government, imitation, and art, necessarily suppose the prevalence of general laws throughout all the objects in nature to which they reach. No being can know itself, project or pursue any scheme, or lay down any maxims for its conduct; but so far as its own constitution is certain; and the connexion of things relative to it are fixed and constant; for so far only, are things ascertainable; and therefore so far only, can rules be drawn from them.

'Nature's operating according to general laws (says a very ingenious philosopher [Berkeley]) is so necessary for letting us into the secret of nature, and for our guidance in the affairs of life, that without it, all reach and compass of thought, all human sagacity could serve to no manner of purpose: it were even impossible there should be any such faculties or powers in the mind'. It is 'this alone, give us that foresight which enables us to regulate our actions for the benefit of life: and without this, we should be eternally at a loss; we could not know how to act any thing that might procure us the least pleasure, or save us from the least pain. That food nourishes, sleep refreshes, and fire warms us; that to sow in the seed-time, is the way to reap in harvest; that to give application is the way to improve and arrive at perfection in knowledge, or in any moral virtue; and in general, that to obtain such or such ends, such or such means are conducive; all this we know, and only can know, by the observation of the settled laws of nature, without which we should be all in uncertainty and confusion, and a grown man no more know how to manage himself in the affairs of life, than an infant just born'.

This first principle in natural philosophy, is therefore indisputable. 'That without the prevalence of general laws there can be no order; and consequently no foresight, no science: and that as all appearances in the corporeal world, which are reducible to general laws are explicable, so such as are not, are utterly inexplicable'. Or in other words, 'such effects as are not always produced in the same way and method, and have always the same consequences and influences, are quite anomalous; they cannot be reduced to any rule or order, and for that reason, no conclusion can be inferred from them'. 'Tis only connexions which take place constantly in the same invariable manner that are ascertainable; or that can lay a foundation for science Theoretical or Practical.

II.   Now those are justly called by philosophers, general laws in the sensible world. To which many effects are conformable. Or which, in other words, are observed to prevail and operate uniformly in it; and regularly to produce like appearances. Thus, for instance, gravitation is concluded to be a general law throughout our mundane system, because all bodies are found to have gravity; not one body within the reach of our observation does not show that quality: but even the most remote ones we are capable of observing, are found to operate according to it; that is, their appearances are reducible to it, as its natural and necessary effects.

This is very justly inferred, because to say, that analogous, or like appearances are not produced according to the same general law; or that they do not proceed from the same general principle, is indeed to say, that they are and are not analogous. Wherever we find analogy, or similarity of effects, there we find the same law prevailing; or so far do we find particular instances of the same property or law; or of the same method of production and operation in nature. All this is really no more [than] asserting, for example, that whatever is produced conformably to a known principle, called gravity, is produced conformably to that principle. This second maxim in natural philosophy is therefore likewise indisputable.

'That those are general laws in a system, which prevail and operate uniformly in that system; or to which many effects in it are reducible and none are repugnant'. Or in other words, 'those effects, however remote from us the objects are, to which they belong, may be justly attributed to that law or property, to which they are reducible, as its natural effects, that is known to be universal, so far as experience can reach; for this very reason that such a known property being sufficient to produce them, is sufficient to account for them' (See Newton's *Principia*, Lib.3. Regulæ philosophandi).

III.   But in the third place, 'Those general laws of the corporeal world are good laws, which by their steady and uniform prevalency produce its good, beauty, and perfection in the whole'. Thus, for instance, gravitation must be a good general law in the sensible or material world, if its uniform operation be conducive to the greatest good, beauty, and perfection of the system. 'Tis needless to define terms to natural philosophers, which are so commonly used by them; and if these terms have any meaning, the following argument must hold good, 'All the interest of intelligent beings require that general laws should prevail, so far as they are concerned; nay, without general laws, there could be no union, no general connexion, and consequently no general beauty, good, or perfection, but all must be tumult, incoherence, and disorder'. It is therefore absolutely good and fit, that general laws should take place; and those laws must be good in a system, which produce in the sum of things, the greater coherence, order, beauty, good, and perfection of that system.

Now from this it necessarily follows, that no particular effects, which flow from good general laws, can be evils absolutely considered, that is, with regard to the whole. No effect, for example, of gravitation can be evil, if gravitation be a good general law in the sense above explained.

There is therefore a third maxim in philosophy, which is beyond all doubt; 'that all the effects of general laws which are good with respect to a whole, are good absolutely considered, or referred to that whole'.

We may then very justly conclude in general, that all effects or appearances in the natural world, are sufficiently explained and accounted for in natural philosophy, which are reduced to good general laws, as so many particular instances of their uniform operation; and that both physically and morally. They are sufficiently explained and accounted for in the physical sense, by being reduced to general laws: for what else is the physical knowledge of a fact in the sensible world, but the knowledge of an effect itself, in its progress, qualities, and influences: or in other words, the knowledge of the manner or order in which it is produced, and in which it operates on other things relating to it; the knowledge of the laws according to which it is produced, works, and is worked upon?

'All philosophers acknowledge (says an excellent one) that the first cause, or producer of the sensible world, must be a mind, whose will gives subsistence and efficacy to all its laws and connexions. The difference there is between natural philosophers and other men with regard to their knowledge of natural phenomena, consists not in an exacter knowledge of the efficient cause, that produces them; for that can be no other than the will of a spirit: but only in a greater largeness of comprehension whereby analogies, harmonies, and agreements are discovered in the works of nature and the particular effects are explained, that is, reduced to general laws'.

But it is needless to dwell longer on this conclusion, since in the language of all natural philosophers (see Sir Isaac Newton's *Principia*. Dr. John Clark's sermons on the origin of evil. The characteristics, &c.), those effects are reckoned to be fully explained in the physical way, which are shown to be particular instances of a general law that had been already inferred from a sufficient variety of fair and unexceptional experiments: and those effects only are said to be unexplained, which are not yet reduced to any known law, or the law of which is not yet understood and ascertained.

Such effects are sufficiently explained, and accounted for morally, when they are reduced to general laws which are proved to be good in the whole; because they are thus shown to proceed from laws that are morally good and just.

Tho' physiology be distinguished from moral philosophy, yet it was needless to suggest to any class of readers, before we used the words, *beauty, order, good* and *perfection*, that these are terms relative to beings capable of pleasure and pain, and of perceiving good order and beauty; or that laws cannot be said to be good or bad, right or wrong, beautiful or imperfect, but with respect to minds or perceiving beings: for pain or pleasure, good or ill, convenience or inconvenience, beauty or deformity, evidently presuppose perceptive faculties. On the one hand, an unperceivable world cannot be the object of knowledge, or enjoyment of any kind; and, on the other, 'tis perceiving beings alone that can enjoy, or to whom existence can be happiness. But from this, it follows, that tho' natural philosophy be commonly distinguished from moral; all the conclusions in natural philosophy, concerning the order, beauty, and perfection of the material world, belong properly to moral philosophy; being inferences that respect the contriver, maker, and governor of the world, and other moral beings capable of understanding its wise, good and beautiful administration, and of being variously affected by its laws and connexions.

In reality, when natural philosophy is carried so far as to reduce phenomena to good general laws, it becomes moral philosophy; and when it stops short of this chief end of all enquiries into the sensible or material world, which is, to be satisfied with regard to the wisdom of its structure and economy; it hardly deserves the name of philosophy in the sense of Socrates, Plato, Lord Verulam, Boyle, Newton, and the other best moral or natural philosophers (see Sir Isaac Newton's *Optics* l.3. p. 345. and Plato's *Pædon*; where we see what Socrates thought natural philosophy ought to aim at, by what he says of the vanity of the natural philosophy of Anaxagoras).

Having thus briefly shown what natural philosophy proposes to do, and upon what foundations it proceeds in establishing any conclusions; let us now see what moral philosophy must be. It is distinguished from physiology (as has been observed), because it enquires chiefly about objects not perceivable by means of our outward organs of sense, but by internal feeling or experience; such as are all our moral powers and faculties, dispositions and affections, the power of comparing ideas, of reasoning or inferring consequences, the power of contracting habits, our sense of beauty and harmony, natural or moral, the desire of society, &c. Even these, however, may very properly be called parts of nature; and by whatever name, they, or the knowledge of them be called, 'tis obvious, that an enquiry about any of them, and the laws and connexions established by the author of nature, with regard to any of them, is as much a question of natural history or of fact, as an enquiry about any of our organs of sense, or about the constitution of any material object whatsoever, and the laws relating to it. And therefore the same principles just mentioned as the foundation of all enquiries and reasonings in natural philosophy, must likewise take place, and be admitted in moral philosophy; that is, in all enquiries and reasonings concerning the human mind, its powers, faculties, dispositions and affections, and the laws relative to them, as well as in all enquiries into the properties of a body.

In truth, these principles must necessarily take place in the explication of any piece of nature that can be understood or explained. They are principles of general nature, which, if they be true in any case, must be universally true; and therefore they must be universally admitted, with regard to every constitution, system or whole, corporeal or incorporeal, natural or moral, that is, body or mind. Whence it results, that with respect to the human mind; to the frame of any mind whatsoever, or in general with respect to any moral system it must be true.

I.   That unless it be so constituted and governed, that all the effects and appearances belonging to it, are the effects of general laws, it must be absolutely unintelligible; it must be complete confusion, irregularity and disorder; it cannot have a certain and determinate nature, but must be made up of analogous, separate, incoherent parts, and operate in a desultory, inconstant manner: that is, it is not a whole; and cannot be the object of government or art, because it cannot be the object of knowledge: for all that can be known of it in such a case, is, that nothing can be ascertained about it; or that it is a *Proteus*, whose changes are without rule, and therefore are absolutely unascertainable.

II. Those must be received as general laws or principles in a moral frame or constitution, which are found by experience to operate uniformly or invariably in that system. Thus, for instance, that habits are contracted by repeated acts, may be justly said to be a general law in our frame, because this law has its effects uniformly and invariably in our natures; or many effects do evidently show a relation to that law as their common source and principle; and not one effect in human nature is repugnant to it; for, in like manner, is gravitation concluded to be a general law in the sensible world.

III. Those must be good principles or laws in the constitution of a mind, or in any moral whole, which are conducive by their steady and uniform operation and prevalency to the greater good, beauty, and perfection of that whole in the sum of things. And therefore no effects which flow from such laws can be evils absolutely considered, or with respect to the whole. Thus the above-mentioned law of habits, must be a good general law in the constitution of the human mind, if its general tendency or influence be contributive to the greater good of the human mind in the sum of things; and no effects of that principle can be absolutely evil; because it is fit and good, that general laws should take place; and those must be good general laws, which are good in the whole, or conducive to the greater order, beauty, and perfection of a whole.

From all which it must necessarily follow, that all those effects, with regard to any moral constitution, are fully explained and accounted for physically and morally, which are reduced to such general laws as have been mentioned, as so many particular instances of their uniform and general prevalency.

To know any moral object physically, can be nothing else but to know what it is, and how it is constituted; or to know its parts, and those references of parts to one another, which make it a certain determinate whole, that works and is operated upon in certain determinable ways.

And to know the final cause, or moral fitness of any constitution, can be nothing else, but to know what good end in the sum of things, all its parts, and all their mutual respects, with all the laws and connexions relative to it, tend to produce. In fine, as different beings as a man and a tree are, yet the knowledge of man and the knowledge of a tree must mean the same kind of knowledge; in either case it is to know what the being is, and to what end it is adapted by its make and texture, and in consequence of the laws and connexions upon which it any wise depends.

All this is too evident to be longer insisted upon. And what is the result of all that has been said? Is it not, that such moral appearances as are reducible to good general laws, will stand upon that same footing in moral philosophy, that those appearances in the natural world do in natural philosophy, which are reducible to good general laws? And that in order to bring moral philosophy, or the knowledge of the moral world, upon the same footing with natural philosophy, or the knowledge of the material world, as it now stands; we must enquire into moral phenomena, in the same manner as we do into physical ones: that is, we must endeavour to find out by experience the good general laws to which they are reducible. For this must hold good in general, that so far as we are able to reduce appearances to a good general law, so far are we able to explain them or account for them. As phenomena which are not the effects of general laws, are in the nature of things absolutely inexplicable; so those which are, can only be explained by reducing them to the general laws of which they are the effects. 'Explaining or accounting for phenomena can mean nothing else; it is not indeed now pretended by any philosopher to mean anything else'.

This conclusion manifestly ensues from what has been said. But lest anyone should be startled at an attempt to treat effects in the same manner, which are evidently of so different natures, as corporeal and moral effects certainly are; or lest any one should have imagined that general laws can only take place with regard to matter and motion, and consequently, that an essay to explain moral appearances by general laws, must involve in it all the absurdity of an attempt to handle effects, which are not mechanical or material, as if they were such: to prevent all such objections, and to proceed more distinctly and surely in this essay, let us just observe here, that though no two things can be more different than a thinking being and a corporeal one; or than moral powers and operations are from passive unperceiving objects, and their qualities and effects; yet the exercises of all the moral powers, dispositions and affections of minds, as necessarily presuppose an established order of nature, or general laws settled by the Author of nature with respect to them; as the exercises of our bodily senses about qualities and effects of corporeal beings, do with regard to them. As we could neither procure nor avoid, by our will and choice, any sensation of our sight, touch, or any other of our senses, had not nature established a certain order, with respect to the succession or conveyance of our sensations, or the methods in which they are produced in us; so in like manner, we could neither acquire knowledge of any kind; contract habits, or attain to any moral perfection whatsoever; unless the Author of our nature had fixed and appointed certain laws relating to our moral powers, and their exercises and acquisitions. Being able to attain to science, to arts, to virtues, as necessarily presupposes a fixed and appointed road to virtue, &c. as being able to move our hands or limbs, does an established order of nature, with respect to these motions, and sensations resulting from them, or attainable by them.

We are not more certain, that sensations are conveyed into or impressed upon our minds, by means of certain organs of sensation in a certain order, than we are sure that we have a certain extent of dominion, or a certain sphere of activity and power allotted to us by nature: that is to say that certain effects, both in the corporeal and moral world, are made to depend, as to their existence or non-existence, upon our will, that they should exist or not exist. That we have such a power, both with regard to several actions of our body and of our mind, is plain matter of experience . . .

But before I proceed to enquire into any of the general laws relative to human nature, and their effects and final causes; it is necessary, in order to give a clear view of the manner in which it is proposed to carry on that enquiry, and of the strict analogy between natural and moral philosophy, to observe:

That as in natural philosophy, though it would be but building a fine visionary Theory or Fable, to draw out a system of consequences the most accurately connected from mere hypotheses, or upon supposition of the existence and operation of properties, and their laws, which experience does not show to be really existent; yet the whole of true natural philosophy is not, for that reason, no more than a system of facts discovered by experiment and observation; but it is a mixture of experiments, with reasonings from experiments: so in the same manner, in moral philosophy, though it would be but to contrive a beautiful, elegant romance, to deduce the best coupled system of conclusions concerning human nature from imaginary suppositions, that have no foundation in nature; yet the whole of true moral philosophy, will not, for that reason, be no more than a collection of facts discovered by experience; but it likewise will be a mixed science of observations, and reasonings from principles known by experience to take place in, or belong to human nature.

In neither case are hypotheses to be any further admitted, than as questions, about the truth or reality of which it is worth while to enquire; but in both we may proceed in the double method of analysis and synthesis: by the former endeavouring to deduce from some certain select effects, the simple powers of nature, and their laws and proportions; from which, by the latter method, we may infer or resolve the nature of other effects. In both cases equally, as soon as certain powers or laws of nature are inferred from experience, we may consider them, reason about them, compare them with other properties, powers and laws; and these powers being found to be real, whatever conclusions necessarily result from such comparisons or reasonings, must be true concerning them; and do therefore denote as certainly some qualities, properties, attendants or consequents of them, as if these had been immediately discovered by experiment, instead of being deduced by strict reasoning, and necessary inference from principles known to be really true by experience . . .

The thing will be sufficiently plain if we take an example. One may draw several conclusions concerning gravity from the nature of the thing, without knowing that it is an universal law of nature; but the moment it is known to be such, all these abstract conclusions concerning the necessary effects of it in certain circumstances, become instead of mere theories, real truths, that is, real parts of the law of gravity, as far as it extends: or though one had never considered gravity in abstract, or made any necessary deductions from its nature and idea, before it was known to be an universal law of bodies; yet after it is found by experience to be such, if any properties, effects or consequences can be drawn from the very consideration of gravity itself, compared with other properties; all such conclusions, the moment they are found out, may be placed to the account of nature, and deemed parts of the natural law of gravity. Thus the laws of centripedal forces have been determined with regard to an ellipsis, parabola, hyperbola, &c. It immediately follows, that if bodies move in such or such a curve, such and such must be the laws of their centripedal forces; and *vice versa*, if the laws of the centripedal forces of bodies are found to be such and such, it immediately follows, that such and such must be the nature of the orbits described by bodies that have such and such centripedal forces.

In like manner in moral philosophy, whatever can be proved to belong to, result from; or contrary wise, to be repugnant to the very definition of intelligence, volition, affection, habit, or any moral power; and a supposed law of such power will become a part of moral philosophy, so soon as such power is known to exist: or *vice versa*, any effects that can only result from such a law, being found by experience to take place, the law itself must be inferred; and so of course all belonging to that law will come into philosophy, as appertaining to it, and be a key to moral nature and its phenomena, as such. Now of this kind of reasonings in moral philosophy, many instances occur in the following enquiry, almost in every chapter, which for that reason above-mentioned, have the same relation to moral philosophy, that abstract mathematical truths have to natural philosophy, and make part of it in the same way as these do of the latter.

In fine, the only thing in enquiries into any part of nature, moral or corporeal, is not to admit any hypothesis as the real solution of appearances, till it is found really to take place in nature, either by immediate experiment, or by necessary reasonings from effects, that unavoidably lead to it as their sole cause, law, or principle. But all demonstrations which show that certain moral ideas must have certain relations, that is, certain agreements and disagreements, are in the same way a key to moral nature, that demonstrations relative to the agreements and disagreements of sensible ideas, as gravity, elasticity, circles, triangles, &c. belong, are applicable, or a key to natural philosophy. So that as the explication of the mundane system, being mixed of reasonings and observations, is properly called mixed mathematics, or mixed natural philosophy; so an account of human nature, mixed of principles inferred from immediate observation, and others deduced from such principles, by reasoning from ideas or definitions, may be called mixed moral philosophy, or mixed metaphysics; for demonstrations about moral ideas are commonly called metaphysical. But the word metaphysic having fallen into contempt, instead of calling this treatise mixed principles, or metaphysical principles, I have simply termed it *The principles of moral philosophy*. I shall not now enquire into the causes that have brought metaphysical reasonings, the name at least, into disrepute: but certainly no one will say, that intelligence, will, affections, or in one word, moral powers, and their relations, are not worth enquiring into, or collecting experiments and reasonings about.

Four

David Hume

1711-1776

David Hume was born in Edinburgh on 26 April 1711. He matriculated at Edinburgh University on 27 February 1723, at the age of eleven, and probably left the University as late as 1726. He took up law, which he abandoned in 1729, worked for a while for a Bristol sugar merchant, and then went to study in France. On his return to Britain he published his first book, *A Treatise of Human Nature*. Since the *Treatise* went almost unnoticed, Hume recast it in a more accessible form and in 1741 and 1742 published two volumes of essays. These were a success and resulted in his work being much more widely read. In 1745 he applied for the Chair of Moral Philosophy at the University of Edinburgh. Though his application was unsuccessful, the events surrounding it made his writings better known, and he became a figure of controversy, whose views on religion, morality and philosophy were regarded by many as dangerous.

In 1745 he accepted a post as tutor to the Marquess of Annandale. But the Marquess was insane and so in May 1746, Hume relinquished this position to become secretary to Lieutenant-General James St Clair, whom he served in England and on the Continent for two years.

In 1748, a new edition of his essays appeared, as well as his *Philosophical Essays Concerning Human Understanding* (he changed the first part of the title to 'An Enquiry' in 1758). In 1751, he published his *Enquiry concerning the Principles of Morals*, and in 1752 his *Political Discourses*. The first collected edition of his *Essays and Treatises on Various Subjects* appeared in 1753 and the first of what was eventually to be six volumes of his *History of England* came out in 1754.

From 1758 to 1763, Hume divided his time between Edinburgh and London, but in 1763, he was appointed Secretary to Lord Hertford in the British Embassy in Paris. He was made Under-Secretary of State, Northern Department in 1767, a post he held until January 1768, returning in the following year to spend the remainder of his life in Edinburgh preparing new editions of his writings. He died there on 25 August 1776.

The account of Hume's sceptical doubts reprinted here, together with the solutions he proposed to them, first appeared in the *Enquiry Concerning Human Understanding*, where he attempted to generate greater interest in his philosophical work by sharpening up the arguments of the earlier *Treatise*, which, in a famous phrase of his, had 'fallen stillborn from the press'. The essay on miracles which appeared in the same place, had no precursor in the *Treatise*. It was an even more obvious attempt to cause an intellectual stir, which it did, but may have been written more to attract attention than to discover the truth. Hume's essay on tragedy, in which he raises the question of how we can take pleasure in the recounting of distressing events, comes from the period in which his writings were more literary than philosophical, but it has been hugely influential in aesthetics and the philosophy of art.

Biographical information: John Vladimir Price, *Thoemmes Dictionary of C18th British Philosophers*.

READING IV
Sceptical Doubts[1]

I

All the objects of human reason or enquiry may naturally be divided into two kinds, to wit, *Relations of Ideas*, and *Matters of Fact*. Of the first kind are the sciences of Geometry, Algebra, and Arithmetic; and in short, every affirmation which is either intuitively or demonstratively certain. *That the square of the hypotenuse is equal to the square of the two sides*, is a proposition which expresses a relation between these figures. *That three times five is equal to the half of thirty*, expresses a relation between these numbers. Propositions of this kind are discoverable by the mere operation of thought, without dependence on what is anywhere existent in the universe. Though there never were a circle or triangle in nature, the truths demonstrated by Euclid would forever retain their certainty and evidence.

Matters of fact, which are the second objects of human reason, are not ascertained in the same manner; nor is our evidence of their truth, however great, of a like nature with the foregoing. The contrary of every matter of fact is still possible; because it can never imply a contradiction, and is conceived by the mind with the same facility and distinctness, as if ever so conformable to reality. *That the sun will not rise tomorrow* is no less intelligible a proposition, and implies no more contradiction than the affirmation, *that it will rise*. We should in vain, therefore, attempt to dem-

---

[1] Extracted from *An Enquiry Concerning Human Understanding*, ed. L.A. Selby-Bigge, Oxford: Clarendon Press, 1902, pp. 25–55.

onstrate its falsehood. Were it demonstratively false, it would imply a contradiction, and could never be distinctly conceived by the mind.

It may, therefore, be a subject worthy of curiosity, to enquire what is the nature of that evidence which assures us of any real existence and matter of fact, beyond the present testimony of our senses, or the records of our memory. This part of philosophy, it is observable, has been little cultivated, either by the ancients or moderns; and therefore our doubts and errors, in the prosecution of so important an enquiry, may be the more excusable; while we march through such difficult paths without any guide or direction. They may even prove useful, by exciting curiosity, and destroying that implicit faith and security, which is the bane of all reasoning and free enquiry. The discovery of defects in the common philosophy, if any such there be, will not, I presume, be a discouragement, but rather an incitement, as is usual, to attempt something more full and satisfactory than has yet been proposed to the public.

All reasonings concerning matter of fact seem to be founded on the relation of *Cause and Effect*. By means of that relation alone we can go beyond the evidence of our memory and senses. If you were to ask a man, why he believes any matter of fact, which is absent; for instance, that his friend is in the country, or in France; he would give you a reason; and this reason would be some other fact; as a letter received from him, or the knowledge of his former resolutions and promises. A man finding a watch or any other machine in a desert island, would conclude that there had once been men in that island. All our reasonings concerning fact are of the same nature. And here it is constantly supposed that there is a connexion between the present fact and that which is inferred from it. Were there nothing to bind them together, the inference would be entirely precarious. The hearing of an articulate voice and rational discourse in the dark assures us of the presence of some person: Why? Because these are the effects of the human make and fabric, and closely connected with it. If we anatomise all the other reasonings of this nature, we shall find that they are founded on the relation of cause and effect, and that this relation is either near or remote, direct or collateral. Heat and light are collateral effects of fire, and the one effect may justly be inferred from the other.

If we would satisfy ourselves, therefore, concerning the nature of that evidence, which assures us of matters of fact, we must enquire how we arrive at the knowledge of cause and effect.

I shall venture to affirm, as a general proposition, which admits of no exception, that the knowledge of this relation is not, in any instance, attained by reasonings *a priori*; but arises entirely from experience, when we find that any particular objects are constantly conjoined with each other. Let an object be presented to a man of ever so strong natural reason and abilities; if that object be entirely new to him, he will not be able, by the most accurate examination of its sensible qualities, to discover any of its causes or effects. Adam, though his rational faculties be supposed, at the very first, entirely perfect, could not have inferred from the fluidity and transparency of water that it would suffocate him, or from the light and warmth of fire that it would consume him. No object ever discovers, by the qualities which appear to the senses, either the causes which produced it, or the effects which will arise from it; nor can our reason, unassisted by experience, ever draw any inference concerning real existence and matter of fact.

This proposition, *that causes and effects are discoverable, not by reason but by experience*, will readily be admitted with regard to such objects, as we remember to have once been altogether unknown to us; since we must be conscious of the utter inability, which we then lay under, of foretelling what would arise from them. Present two smooth pieces of marble to a man who has no tincture of natural philosophy; he will never discover that they will adhere together in such a manner as to require great force to separate them in a direct line, while they make so small a resistance to a lateral pressure. Such events, as bear little analogy to the common course of nature, are also readily confessed to be known only by experience; nor does any man imagine that the explosion of gunpowder, or the attraction of a loadstone, could ever be discovered by arguments *a priori*. In like manner, when an effect is supposed to depend upon an intricate machinery or secret structure of parts, we make no difficulty in attributing all our knowledge of it to experience. Who will assert that he can give the ultimate reason, why milk or bread is proper nourishment for a man, not for a lion or a tiger?

But the same truth may not appear, at first sight, to have the same evidence with regard to events, which have become familiar to us from our first appearance in the world, which bear a close analogy to the whole course of nature, and which are supposed to depend on the simple qualities of objects, without any secret structure of parts. We are apt to imagine that we could discover these effects by the mere operation of our reason, without experience. We fancy, that were we brought on a sudden into this world, we could at first have inferred that one billiard-ball would communicate motion to another upon impulse; and that we needed not to have waited for the event, in order to pronounce with certainty concerning it. Such is the influence of custom, that, where it is strongest, it not only covers our natural ignorance, but even conceals itself, and seems not to take place, merely because it is found in the highest degree.

But to convince us that all the laws of nature, and all the operations of bodies without exception, are known only by experience, the following reflections may, perhaps, suffice. Were any object presented to us, and were we required to pronounce concerning the effect, which will result from it, without consulting past observation; after what manner, I beseech you, must the mind proceed in this operation? It must invent or imagine some event, which it ascribes to the object as its effect; and it is plain that this invention must be entirely arbitrary. The mind can never possibly find the effect in the supposed cause, by the most accurate scrutiny and examination. For the effect is totally different from the cause, and consequently can never be discovered in it. Motion in the second billiard-ball is a quite distinct event from motion in the first; nor is there anything in the one to suggest the smallest hint of the other. A stone or piece of metal raised into the air, and left without any support, immediately falls: but to consider the matter *a priori*, is there anything we discover in this situation which can beget the idea of a downward, rather than an upward, or any other motion, in the stone or metal?

And as the first imagination or invention of a particular effect, in all natural operations, is arbitrary, where we consult not experience; so must we also esteem the supposed tie or connexion between the cause and effect, which binds them together, and renders it impossible that any other effect could result from the operation of that cause. When I see, for instance, a billiard-ball moving in a straight line towards another; even suppose motion in the second ball should by accident be suggested to me, as the result of their contact or impulse; may I not conceive, that a hundred different events might as well follow from that cause? May not both these balls remain at absolute rest? May not the first ball return in a straight line, or leap off from the second in any line or direction? All these suppositions are consistent and conceivable. Why then should we give the preference to one, which is no more consistent or conceivable than the rest? All our reasonings *a priori*, will never be able to show us any foundation for this preference.

In a word, then, every effect is a distinct event from its cause. It could not, therefore, be discovered in the cause, and the first invention or conception of it, *a priori*, must be entirely arbitrary. And even after it is suggested, the conjunction of it with the cause must appear equally arbitrary; since there are always many other effects, which, to reason, must seem fully as consistent and natural. In vain, therefore, should we pretend to determine any single event, or infer any cause or effect, without the assistance of observation and experience.

Hence we may discover the reason why no philosopher, who is rational and modest, has ever pretended to assign the ultimate cause of any natural operation, or to show distinctly the action of that power, which produces any single effect in the universe. It is confessed, that the utmost effort of human reason is to reduce the principles, productive of natural phenomena, to a greater simplicity, and to resolve the many particular effects into a few general causes, by means of reasonings from analogy, experience, and observation. But as to the causes of these general causes, we should in vain attempt their discovery; nor shall we ever be able to satisfy ourselves, by any particular explication of them. These ultimate springs and principles are totally shut up from human curiosity and enquiry. Elasticity, gravity, cohesion of parts, communication of motion by impulse; these are probably the ultimate causes and principles which we shall ever discover in nature; and we may esteem ourselves sufficiently happy, if, by accurate enquiry and reasoning, we can trace up the particular phenomena to, or near to, these general principles. The most perfect philosophy of the natural kind only staves off our ignorance a little longer: as perhaps the most perfect philosophy of the moral or metaphysical kind serves only to discover larger portions of it. Thus the observation of human blindness and weakness is the result of all philosophy, and meets us at every turn, in spite of our endeavours to elude or avoid it.

Nor is geometry, when taken into the assistance of natural philosophy, ever able to remedy this defect, or lead us into the knowledge of ultimate causes, by all the accuracy of reasoning for which it is so justly celebrated. Every part of mixed mathematics proceeds upon the supposition that certain laws are established by nature in her operations; and abstract reasonings are employed, either to assist experience in the discovery of these laws, or to determine their influence in particular instances, where it depends upon any precise degree of distance and quantity. Thus, it is a law of motion, discovered by experience, that the moment or force of any body in motion is in the compound ratio or proportion of its solid contents and its velocity; and consequently, that a small force may remove the greatest obstacle or raise the greatest weight, if, by any contrivance or machinery, we can increase the velocity of that force, so as to make it an overmatch for its antagonist. Geometry assists us in the application of this law, by giving us the just dimensions of all the parts and figures which can enter into any species of machine; but still the discovery of the law itself is owing merely to experience, and all the abstract reasonings in the world could never lead us one step towards the knowledge of it. When we reason *a priori*, and consider merely any object or cause, as it appears to the mind, independent of all observation, it never could suggest to us the notion of any distinct object, such as its effect; much less, show us the inseparable and inviolable connexion between them. A man must be very sagacious who could discover by reasoning that crystal is the effect of heat, and ice of cold, without being previously acquainted with the operation of these qualities.

II

But we have not yet attained any tolerable satisfaction with regard to the question first proposed. Each solution still gives rise to a new question as difficult as the foregoing, and leads us on to farther enquiries. When it is asked, *What is the nature of all our reasonings concerning matter of fact?* the proper answer seems to be, that they are founded on the relation of cause and effect. When again it is asked, *What is the foundation of all our reasonings and conclusions concerning that relation?* it may be replied in one word, Experience. But if we still carry on our sifting humour, and ask, *What is the foundation of all conclusions from experience?* this implies a new question, which may be of more difficult solution and explication. Philosophers, that give themselves airs of superior wisdom and sufficiency, have a hard task when they encounter persons of inquisitive dispositions, who push them from every corner to which they retreat, and who are sure at last to bring them to some dangerous dilemma. The best expedient to prevent this confusion, is to be modest in our pretensions; and even to discover the difficulty ourselves before it is objected to us. By this means, we may make a kind of merit of our very ignorance.

I shall content myself, in this section, with an easy task, and shall pretend only to give a negative answer to the question here proposed. I say then, that, even after we have experience of the operations of cause and effect, our conclusions from that experience are *not* founded on reasoning, or any process of the understanding. This answer we must endeavour both to explain and to defend.

It must certainly be allowed, that nature has kept us at a great distance from all her secrets, and has afforded us only the knowledge of a few superficial qualities of objects; while she conceals from us those powers and principles on which the influence of those objects entirely depends. Our senses inform us of the colour, weight, and consistence of bread; but neither sense nor reason can ever inform us of those qualities which fit it for the nourishment and support of a human body. Sight or feeling conveys an idea of the actual motion of bodies; but as to that wonderful force or power, which would carry on a moving body forever in a continued change of place, and which bodies never lose but by communicating it to others; of this we cannot form the most distant conception. But notwithstanding this ignorance of natural powers and principles, we always presume, when we see like sensible qualities, that they have like secret powers, and expect that effects, similar to those which we have experienced, will follow from them. If a body of like colour and consistence with that bread, which we have formerly eaten, be presented to us, we make no scruple of repeating the experiment, and foresee, with certainty, like nourishment and support. Now this is a process of the mind or thought, of which I would willingly know the foundation. It is allowed on all hands that there is no known connexion between the sensible qualities and the secret powers; and consequently, that the mind is not led to form such a conclusion concerning their constant and regular conjunction, by anything which it knows of their nature. As to past *experience*, it can be allowed to give *direct* and *certain* information of those precise objects only, and that precise period of time, which fell under its cognisance: but why this experience should be extended to future times, and to other objects, which for aught we know, may be only in appearance similar; this is the main question on which I would insist. The bread, which I formerly ate, nourished me; that is, a body of such sensible qualities was, at that time, endued with such secret powers: but does it follow, that other bread must also nourish me at another time, and that like sensible qualities must always be attended with like secret powers? The consequence seems nowise necessary. At least, it must be acknowledged that there is here a consequence drawn by the mind; that there is a certain step taken; a process of thought, and an inference, which wants to be explained. These two propositions are far from being the same, *I have found that such an object has always been attended with such an effect*, and *I foresee, that other objects, which are, in appearance, similar, will be attended with similar effects*. I shall allow, if you please, that the one proposition may justly be inferred from the other: I know, in fact, that it always is inferred. But if you insist that the inference is made by a chain of reasoning, I desire you to produce that reasoning. The connexion between these propositions is not intuitive. There is required a medium, which may enable the mind to draw such an inference, if needed it be drawn by reasoning and argument. What that medium is, I must confess, passes my comprehension; and it is incumbent on those to produce it, who assert that it really exists, and is the origin of all our conclusions concerning matter of fact.

This negative argument must certainly, in process of time, become altogether convincing, if many penetrating and able philosophers shall turn their enquiries this way and no one be ever able to discover any connecting proposition or intermediate step, which supports the understanding in this conclusion. But as the question is yet new, every reader may not trust so far to his own penetration, as to conclude, because an argument escapes his enquiry, that therefore it does not really exist. For this reason it may be requisite to venture upon a more difficult task, and enumerating all the branches of human knowledge, endeavour to show that none of them can afford such an argument.

All reasonings may be divided into two kinds, namely, demonstrative reasoning, or that concerning relations of ideas, and moral reasoning, or that concerning matter of fact and existence. That there are no demonstrative arguments in the case seems evident, since it implies no contradiction that the course of nature may change, and that an object, seemingly like those which we have experienced, may be attended with different or contrary effects. May I not clearly and distinctly conceive that a body, falling from the clouds, and which, in all other respects, resembles snow, has yet the taste of salt or feeling of fire? Is there any more intelligible proposition than to affirm, that all the trees will flourish in December and January, and decay in May and June? Now whatever is intelligible, and can be distinctly conceived, implies no contradiction, and can never be proved false by any demonstrative argument or abstract reasoning *a priori*.

If we be, therefore, engaged by arguments to put trust in past experience, and make it the standard of our future judgement, these arguments must be probable only, or such as regard matter of fact and real existence, according to the division above mentioned. But that there is no argument of this kind, must appear, if our explication of that species of reasoning be admitted as solid and satisfactory. We have said that all arguments concerning existence are founded on the relation of cause and effect; that our knowledge of that relation is derived entirely from experience; and that all our experimental conclusions proceed upon the supposition that the future will be conformable to the past. To endeavour, therefore, the proof of this last supposition by probable arguments, or arguments regarding existence, must be evidently going in a circle, and taking that for granted, which is the very point in question.

In reality, all arguments from experience are founded on the similarity which we discover among natural objects, and by which we are induced to expect effects similar to those which we have found to follow from such objects. And though none but a fool or madman will ever pretend to dispute the authority of experience, or to reject that great guide of human life, it may surely be allowed a philosopher to have so much curiosity at least as to examine the principle of human nature, which gives this mighty authority to experience, and makes us draw advantage from that similarity which nature has placed among different objects. From causes which appear *similar* we expect similar effects. This is the sum of all our experimental conclusions. Now it seems evident that, if this conclusion were formed by reason, it would be as perfect at first, and upon one instance, as after ever so long a course of experience. But the case is far otherwise. Nothing is so like as eggs; yet no one, on account of this appearing similarity, expects the same taste and relish in all of them. It is only after a long course of uniform experiments in any kind, that we attain a firm reliance and security with regard to a particular event. Nowhere is that process of reasoning which, from one instance, draws a conclusion, so different from that which it infers from a hundred instances that are nowise different from that single one? This question I propose as much for the sake of information, as with an intention of raising difficulties. I cannot find, I cannot imagine any such reasoning. But I keep my mind still open to instruction, if any one will vouchsafe to bestow it on me.

Should it be said that, from a number of uniform experiments, we *infer* a connexion between the sensible qualities and the secret powers; this, I must confess seems the same difficulty, couched in different terms. The question still recurs, on what process of argument this *inference* is founded? Where is the medium, the interposing ideas, which join propositions so very wide of each other? It is confessed that the colour, consistence, and other sensible qualities of bread appear not, of themselves, to have any connexion with the secret powers of nourishment and support. For otherwise we could infer these secret powers from the first appearance of these sensible qualities, without the aid of experience; contrary to the sentiment of all philosophers, and contrary to plain matter of fact. Here, then, is our natural state of ignorance with regard to the powers and influence of all objects. How is this remedied by experience? It only shows us a number of uniform effects, resulting from certain objects, and teaches us that those particular objects, at that particular time, were endowed with such powers and forces. When a new object, endowed with similar sensible qualities, is produced, we expect similar powers and forces, and look for a like effect. From a body of like colour and consistence with bread we expect like nourishment and support. But this surely is a step or progress of the mind, which wants to be explained. When a man says, *I have found, in all past instances, such sensible qualities conjoined with such secret powers*: And when he says, *Similar sensible qualities will always be conjoined with similar secret powers*, he is not guilty of a tautology, nor are these propositions in any respect the same. You say that the one proposition is an inference from the other. But you must confess that the inference is not intuitive; neither is it demonstrative: Of what nature is it, then? To say it is experimental, is begging the question. For all inferences from experience suppose, as their foundation, that the future will resemble the past, and that similar powers will be conjoined with similar sensible qualities. If there be any suspicion that the course of nature may change, and that the past may be no rule for the future, all experience becomes useless, and can give rise to no inference or conclusion. It is impossible, therefore, that any arguments from experience can prove this resemblance of the past to the future; since all these arguments are founded on the supposition of that resemblance. Let the course of things be allowed hitherto ever so regular; that alone, without some new argument or inference, proves not that, for the future, it will continue so. In vain do you pretend to have learned the nature of bodies from your past experience. Their secret nature, and consequently all their effects and influence, may change, without any change in their sensible qualities. This happens sometimes, and with regard to some objects: Why may it not happen always, and with regard to all objects? What logic, what process of argument secures you against this supposition? My practice, you say, refutes my doubts. But you mistake the purport of my question. As an agent, I am quite satisfied in the point; but as a philosopher, who has some share of curiosity, I will not say scepticism, I want to learn the foundation of this inference. No reading, no enquiry has yet been able to remove my difficulty, or give me satisfaction in a matter of such importance. Can I do better than propose the difficulty to the public, even though, perhaps, I shall have small hopes of obtaining a solution? We shall at least, by this means, be sensible of our ignorance, if we do not augment our knowledge.

I must confess that a man is guilty of unpardonable arrogance who concludes, because an argument has escaped his own investigation, that therefore it does not really exist. I must also confess that, though all the learned, for several ages, should have employed themselves in fruitless search upon any subject, it may still, perhaps, be rash to conclude positively that the subject must, therefore, pass all human comprehension. Even though we examine all the sources of our knowledge, and conclude them unfit for such a subject, there may still remain a suspicion, that the enumeration is not complete, or the examination not accurate.

But with regard to the present subject, there are some considerations which seem to remove all this accusation of arrogance or suspicion of mistake.

It is certain that the most ignorant and stupid peasants — nay infants, nay even brute beasts — improve by experience, and learn the qualities of natural objects, by observing the effects which result from them. When a child has felt the sensation of pain from touching the flame of a candle, he will be careful not to put his hand near any candle; but will expect a similar effect from a cause which is similar in its sensible qualities and appearance. If you assert, therefore, that the understanding of the child is led into this conclusion by any process of argument or ratiocination, I may justly require you to produce that argument; nor have you any pretence to refuse so equitable a demand. You cannot say that the argument is abstruse, and may possibly escape your enquiry; since you confess that it is obvious to the capacity of a mere infant. If you hesitate, therefore, a moment, or if, after reflection, you produce any intricate or profound argument, you, in a manner, give up the question, and confess that it is not reasoning which engages us to suppose the past resembling the future, and to expect similar effects from causes which are, to appearance, similar. This is the proposition which I intended to enforce in the present section. If I be right, I pretend not to have made any mighty discovery. And if I be wrong, I must acknowledge myself to be indeed a very backward scholar; since I cannot now discover an argument which, it seems, was perfectly familiar to me long before I was out of my cradle.

Sceptical Solution of These Doubts

I

The passion for philosophy, like that for religion, seems liable to this inconvenience, that, though it aims at the correction of our manners, and extirpation of our vices, it may only serve, by imprudent management, to foster a predominant inclination, and push the mind, with more determined resolution, towards that side which already *draws* too much, by the bias and propensity of the natural temper. It is certain that, while we aspire to the magnanimous firmness of the philosophic sage, and endeavour to confine our pleasures altogether within our own minds, we may, at last, render our philosophy like that of Epictetus, and other Stoics, only a more refined system of selfishness, and reason ourselves out of all virtue as well as social enjoyment. While we study with attention the vanity of human life, and turn all our thoughts towards the empty and transitory nature of riches and honours, we are, perhaps, all the while flattering our natural indolence, which, hating the bustle of the world, and drudgery of business, seeks a pretence of reason to give itself a full and uncontrolled indulgence. There is, however, one species of philosophy which seems little liable to this inconvenience, and that because it strikes in with no disorderly passion of the human mind, nor can mingle itself with any natural affection or propensity; and that is the Academic or Sceptical philosophy. The academics always talk of doubt and suspense of judgement, of danger in hasty determinations, of confining to very narrow bounds the enquiries of the understanding, and of renouncing all speculations which lie not within the limits of common life and practice. Nothing, therefore, can be more contrary than such a philosophy to the supine indolence of the mind, its rash arrogance, its lofty pretensions, and it superstitious credulity. Every passion is mortified by it, except the love of truth; and that passion never is, nor can be, carried to too high a degree. It is surprising, therefore, that this philosophy, which, in almost every instance, must be harmless and innocent, should be the subject of so much groundless reproach and obloquy. But, perhaps, the very circumstance which renders it so innocent is what chiefly exposes it to the public hatred and resentment. By flattering no irregular passion, it gains few partisans: By opposing so many vices and follies, it raises to itself abundance of enemies, who stigmatise it as libertine, profane, and irreligious.

Nor need we fear that this philosophy, while it endeavours to limit our enquiries to common life, should ever undermine the reasonings of common life, and carry its doubts so far as to destroy all action, as well as speculation. Nature will always maintain her rights, and prevail in the end over any abstract reasoning whatsoever. Though we should conclude, for instance, as in the foregoing section, that, in all reasonings from experience, there is a step taken by the mind which is not supported by any argument or process of the understanding; there is no danger that these reasonings, on which almost all knowledge depends, will ever be affected by such a discovery. If the mind be not engaged by argument to make this step, it must be induced by some other principle of equal weight and authority; and that principle will preserve its influence as long as human nature remains the same. What that principle is may well be worth the pains of enquiry.

Suppose a person, though endowed with the strongest faculties of reason and reflection, to be brought on a sudden into this world; he would, indeed, immediately observe a continual succession of objects, and one event following another; but he would not be able to discover anything farther. He would not, at first, by any reasoning, be able to reach the idea of cause and effect; since the particular powers, by which all natural operations are performed, never appear to the senses; nor is it reasonable to conclude, merely because one event, in one instance, precedes another, that therefore the one is the cause, the other the effect. Their conjunction may be arbitrary and casual. There may be no reason to infer the existence of one from the appearance of the other. And in a word, such a person, without more experience, could never employ his conjecture or reasoning concerning any matter of fact, or be assured of anything beyond what was immediately present to his memory and senses.

Suppose, again, that he has acquired more experience, and has lived so long in the world as to have observed familiar objects or events to be constantly conjoined together; what is the consequence of this experience? He immediately infers the existence of one object from the appearance of the other. Yet he has not, by all his experience, acquired any idea or knowledge of the secret power by which the one object produces the other; nor is it, by any process of reasoning, he is engaged to draw this inference. But still he finds himself determined to draw it: And though he should be convinced that his understanding has no part in the operation, he would nevertheless continue in the same course of thinking. There is some other principle which determines him to form such a conclusion.

This principle is Custom or Habit. For wherever the repetition of any particular act or operation produces a propensity to renew the same act or operation, without being impelled by any reasoning or process of the understanding, we always say, that this propensity is the effect of *Custom*. By employing that word, we pretend not to have given the ultimate reason of such a propensity. We only point out a principle of human nature, which is universally acknowledged, and which is well known by its effects. Perhaps we can push our enquiries no farther, or pretend to give the cause of this cause; but must rest contented with it as the ultimate principle, which we can assign, of all our conclusions from experience. It is sufficient satisfaction, that we can go so far, without repining at the narrowness of our faculties because they will carry us no farther. And it is certain we here advance a very intelligible proposition at least, if not a true one, when we assert that, after the constant conjunction of two objects — heat and flame, for instance, weight and solidity — we are determined by custom alone to expect the one from the appearance of the other. This hypothesis seems even the only one which explains the difficulty, why we draw, from a thousand instances, an inference which we are not able to draw from one instance, that is, in no respect, different from them. Reason is incapable of any such variation. The conclusions which it draws from considering one circle are the same which it would form upon surveying all the circles in the universe. But no man, having seen only one body move after being impelled by another, could infer that every body will move after a like impulse. All inferences from experience, therefore, are effects of custom, not of reasoning.

Custom, then, is the great guide of human life. It is that principle alone which renders our experience useful to us, and makes us expect, for the future, a similar train of events with those which have appeared in the past. Without the influence of custom, we should be entirely ignorant of every matter of fact beyond what is immediately present to the memory and senses. We should never know how to adjust means to ends, or to employ our natural powers in the production of any effect. There would be an end at once of all action, as well as of the chief part of speculation.

But here it may be proper to remark, that though our conclusions from experience carry us beyond our memory and senses, and assure us of matters of fact which happened in the most distant places and most remote ages, yet some fact must always be present to the senses or memory, from which we may first proceed in drawing these conclusions. A man, who should find in a desert country the remains of pompous buildings, would conclude that the country had, in ancient times, been cultivated by civilized inhabitants; but did nothing of this nature occur to him, he could never form such an inference. We learn the events of former ages from history; but then we must peruse the volumes in which this instruction is contained, and thence carry up our inferences from one testimony to another, till we arrive at the eyewitnesses and spectators of these distant events. In a word, if we proceed not upon some fact, present to the memory or senses, our reasonings would be merely hypothetical; and however the particular links might be connected with each other, the whole chain of inferences would have nothing to support it, nor could we ever, by its means, arrive at the knowledge of any real existence. If I ask why you believe any particular matter of fact, which you relate, you must tell me some reason; and this reason will be some other fact, connected with it. But as you cannot proceed after this manner, *in infinitum*, you must at last terminate in some fact, which is present to your memory or senses; or must allow that your belief is entirely without foundation.

What, then, is the conclusion of the whole matter? A simple one; though, it must be confessed, pretty remote from the common theories of philosophy. All belief of matter of fact or real existence is derived merely from some object, present to the memory or senses, and a customary conjunction between that and some other object. Or in other words; having found, in many instances, that any two kinds of objects — flame and heat, snow and cold — have always been conjoined together; if flame or snow be presented anew to the senses, the mind is carried by custom to expect heat or cold, and to *believe* that such a quality does exist, and will discover itself upon a nearer approach. This belief is the necessary result of placing the mind in such circumstances. It is an operation of the soul, when we are so situated, as unavoidable as to feel the passion of love, when we receive benefits; or hatred, when we meet with injuries. All these operations are a species of natural instincts, which no reasoning or process of the thought and understanding is able either to produce or to prevent.

At this point, it would be very allowable for us to stop our philosophical researches. In most questions we can never make a single step farther; and in all questions we must terminate here at last, after our most restless and curious enquiries. But still our curiosity will be pardonable, perhaps commendable, if it carry us on to still farther researches, and make us examine more accurately the nature of this *belief*, and of the *customary conjunction*, whence it is derived. By this means we may meet with some explications and analogies that will give satisfaction; at least to such as love the abstract sciences, and can be entertained with speculations, which, however accurate, may still retain a degree of doubt and uncertainty. As to readers of a different taste; the remaining part of this section is not calculated for them, and the following enquiries may well be understood, though it be neglected.

II

Nothing is more free than the imagination of man, and though it cannot exceed that original stock of ideas furnished by the internal and external senses, it has unlimited power of mixing, compounding, separating, and dividing these ideas, in all the varieties of fiction and vision. It can feign a train of events, with all the appearance of reality, ascribe to them a particular time and place, conceive them as existent, and paint them out to itself with every circumstance, that belongs to any historical fact, which it believes with the greatest certainty. Wherein, therefore, consists the difference between such a fiction and belief? It lies not merely in any peculiar idea, which is annexed to such a conception as commands our assent, and which is wanting to every known fiction. For as the mind has authority over all its ideas, it could voluntarily annex this particular idea to any fiction, and consequently be able to believe whatever it pleases, contrary to what we find by daily experience. We can, in our conception, join the head of a man to the body of a horse; but it is not in our power to believe that such an animal has ever really existed.

It follows, therefore, that the difference between *fiction* and *belief* lies in some sentiment or feeling, which is annexed to the latter, not to the former, and which depends not on the will, nor can be commanded at pleasure. It must be excited by nature, like all other sentiments, and must arise from the particular situation, in which the mind is placed at any particular juncture. Whenever any object is presented to the memory or senses, it immediately, by the force of custom, carries the imagination to conceive that object, which is usually conjoined to it; and this conception is attended with a feeling or sentiment, different from the loose reveries of the fancy. In this consists the whole nature of belief. For as there is no matter of fact which we believe so firmly that we cannot conceive the contrary, there would be no difference between the conception assented to and that which is rejected, were it not for some sentiment which distinguishes the one from the other. If I see a billiard-ball moving towards another, on a smooth table, I can easily conceive it to stop upon contact. This conception implies no contradiction; but still it feels very differently from that conception by which I represent to myself the impulse and the communication of motion from one ball to another.

Were we to attempt a *definition* of this sentiment, we should, perhaps, find it a very difficult, if not an impossible task; in the same manner as if we should endeavour to define the feeling of cold or passion of anger, to a creature who never had any experience of these sentiments. Belief is the true and proper name of this feeling; and no one is ever at a loss to know the meaning of that term; because every man is every moment conscious of the sentiment represented by it. It may not, however, be improper to attempt a *description* of this sentiment; in hopes we may, by that means, arrive at some analogies, which may afford a more perfect explication of it. I say, then, that belief is nothing but a more vivid, lively, forcible, firm, steady conception of an object, than what the imagination alone is ever able to attain. This variety of terms, which may seem so unphilosophical, is intended only to express that act of mind, which renders realities, or what is taken for such, more present to us than fictions, causes them to weigh more in the thought, and gives them a superior influence on the passions and imagination. Provided we agree about the thing, it is needless to dispute about the terms. The imagination has the command over all its ideas, and can join and mix and vary them, in all the ways possible. It may conceive fictitious objects with all the circumstances of place and time. It may set them, in a manner, before our eyes, in their true colours, just as they might have existed. But as it is impossible that this faculty of imagination can ever, of itself, reach belief, it is evident that belief consists not in the peculiar nature or order of ideas, but in the *manner* of their conception, and in their *feeling* to the mind. I confess, that it is impossible perfectly to explain this feeling or manner of conception. We may make use of words which express something near it. But its true and proper name, as we observed before, is *belief*; which is a term that everyone sufficiently understands in common life. And in philosophy, we can go no farther than assert, that *belief* is something felt by the mind, which distinguishes the ideas of the judgement from the fictions of the imagination. It gives them more weight and influence; makes them appear of greater importance; enforces them in the mind; and render them the governing principle of our actions. I hear at present, for instance, a person's voice, with whom I am acquainted; and the sound comes as from the next room. This impression of my senses immediately conveys my thought to the person, together with all the surrounding objects. I paint them out to myself as existing at present, with the same qualities and relations, of which I formerly knew them possessed. These ideas take faster hold of my mind than ideas of an enchanted castle. They are very different to the feeling, and have a much greater influence of every kind, either to give pleasure or pain, joy or sorrow.

Let us, then, take in the whole compass of this doctrine, and allow, that the sentiment of belief is nothing but a conception more intense and steady than what attends the mere fictions of the imagination, and that this *manner* of conception arises from a customary conjunction of the object with something present to the memory or senses: I believe that it will not be difficult, upon these suppositions, to find other operations of the mind analogous to it, and to trace up these phenomena to principles still more general.

We have already observed that nature has established connexions among particular ideas, and that no sooner one idea occurs to our thoughts than it introduces its correlative, and carries our attention towards it, by a gentle and insensible movement. These principles of connexion or association we have reduced to three, namely, *Resemblance, Contiguity,* and *Causation;* which are the only bonds that unite our thoughts together, and beget that regular train of reflection or discourse, which, in a greater or less degree, takes place among all mankind. Now here arises a question, on which the solution of the present difficulty will depend. Does it happen, in all these relations, that, when one of the objects is presented to the sense or memory, the mind is not only carried to the conception of the correlative, but reaches a steadier and stronger conception of it than what otherwise it would have been able to attain? This seems to be the case with that belief which arises from the relation of cause and effect. And if the case be the same with the other relations or principles of associations, this may be established as a general law, which takes place in all the operations of the mind.

We may, therefore, observe, as the first experiment to our present purpose, that, upon the appearance of the picture of an absent friend, our idea of him is evidently enlivened by the *resemblance,* and that every passion, which that idea occasions, whether of joy or sorrow, acquires new force and vigour. In producing this effect, there concur both a relation and a present impression. Where the picture bears him no resemblance, at least was not intended for him, it never so much as conveys our thought to him: And where it is absent, as well as the person, though the mind may pass from the thought of the one to that of the other, it feels its idea to be rather weakened than enlivened by that transition. We take a pleasure in viewing the picture of a friend, when it is set before us; but when it is removed, rather choose to consider him directly than by reflection in an image, which is equally distant and obscure . . .

We may add force to these experiments by others of a different kind, in considering the effects of *contiguity* as well as of *resemblance.* It is certain that distance diminishes the force of every idea, and that, upon our approach to any object, though it does not discover itself to our senses, it operates upon the mind with an influence, which imitates an immediate impression. The thinking on any object readily transports the mind to what is contiguous; but it is only the actual presence of an object, that transports it with a superior vivacity. When I am a few miles from home, whatever relates to it touches me more nearly than when I am two hundred leagues distant; though even at that distance the reflecting on anything in the neighbourhood of my friends or family naturally produces an idea of them. But as in this latter case, both the objects of the mind are ideas; notwithstanding there is an easy transition between them, that transition alone is not able to give a superior vivacity to any of the ideas, for want of some immediate impression.

No one can doubt but causation has the same influence as the other two relations of resemblance and contiguity. Superstitious people are fond of the relics of saints and holy men, for the same reason, that they seek after types or images, in order to enliven their devotion, and give them a more intimate and strong conception of those exemplary lives, which they desire to imitate. Now it is evident, that one of the best relics, which a devotee could procure, would be the handiwork of a saint; and if his clothes and furniture are ever to be considered in this light, it is because they were once at his disposal, and were moved and affected by him; in which respect they are to be considered as imperfect effects, and as connected with him by a shorter chain of consequences than any of those, by which we learn the reality of his existence.

Suppose, that the son of a friend, who had been long dead or absent, were presented to us; it is evident, that this object would instantly revive its correlative idea, and recall to our thoughts all past intimacies and familiarities, in more lively colours than they would otherwise have appeared to us. This is another phenomenon, which seems to prove the principle above mentioned.

We may observe, that, in these phenomena, the belief of the correlative object is always presupposed, without which the relation could have no effect. The influence of the picture supposes, that we *believe* our friend to have once existed. Contiguity to home can never excite our ideas of home, unless we *believe* that it really exists. Now I assert, that this belief, where it reaches beyond the memory or senses, is of a similar nature, and arises from similar causes, with the transition of thought and vivacity of conception here explained. When I throw a piece of dry wood into a fire, my mind is immediately carried to conceive, that it augments, not extinguishes the flame. This transition of thought from the cause to the effect proceeds not from reason. It derives its origin altogether from custom and experience. And as it first begins from an object, present to the senses, it renders the idea or conception of flame more strong and lively than any loose, floating reverie of the imagination. That idea arises immediately. The thought moves instantly towards it, and conveys to it all that force of conception, which is derived from the impression present to the senses. When a sword is levelled at my breast, does not the idea of wound and pain strike me more strongly, than when a glass of wine is presented to me, even though by accident this idea should occur after the appearance of the latter object? But what is there in this whole matter to cause such a strong conception, except only a present object and a customary transition to the idea of another object, which we have been accustomed to conjoin with the former? This is the whole operation of the mind, in all our conclusions concerning matter of fact and existence; and it is a satisfaction to find some analogies, by which it may be explained. The transition from a present object does in all cases give strength and solidity to the related idea.

Here, then, is a kind of pre-established harmony between the course of nature and the succession of our ideas; and though the powers and forces, by which the former is governed, be wholly unknown to us; yet our thoughts and conceptions have still, we find, gone on in the same train with the other works of nature. Custom is that principle, by which this correspondence has been effected; so necessary to the subsistence of our species, and the regulation of our conduct, in every circumstance and occurrence of human life. Had not the presence of an object, instantly excited the idea of those objects, commonly conjoined with it, all our knowledge must have been limited to the narrow sphere of our memory and senses; and we should never have been able to adjust means to ends, or employ our natural powers, either to the producing of good, or avoiding of evil. Those, who delight in the discovery and contemplation of *final causes*, have here ample subject to employ their wonder and admiration.

READING V
Miracles[2]

I

Though experience be our only guide in reasoning concerning matters of fact, it must be acknowledged, that this guide is not altogether infallible, but in some cases is apt to lead us into errors. One who in our climate should expect better weather in any week of June than in one of December, would reason justly and conformably to experience; but it is certain that he may happen, in the event, to find himself mistaken. However, we may observe that, in such a case, he would have no cause to complain of experience, because it commonly informs us beforehand of the uncertainty, by that contrariety of events which we may learn from a diligent observation. All effects follow not with like certainty from their supposed causes. Some events are found, in all countries and all ages, to have been constantly conjoined together: others are found to have been more variable, and sometimes to disappoint our expectations; so that in our reasonings concerning matter of fact, there are all imaginable degrees of assurance, from the highest certainty to the lowest species of moral evidence.

A wise man, therefore, proportions his belief to the evidence. In such conclusions as are founded on an infallible experience, he expects the event with the last degree of assurance, and regards his past experience

---

[2] Extracted from *An Enquiry Concerning Human Understanding*, ed. L.A. Selby-Bigge, Oxford: Clarendon Press, 1902, pp. 109-31.

as a full *proof* of the future existence of that event. In other cases he proceeds with more caution: he weighs the opposite experiments: he considers which side is supported by the greater number of experiments: to
that side he inclines with doubt and hesitation; and when at last he fixes
his judgment, the evidence exceeds not what we properly call *probability*.
All probability, then, supposes an opposition of experiments and observations, where the one side is found to overbalance the other, and to produce a degree of evidence proportioned to the superiority. A hundred
instances or experiments on one side, and fifty on another, afford a
doubtful expectation of any event; though a hundred uniform experiments, with only one that is contradictory, reasonably beget a pretty
strong degree of assurance. In all cases, we must balance the opposite
experiments, where they are opposite, and deduct the smaller number
from the greater, in order to know the exact force of the superior evidence.

To apply these principles to a particular instance; we may observe,
that there is no species of reasoning more common, more useful, and
even necessary to human life, than that which is derived from the testimony of men, and the reports of eyewitnesses and spectators. This species of reasoning, perhaps, one may deny to be founded on the relation
of cause and effect. I shall not dispute about a word. It will be sufficient
to observe, that our assurance in any argument of this kind is derived
from no other principle than our observation of the veracity of human
testimony, and of the usual conformity of facts to the report of witnesses.
It being a general maxim that no objects have any discoverable connection together, and that all the inferences which we can draw from one to
another, are founded merely on our experience of their constant and regular conjunction, it is evident that we ought not to make an exception to
this maxim in favour of human testimony, whose connection with any
event seems, in itself, as little necessary as any other. Were not the memory tenacious to a certain degree; had not men commonly an inclination
to truth and a principle of probity; were they not sensible to shame when
detected in a falsehood: were not these, I say, discovered by *experience* to
be qualities inherent in human nature, we should never repose the least
confidence in human testimony. A man delirious, or noted for falsehood
and villainy, has no manner of authority with us.

And as the evidence derived from witnesses and human testimony is
founded on past experience, so it varies with the experience, and is
regarded either as a *proof* or a *probability*, according as the conjunction
between any particular kind of report, and any kind of object, has been
found to be constant or variable. There are a number of circumstances to
be taken into consideration in all judgments of this kind; and the ultimate standard by which we determine all disputes that may arise concerning them, is always derived from experience and observation.
Where this experience is not entirely uniform on any side, it is attended
with an unavoidable contrariety in our judgments, and with the same

opposition and mutual destruction of argument as in every other kind of evidence. We frequently hesitate concerning the reports of others. We balance the opposite circumstances which cause any doubt or uncertainty; and when we discover a superiority on any side, we incline to it, but still with a diminution of assurance, in proportion to the force of its antagonist.

This contrariety of evidence, in the present case, may be derived from several different causes; from the opposition of contrary testimony; from the character or number of the witnesses; from the manner of their delivering their testimony; or from the union of all these circumstances. We entertain a suspicion concerning any matter of fact when the witnesses contradict each other; when they are but few or of a doubtful character: when they have an interest in what they affirm; when they deliver their testimony with hesitation, or, on the contrary, with too violent asseverations. There are many other particulars of the same kind, which may diminish or destroy the force of any argument derived from human testimony.

Suppose, for instance, that the fact which the testimony endeavours to establish partakes of the extraordinary and the marvellous, in that case, the evidence resulting from the testimony admits of a diminution, greater or less, in proportion as the fact is more or less unusual. The reason why we place any credit in witnesses and historians, is not derived from any *connection* which we perceive *a priori* between testimony and reality, but because we are accustomed to find a conformity between them. But when the fact attested is such a one as has seldom fallen under our observation, here is a contest of two opposite experiences, of which the one destroys the other as far as its force goes, and the superior can only operate on the mind by the force which remains. The very same principle of experience, which gives us a certain degree of assurance in the testimony of witnesses, gives us also, in this case, another degree of assurance against the fact which they endeavour to establish; from which contradiction there necessarily arises a counterpoise, and mutual destruction of belief and authority.

I should not believe such a story were it told me by Cato, was a proverbial saying in Rome, even during the lifetime of that philosophical patriot. The incredibility of a fact, it was allowed, might invalidate so great an authority.

The Indian prince, who refused to believe the first relations concerning the effects of frost, reasoned justly; and it naturally required very strong testimony to engage his assent to facts that arose from a state of nature with which he was acquainted, and which bore so little analogy to those events of which he had had constant and uniform experience.

Though they were not contrary to his experience, they were not conformable to it.[3]

But in order to increase the probability against the testimony of witnesses, let us suppose that the fact which they affirm, instead of being only marvellous, is really miraculous; and suppose also, that the testimony, considered apart and in itself, amounts to an entire proof, in that case there is proof against proof, of which the strongest must prevail, but still with a diminution of its force, in proportion to that of its antagonist.

A miracle is a violation of the laws of nature; and as a firm and unalterable experience has established these laws, the proof against a miracle, from the very nature of the fact, is as entire as any argument from experience can possibly be imagined. Why is it more than probable that all men must die; that lead cannot, of itself, remain suspended in the air; that fire consumes wood, and is extinguished by water; unless it be that these events are found agreeable to the laws of nature, and there is required a violation of these laws, or, in other words, a miracle to prevent them? Nothing is esteemed a miracle, if it ever happen in the common course of nature. It is no miracle that a man, seemingly in good health, should die on a sudden, because such a kind of death, though more unusual than any other, has yet been frequently observed to happen. But it is a miracle that a dead man should come to life, because that has never been observed in any age or country. There must, therefore, be a uniform experience against every miraculous event, otherwise the event would not merit that appellation. And as a uniform experience amounts to a proof, there is here a direct and full *proof*, from the nature of the fact, against the existence of any miracle; nor can such a proof be destroyed, or the miracle rendered credible, but by an opposite proof, which is superior.[4]

---

[3]   No Indian, it is evident, could have experience that water did not freeze in cold climates. This is placing nature in a situation quite unknown to him; and it is impossible for him to tell *a priori* what will result from it. It is making a new experiment, the consequence of which is always uncertain. One may sometimes conjecture from analogy what will follow; but still this is but conjecture. And it must be confessed, that, in the present case of freezing, the event follows contrary to the rules of analogy, and is such as a rational Indian would not look for. The operations of cold upon water are not gradual, according to the degrees of cold; but whenever it comes to the freezing point, the water passes in a moment, from the utmost liquidity to perfect hardness. Such an event, therefore, may be denominated *extraordinary*, and requires a pretty strong testimony, to render it credible to people in a warm climate: but still it is not *miraculous*, nor contrary to uniform experience of the course of nature in cases where all the circumstances are the same. The inhabitants of Sumatra have always seen water fluid in their own climate, and the freezing of their rivers ought to be deemed a prodigy: but they never saw water in Muscovy during the winter; and therefore they cannot reasonably be positive what would there be the consequence.

[4]   Sometimes an event may not, *in itself, seem* to be contrary to the laws of nature, and yet, if it were real, it might, by reason of some circumstances, be denominated a

The plain consequence is (and it is a general maxim worthy of our attention), "That no testimony is sufficient to establish a miracle, unless the testimony be of such a kind, that its falsehood would be more miraculous than the fact which it endeavours to establish: and even in that case there is a mutual destruction of arguments, and the superior only gives us an assurance suitable to that degree of force which remains after deducting the inferior". When any one tells me that he saw a dead man restored to life, I immediately consider with myself whether it be more probable that this person should either deceive or be deceived, or that the fact which he relates should really have happened. I weigh the one miracle against the other; and according to the superiority which I discover, I pronounce my decision, and always reject the greater miracle. If the falsehood of his testimony would be more miraculous than the event which he relates, then, and not till then, can he pretend to command my belief or opinion.

II

In the foregoing reasoning we have supposed, that the testimony upon which a miracle is founded, may possibly amount to an entire proof, and that the falsehood of that testimony would be a real prodigy: but it is easy to show that we have been a great deal too liberal in our concession, and that there never was a miraculous event established on so full an evidence.

For, *first*, there is not to be found, in all history, any miracle attested by a sufficient number of men, of such unquestioned good sense, education, and learning, as to secure us against all delusion in themselves; of such undoubted integrity, as to place them beyond all suspicion of any design to deceive others; of such credit and reputation in the eyes of mankind, as to have a great deal to lose in case of their being detected in any falsehood; and at the same time attesting facts, performed in such a

---

miracle; because, in fact, it is contrary to these laws. Thus if a person, claiming a divine authority, should command a sick person to be well, a healthful man to fall down dead, the clouds to pour rain, the winds to blow; in short, should order many natural events, which immediately follow upon his command; these might justly be esteemed miracles, because they are really, in this case, contrary to the laws of nature. For if any suspicion remain, that the event and command concurred by accident, there is no miracle and no transgression of the laws of nature. If this suspicion be removed, there is evidently a miracle, and a transgression of these laws; because nothing can be more contrary to nature than that the voice or command of a man should have such an influence. A miracle may be accurately defined, *a transgression of a law of nature by a particular volition of the Deity, or by the interposition of some invisible agent*. A Miracle may either be discovered by men or not. This alters not its nature and essence. The raising of a house or ship into the air is a visible miracle. The raising of a feather, when the wind wants ever so little of a force requisite for that purpose, is as real a miracle, though not so sensible with regard to us.

public manner, and in so celebrated a part of the world, as to render the detection unavoidable: all which circumstances are requisite to give us a full assurance in the testimony of men.

Secondly, we may observe in human nature a principle which, if strictly examined, will be found to diminish extremely the assurance, which we might, from human testimony, have in any kind of prodigy. The maxim, by which we commonly conduct ourselves in our reasonings, is, that the objects, of which we have no experience, resemble those of which we have; that what we have found to be most usual is always most probable; and that where there is an opposition of arguments, we ought to give the preference to such as are founded on the greatest number of past observations. But though, in proceeding by this rule, we readily reject any fact which is unusual and incredible in an ordinary degree; yet in advancing further, the mind observes not always the same rule; but when any thing is affirmed utterly absurd and miraculous, it rather the more readily admits of such a fact, upon account of that very circumstance which ought to destroy all its authority. The passion of *surprise* and *wonder*, arising from miracles, being an agreeable emotion, gives a sensible tendency towards the belief of those events from which it is derived. And this goes so far, that even those who cannot enjoy this pleasure immediately, nor can believe those miraculous events of which they are informed, yet love to partake the satisfaction at second hand, or by rebound, and place a pride and delight in exciting the admiration of others.

With what greediness are the miraculous accounts of travellers received, their descriptions of sea and land monsters, their relations of wonderful adventures, strange men, and uncouth manners? But if the spirit of religion join itself to the love of wonder, there is an end of common sense; and human testimony, in these circumstances, loses all pretensions to authority. A religionist may be an enthusiast, and imagine he sees what has no reality: he may know his narrative to be false, and yet persevere in it, with the best intentions in the world, for the sake of promoting so holy a cause: or even where this delusion has not place, vanity, excited by a strong temptation, operates on him more powerfully than on the rest of mankind in any other circumstances; and self-interest with equal force. His auditors may not have, and commonly have not, sufficient judgment to canvass his evidence: what judgment they have, they renounce by principle, in these sublime and mysterious subjects: or if they were ever so willing to employ it, passion and a heated imagination disturb the regularity of its operations. Their credulity increases his impudence; and his impudence overpowers their credulity.

Eloquence, when at its highest pitch, leaves little room for reason or reflection; but addressing itself entirely to the fancy or the affections, captivates the willing hearers, and subdues their understanding. Happily, this pitch it seldom attains. But what a Tully or a Demosthenes could scarcely effect over a Roman or Athenian audience, every *Capu-*

chin, every itinerant or stationary teacher, can perform over the generality of mankind, and in a higher degree, by touching such gross and vulgar passions.

The many instances of forged miracles and prophecies and supernatural events, which, in all ages, have either been detected by contrary evidence, or which detect themselves by their absurdity, prove sufficiently the strong propensity of mankind to the extraordinary and marvellous, and ought reasonably to beget a suspicion against all relations of this kind. This is our natural way of thinking, even with regard to the most common and most credible events. For instance, there is no kind of report which arises so easily, and spreads so quickly, especially in country places and provincial towns, as those concerning marriages; in so much that two young persons of equal condition never see each other twice, but the whole neighbourhood immediately join them together. The pleasure of telling a piece of news so interesting, of propagating it, and of being the first reporters of it, spreads the intelligence; and this is so well known, that no man of sense gives attention to these reports till he find them confirmed by some greater evidence. Do not the same passions, and others still stronger, incline the generality of mankind to believe and report, with the greatest vehemence and assurance, all religious miracles?

Thirdly, It forms a strong presumption against all supernatural and miraculous relations, that they are observed chiefly to abound among ignorant and barbarous nations; or if a civilised people has ever given admission to any of them, that people will be found to have received them from ignorant and barbarous ancestors, who transmitted them with that inviolable sanction and authority which always attend received opinions. When we peruse the first histories of all nations, we are apt to imagine ourselves transported into some new world, where the whole frame of nature is disjointed, and every element performs its operations in a different manner from what it does at present. Battles, revolutions, pestilence, famine, and death, are never the effect of those natural causes which we experience. Prodigies, omens, oracles, judgments, quite obscure the few natural events that are intermingled with them. But as the former grow thinner every page, in proportion as we advance nearer the enlightened ages, we soon learn that there is nothing mysterious or supernatural in the case, but that all proceeds from the usual propensity of mankind towards the marvellous, and that, though this inclination may at intervals receive a check from sense and learning, it can never be thoroughly extirpated from human nature.

It is strange, a judicious reader is apt to say, upon the perusal of these wonderful historians, *that such prodigious events never happen in our days!* But it is nothing strange, I hope, that men should lie in all ages. You must surely have seen instances enough of that frailty. You have yourself heard many such marvellous relations started, which, being treated with scorn by all the wise and judicious, have at last been abandoned even by the vulgar. Be assured, that those renowned lies, which have spread and flourished to such a monstrous height, arose from like beginnings; but being sown in a more proper soil, shot up at last into prodigies almost equal to those which they relate.

It was a wise policy in that false prophet Alexander, who, though now forgotten, was once so famous, to lay the first scene of his impostures in Paphlagonia, where, as Lucian tells us, the people were extremely ignorant and stupid, and ready to swallow even the grossest delusion. People at a distance, who are weak enough to think the matter at all worthy inquiry, have no opportunity of receiving better information. The stories come magnified to them by a hundred circumstances. Fools are industrious in propagating the imposture; while the wise and learned are contented, in general, to deride its absurdity, without informing themselves of the particular facts by which it may be distinctly refuted. And thus the impostor above mentioned was enabled to proceed, from his ignorant Paphlagonians, to the enlisting of votaries, even among the Grecian philosophers, and men of the most eminent rank and distinction in Rome: nay, could engage the attention of that sage emperor Marcus Aurelius, so far as to make him trust the success of a military expedition to his delusive prophecies.

The advantages are so great, of starting an imposture among an ignorant people, that even though the delusion should be too gross to impose on the generality of them, (*which, though seldom, is sometimes the case*), it has a much better chance for succeeding in remote countries, than if the first scene had been laid in a city renowned for arts and knowledge. The most ignorant and barbarous of these barbarians carry the report abroad. None of their countrymen have a large correspondence, or sufficient credit and authority to contradict and beat down the delusion. Men's inclination to the marvellous has full opportunity to display itself. And thus a story, which is universally exploded in the place where it first started, shall pass for certain at a thousand miles distance. But, had Alexander fixed his residence at Athens, the philosophers at that renowned mart of learning had immediately spread, throughout the whole Roman empire, their sense of the matter; which, being supported by so great authority, and displayed by all the force of reason and eloquence, had entirely opened the eyes of mankind. It is true, Lucian, passing by chance through Paphlagonia, had an opportunity of performing this good office. But, though much to be wished, it does not always happen that every Alexander meets with a Lucian, ready to expose and detect his impostures.

I may add, as a *fourth* reason, which diminishes the authority of prodigies, that there is no testimony for any, even those which have not been expressly detected, that is not opposed by an infinite number of witnesses; so that not only the miracle destroys the credit of testimony, but the testimony destroys itself. To make this the better understood, let us consider, that in matters of religion, whatever is different is contrary;

and that it is impossible the religions of ancient Rome, of Turkey, of Siam, and of China, should all of them be established on any solid foundation. Every miracle, therefore, pretended to have been wrought in any of these religions, (and all of them abound in miracles), as its direct scope is to establish the particular system to which it is attributed; so has it the same force, though more indirectly, to overthrow every other system. In destroying a rival system, it likewise destroys the credit of those miracles on which that system was established, so that all the prodigies of different religions are to be regarded as contrary facts, and the evidences of these prodigies, whether weak or strong, as opposite to each other. According to this method of reasoning, when we believe any miracle of Mahomet or his successors, we have for our warrant the testimony of a few barbarous Arabians: and, on the other hand, we are to regard the authority of Titus Livius, Plutarch, Tacitus, and, in short, of all the authors and witnesses, Grecian, Chinese, and Roman Catholic, who have related any miracle in their particular religion; I say, we are to regard their testimony in the same light as if they had mentioned the Mohametan miracle, and had in express terms contradicted it, with the same certainty as they have for the miracle they relate. This argument may appear over subtle and refined, but is not in reality different from the reasoning of a judge, who supposes that the credit of two witnesses, maintaining a crime against any one, is destroyed by the testimony of two others, who affirm him to have been two hundred leagues distant at the same instant when the crime is said to have been committed.

One of the best attested miracles in all profane history, is that which Tacitus reports of Vespasian, who cured a blind man in Alexandria by means of his spittle, and a lame man by the mere touch of his foot; in obedience to a vision of the god Serapis, who had enjoined them to have recourse to the Emperor for these miraculous cures. The story may be seen in that fine historian; where every circumstance seems to add weight to the testimony, and might be displayed at large with all the force of argument and eloquence, if any one were now concerned to enforce the evidence of that exploded and idolatrous superstition. The gravity, solidity, age, and probity of so great an Emperor, who, through the whole course of his life conversed in a familiar manner with his friends and courtiers, and never affected those extraordinary airs of divinity assumed by Alexander and Demetrius: the historian, a contemporary writer, noted for candour and veracity, and withal, the greatest and most penetrating genius perhaps of all antiquity; and so free from any tendency to credulity, that he even lies under the contrary imputation of atheism and profaneness: the persons, from whose authority he related the miracle, of established character for judgment and veracity, as we may well presume; eyewitnesses of the fact, and confirming their testimony, after the Flavian family was despoiled of the empire, and could no longer give any reward as the price of a lie. ... [I]f we add the public nature of the facts, as related, it will appear that no evidence can well be supposed stronger for so gross and so palpable a falsehood.

There is also a memorable story related by Cardinal De Retz, which may well deserve our consideration. When that intriguing politician fled into Spain to avoid the persecution of his enemies, he passed through Saragossa, the capital of Arragon, where he was shown, in the cathedral, a man who had served seven years as a door-keeper, and was well known to everybody in town that had ever paid his devotions at that church. He had been seen for so long a time wanting a leg, but recovered that limb by the rubbing of holy oil upon the stump; and the Cardinal assures us that he saw him with two legs. This miracle was vouched by all the canons of the church; and the whole company in town were appealed to for a confirmation of the fact; whom the Cardinal found, by their zealous devotion, to be thorough believers of the miracle. Here the relater was also contemporary to the supposed prodigy, of an incredulous and libertine character, as well as of great genius; the miracle of so *singular* a nature as could scarcely admit of a counterfeit, and the witnesses very numerous, and all of them, in a manner, spectators of the fact to which they gave their testimony. And what adds mightily to the force of the evidence, and may double our surprise on this occasion, is, that the Cardinal himself, who relates the story, seems not to give any credit to it, and consequently cannot be suspected of any concurrence in the holy fraud. He considered justly, that it was not requisite, in order to reject a fact of this nature, to be able accurately to disprove the testimony, and to trace its falsehood through all the circumstances of knavery and credulity which produced it. He knew that, as this was commonly altogether impossible at any small distance of time and place, so was it extremely difficult, even where one was immediately present, by reason of the bigotry, ignorance, cunning, and roguery of a great part of mankind. He therefore concluded, like a just reasoner, that such an evidence carried falsehood upon the very face of it, and that a miracle, supported by any human testimony, was more properly a subject of derision than of argument.

There surely never was a greater number of miracles ascribed to one person than those which were lately said to have been wrought in France upon the tomb of Abbé Paris, the famous Jansenist, with whose sanctity the people were so long deluded. The curing of the sick, giving hearing to the deaf, and sight to the blind, were everywhere talked of as the usual effects of that holy sepulchre. But what is more extraordinary, many of the miracles were immediately proved upon the spot, before judges of unquestioned integrity, attested by witnesses of credit and distinction, in a learned age, and on the most eminent theatre that is now in the world. Nor is this all: a relation of them was published and dispersed everywhere; nor were the *Jesuits*, though a learned body, supported by the civil magistrate, and determined enemies to those opinions in whose favour the miracles were said to have been wrought, ever able distinctly to refute them.

Where shall we find such a number of circumstances agreeing to the corroboration of one fact? And what have we to oppose to such a cloud of witnesses, but the absolute impossibility or miraculous nature of the events which they relate? And this, surely, in the eyes of all reasonable people, will alone be regarded as a sufficient refutation.

Is the consequence just, because some human testimony has the utmost force and authority in some cases, when it relates the battles of Philippi or Pharsalia for instance, that therefore all kinds of testimony must, in all cases, have equal force and authority? Suppose that the Cæsarean or Pompeian factions had, each of them, claimed the victory in these battles, and that the historians of each party had uniformly ascribed the advantage to their own side, how could mankind, at this distance, have been able to determine between them? The contrariety is equally strong between the miracles related by Herodous or Plutarch, and those delivered by Mariana, Bede, or any monkish historian.

The wise lend a very academic faith to every report which favours the passion of the reporter, whether it magnifies his country, his family, or himself, or in any other way strikes in with his natural inclinations and propensities. But what greater temptation than to appear a missionary, a prophet, an ambassador from heaven? Who would not encounter many dangers and difficulties in order to obtain so sublime a character? Or if, by the help of vanity and a heated imagination, a man has first made a convert of himself, and entered seriously into the delusion, who ever scruples to make use of pious frauds in support of so holy and meritorious cause?

The smallest spark may here kindle into the greatest flame, because the materials are always prepared for it. The *avidum genus auricularum* [Lucretius], the gazing populace, receive greedily, without examination, whatever soothes superstition and promotes wonder.

How many stories of this nature have, in all ages, been detected and exploded in their infancy? How many more have been celebrated for a time, and have afterwards sunk into neglect and oblivion? Where such reports, therefore, fly about, the solution of the phenomenon is obvious; and we judge in conformity to regular experience and observation, when we account for it by the known and natural principles of credulity and delusion. And shall we, rather than have recourse to so natural a solution, allow of a miraculous violation of the most established laws of nature?

I need not mention the difficulty of detecting a falsehood in any private or even public history, at the place where it is said to happen; much more when the scene is removed to ever so small a distance. Even a court of judicature, with all the authority, accuracy, and judgment, which they can employ, find themselves often at a loss to distinguish between truth and falsehood in the most recent actions. But the matter never comes to any issue, if trusted to the common method of altercation and debate, and flying rumours, especially when men's passions have taken part on either side.

In the infancy of new religions, the wise and learned commonly esteem the matter too inconsiderable to deserve their attention or regard. And when afterwards they would willingly detect the cheat, in order to undeceive the deluded multitude, the season is now past, and the records and witnesses, which might clear up the matter, have perished beyond recovery.

No means of detection remain but those which must be drawn from the very testimony itself of the reporters: and these, though always sufficient with the judicious and knowing, are commonly too fine to fall under the comprehension of the vulgar.

Upon the whole, then, it appears, that no testimony for any kind of miracle has ever amounted to a probability, much less to a proof; and that, even supposing it amounted to a proof, it would be opposed by another proof, derived from the very nature of the fact which it would endeavour to establish. It is experience only which gives authority to human testimony; and it is the same experience which assures us of the laws of nature. When, therefore, these two kinds of experience are contrary, we have nothing to do but to subtract the one from the other, and embrace an opinion either on one side or the other, with that assurance which arises from the remainder. But according to the principle here explained, this subtraction with regard to all popular religions amounts to an entire annihilation; and therefore we may establish it as a maxim, that no human testimony can have such force as to prove a miracle, and make it a just foundation for any such system of religion.

I beg the limitations here made may be remarked, when I say, that a miracle can never be proved so as to be the foundation of a system of religion. For I own, that otherwise there may possibly be miracles, or violations of the usual course of nature, of such a kind as to admit of proof from human testimony; though perhaps it will be impossible to find any such in all the records of history. Thus, suppose all authors, in all languages, agree, that, from the 1st of January, 1600, there was a total darkness over the whole earth for eight days: suppose that the tradition of this extraordinary event is still strong and lively among the people: that all travellers who return from foreign countries bring us accounts of the same tradition, without the least variation or contradiction: it is evident that our present philosophers, instead of doubting the fact, ought to receive it as certain, and ought to search for the causes whence it might be derived. The decay, corruption, and dissolution of nature, is an event rendered probable by so many analogies, that any phenomenon, which seems to have a tendency towards that catastrophe, comes within the reach of human testimony, if that testimony be very extensive and uniform.

But suppose that all the historians who treat of England should agree, that on the first of January, 1600, Queen Elizabeth died; that both before and after her death, she was seen by her physicians and the whole court, as is usual with persons of her rank; that her successor was acknowledged and proclaimed by the Parliament; and that, after being interred for a month, she again appeared, resumed the throne, and governed England for three years; I must confess that I should be surprised at the concurrence of so many odd circumstances, but should not have the least inclination to believe so miraculous an event. I should not doubt of her pretended death, and of those other public circumstances that followed it: I should only assert it to have been pretended, and that it neither was, nor possibly could be, real. You would in vain object to me the difficulty, and almost impossibility of deceiving the world in an affair of such consequence; the wisdom and solid judgment of that renowned Queen; with the little or no advantage which she could reap from so poor an artifice: all this might astonish me; but I would still reply, that the knavery and folly of men are such common phenomena, that I should rather believe the most extraordinary events to arise from their concurrence, than admit of so signal a violation of the laws of nature.

But should this miracle be ascribed to any new system of religion; men, in all ages, have been so much imposed on by ridiculous stories of that kind, that this very circumstance would be a full proof of a cheat, and sufficient, with all men of sense, not only to make them reject the fact, but even reject it without further examination. Though the being to whom the miracle is ascribed, be in this case Almighty, it does not, upon that account, become a whit more probable; since it is impossible for us to know the attributes or actions of such a Being, otherwise than from the experience which we have of his productions in the usual course of nature. This still reduces us to past observation, and obliges us to compare the instances of the violation of truth in the testimony of men, with those of the violation of the laws of nature by miracles, in order to judge which of them is most likely and probable. As the violations of truth are more common in the testimony concerning religious miracles than in that concerning any other matter of fact; this must diminish very much the authority of the former testimony, and make us form a general resolution never to lend any attention to it, with whatever specious pretence it may be covered.

Lord Bacon seems to have embraced the same principles of reasoning. 'We ought', says he, 'to make a collection or particular history of all monsters and prodigious births or productions; and in a word, of every thing new, rare, and extraordinary in nature. But this must be done with the most severe scrutiny, lest we depart from truth. Above all, every relation must be considered as suspicious which depends in any degree upon religion, as the prodigies of Livy: and no less so every thing that is to be found in the writers on natural magic or alchemy, or such authors who seem all of them to have an unconquerable appetite for falsehood and fable'.[5]

I am the better pleased with the method of reasoning here delivered, as I think it may serve to confound those dangerous friends, or disguised enemies to the *Christian religion*, who have undertaken to defend it by the principles of human reason. Our most holy religion is founded on *Faith*, not on reason; and it is a sure method of exposing it to put it to such a trial as it is by no means fitted to endure. To make this more evident, let us examine those miracles related in Scripture; and, not to lose ourselves in too wide a field, let us confine ourselves to such as we find in the *Pentateuch*, which we shall examine, according to the principles of these pretended Christians, not as the word or testimony of God himself, but as the production of a mere human writer and historian. Here, then, we are first to consider a book, presented to us by a barbarous and ignorant people, written in an age when they were still more barbarous, and, in all probability, long after the facts which it relates, corroborated by no concurring testimony, and resembling those fabulous accounts which every nation gives of its origin. Upon reading this book, we find it full of prodigies and miracles. It gives an account of a state of the world and of human nature entirely different from the present: of our fall from that state: of the age of man, extended to near a thousand years: of the destruction of the world by a deluge: of the arbitrary choice of one people as the favourites of heaven; and that people the countrymen of the author: of their deliverance from bondage by prodigies the most astonishing imaginable: I desire any one to lay his hand upon his heart, and, after a serious consideration, declare whether he thinks that the falsehood of such a book, supported by such a testimony, would be more extraordinary and miraculous than all the miracles it relates; which is, however, necessary to make it be received, according to the measures of probability above established.

What we have said of miracles, may be applied without any variation to prophecies; and, indeed, all prophecies are real miracles, and as such, only can be admitted as proofs of such revelation. If it did not exceed the capacity of human nature to foretell future events, it would be absurd to employ any prophecy as an argument for a divine mission or authority from heaven. So that, upon the whole, we may conclude, that the *Christian Religion* not only was at first attended with miracles, but even at this day cannot be believed by any reasonable person without one. Mere reason is insufficient to convince us of its veracity: and whoever is moved by *Faith* to assent to it, is conscious of a continued miracle in his own person, which subverts all the principles of his understanding, and gives him a determination to believe what is most contrary to custom and experience.

[5]   *Nov. Org.* lib. ii. aph. 29.

READING VI
Tragedy[6]

It seems an unaccountable pleasure which the spectators of a well-written tragedy receive from sorrow, terror, anxiety, and other passions that are in themselves disagreeable and uneasy. The more they are touched and affected, the more are they delighted with the spectacle; and as soon as the uneasy passions cease to operate, the piece is at an end. One scene of full joy and contentment and security is the utmost that any composition of this kind can bear; and it is sure always to be the concluding one. If in the texture of the piece there be interwoven any scenes of satisfaction, they afford only faint gleams of pleasure, which are thrown in by way of variety, and in order to plunge the actors into deeper distress by means of that contrast and disappointment. The whole art of the poet is employed in rousing and supporting the compassion and indignation, the anxiety and resentment, of his audience. They are pleased in proportion as they are afflicted, and never are so happy as when they employ tears, sobs, and cries, to give vent to their sorrow, and relieve their heart swollen with the tenderest sympathy and compassion.

The few critics who have had some tincture of philosophy have remarked this singular phenomenon, and have endeavoured to account for it.

L'Abbé Dubos, in his *Reflections on Poetry and Painting*, asserts, that nothing is in general so disagreeable to the mind as the languid, listless state of indolence into which it falls upon the removal of all passion and occupation. To get rid of this painful situation, it seeks every amusement and pursuit; business, gaming, shows, executions; whatever will rouse the passions and take its attention from itself. No matter what the passion is; let it be disagreeable, afflicting, melancholy, disordered; it is still better than that insipid languor which arises from perfect tranquillity and repose.

It is impossible not to admit this account as being, at least in part, satisfactory. You may observe, when there are several tables of gaming, that all the company run to those where the deepest play is, even though they find not there the best players. The view, or, at least, imagination of high passions, arising from great loss or gain, affects the spectator by sympathy, gives him some touches of the same passions, and serves him for a momentary entertainment. It makes the time pass the easier with him, and is some relief to that oppression under which men commonly labour when left entirely to their own thoughts and meditations.

We find that common liars always magnify, in their narrations, all kinds of danger, pain, distress, sickness, deaths, murders, and cruelties,

---

[6]   Extracted from *Essays Moral, Political and Literary*, Oxford: University Press, 1963, pp. 221–30.

as well as joy, beauty, mirth, and magnificence. It is an absurd secret which they have for pleasing their company, fixing their attention, and attaching them to such marvellous relation by the passions and emotions which they excite.

There is, however, a difficulty in applying to the present subject, in its full extent, this solution, however ingenious and satisfactory it may appear. It is certain that the same object of distress, which pleases in a tragedy, were it really set before us, would give the most unfeigned uneasiness, though it be then the most effectual cure to languor and indolence. Monsieur Fontenelle seems to have been sensible of this difficulty, and accordingly attempts another solution of the phenomenon, at least makes some addition to the theory above mentioned.

'Pleasure and pain', says he, 'which are two sentiments so different in themselves, differ not so much in their cause. From the instance of tickling it appears, that the movement of pleasure, pushed a little too far, becomes pain, and that the movement of pain, a little moderate, becomes pleasure. Hence it proceeds, that there is such a thing as a sorrow, soft and agreeable: it is a pain weakened and diminished. The heart likes naturally to be moved and affected. Melancholy objects suit it, and even disastrous and sorrowful, provided they are softened by some circumstance. It is certain, that, on the theatre, the representation has almost the effect of reality; yet it has not altogether that effect. However we may be hurried away by the spectacle, whatever dominion the senses and imagination may usurp over the reason, there still lurks at the bottom a certain idea of falsehood in the whole of what we see. This idea, though weak and disguised, suffices to diminish the pain which we suffer from the misfortunes of those whom we love, and to reduce that affliction to such a pitch as converts it into pleasure. We weep for the misfortune of a hero to whom we are attached. In the same instant we comfort ourselves by reflecting, that it is nothing but a fiction: and it is precisely that mixture of sentiments which composes an agreeable sorrow, and tears that delight us. But as that affliction which is caused by exterior and sensible objects is stronger than the consolation which arises from an internal reflection, they are the effects and symptoms of sorrow that ought to predominate in the composition'.

This solution seems just and convincing: but perhaps it wants still some new addition, in order to make it answer fully the phenomenon which we here examine. All the passions, excited by eloquence, are agreeable in the highest degree, as well as those which are moved by painting and the theatre. The Epilogues of Cicero are, on this account chiefly, the delight of every reader of taste; and it is difficult to read some of them without the deepest sympathy and sorrow. His merit as an orator, no doubt depends much on his success in this particular. When he had raised tears in his judges and all his audience, they were then the most highly delighted, and expressed the greatest satisfaction with the pleader. The pathetic description of the butchery made by Verres of the

Sicilian captains, is a masterpiece of this kind but I believe none will affirm, that the being present at a melancholy scene of that nature would afford any entertainment. Neither is the sorrow here softened by fiction; for the audience were convinced of the reality of every circumstance. What is it then which in this case raises a pleasure from the bosom of uneasiness, so to speak, and a pleasure which still retains all the features and outward symptoms of distress and sorrow?

I answer: this extraordinary effect proceeds from that very eloquence with which the melancholy scene is represented. The genius required to paint objects in a lively manner, the art employed in collecting all the pathetic circumstances, the judgement displayed in disposing them; the exercise, I say, of these noble talents, together with the force of expression, and beauty of oratorial numbers, diffuse the highest satisfaction on the audience, and excite the most delightful movements. By this means, the uneasiness of the melancholy passions is not only overpowered and effaced by something stronger of an opposite kind, but the whole impulse of those passions is converted into pleasure, and swells the delight which the eloquence raises in us. The same force of oratory, employed on an uninteresting subject, would not please half so much, or rather would appear altogether ridiculous; and the mind, being left in absolute calmness and indifference, would relish none of those beauties of imagination or expression, which, if joined to passion, give it such exquisite entertainment. The impulse or vehemence arising from sorrow, compassion, indignation, receives a new direction from the sentiments of beauty. The latter, being the predominant emotion, seize the whole mind, and convert the former into themselves, at least tincture them so strongly as totally to alter their nature. And the soul being at the same time roused by passion and charmed by eloquence, feels on the whole a strong movement, which is altogether delightful.

The same principle takes place in tragedy; with this addition, that tragedy is an imitation, and imitation is always of itself agreeable. This circumstance serves still further to smooth the motions of passion, and convert the whole feeling into one uniform and strong enjoyment. Objects of the greatest terror and distress please in painting, and please more than the most beautiful objects that appear calm and indifferent.[7] The affection, rousing the mind, excites a large stock of spirit and vehemence; which is all transformed into pleasure by the force of the prevailing movement. It is thus the fiction of tragedy softens the passion, by an

---

[7] Painters make no scruple of representing distress and sorrow, as well as any other passion; but they seem, not to dwell so much on these melancholy affections as the poets, who, though they copy every motion of the human breast, yet pass quickly over the agreeable sentiments. A painter represents only one instant; and if that be passionate enough, it is sure to affect and delight the spectator; but nothing can furnish to the poet a variety of scenes, and incidents, and sentiments, except distress, terror, or anxiety. Complete joy and satisfaction is attended with security, and leaves no further room for action.

infusion of a new feeling, not merely by weakening or diminishing the sorrow. You may by degrees weaken a real sorrow, till it totally disappears; yet in none of its gradations will it ever give pleasure; except, perhaps, by accident, to a man sunk under lethargic indolence, whom it rouses from that languid state.

To confirm this theory, it will be sufficient to produce other instances, where the subordinate movement is converted into the predominant, and gives force to it, though of a different, and even sometimes though of a contrary nature.

Novelty naturally rouses the mind, and attracts our attention; and the movements which it causes are always converted into any passion belonging to the object, and join their force to it. Whether an event excite joy or sorrow, pride or sham, anger or good-will, it is sure to produce a stronger affection, when new or unusual. And though novelty of itself be agreeable, it fortifies the painful, as well as agreeable passions.

Had you any intention to move a person extremely by the narration of any event, the best method of increasing its effect would be artfully to delay informing him of it, and first to excite his curiosity and impatience before you let him into the secret. This is the artifice practised by Iago in the famous scene of Shakespeare; and every spectator is sensible, that Othello's jealousy acquires additional force from his preceding impatience, and that the subordinate passion is here readily transformed into the predominant one.

Difficulties increase passions of every kind; and by rousing our attention, and exciting our active powers, they produce an emotion which nourishes the prevailing affection.

Parents commonly love that child most whose sickly infirm frame of body has occasioned them the greatest pains, trouble, and anxiety, in rearing him. The agreeable sentiment of affection here acquires force from sentiments of uneasiness.

Nothing endears so much a friend as sorrow for his death. The pleasure of his company has not so powerful an influence.

Jealousy is a painful passion; yet without some share of it, the agreeable affection of love has difficulty to subsist in its full force and violence. Absence is also a great source of complaint among lovers, and gives them the greatest uneasiness: yet nothing is more favourable to their mutual passion than short intervals of that kind. And if long intervals often prove fatal, it is only because, through time, men are accustomed to them, and they cease to give uneasiness. Jealousy and absence in love compose the *dolce peccante* of the Italians, which they suppose so essential to all pleasure.

There is a fine observation of the elder Pliny, which illustrates the principle here insisted on. 'It is very remarkable', says he, 'that the last works of celebrated artists, which they left imperfect, are always the most prized, such as the Iris of Aristides, the Tyndarides of Nicomachus, the Medea of Timomachus, and the Venus of Apelles. These are valued even above their finished productions. The broken lineaments of the piece, and the half-formed idea of the painter, are carefully studied; and our very grief for that curious hand, which had been stopped by death, is an additional increase to our pleasure'.

These instances (and many more might be collected) are sufficient to afford us some insight into the analogy of nature, and to show us, that the pleasure which poets, orators, and musicians give us, by exciting grief, sorrow, indignation, compassion, is not so extraordinary or paradoxical as it may at first sight appear. The force of imagination, the energy of expression, the power of numbers, the charms of imitation; all these are naturally, of themselves, delightful to the mind: and when the object presented lays also hold of some affection, the pleasure still gives rise upon us, by the conversion of this subordinate movement into that which is predominant. The passion, though perhaps naturally, and when excited by the simple appearance of a real object, it may be painful; yet is so smoothed, and softened, and mollified, when raised by the finer arts, that it affords the highest entertainment.

To confirm this reasoning, we may observe, that if the movements of the imagination be not predominant above those of the passion, a contrary effect follows; and the former, being now subordinate, is converted into the latter, and still further increases the pain and affliction of the sufferer.

Who could ever think of it as a good expedient for comforting an afflicted parent, to exaggerate, with all the force of elocution, the irreparable loss which he has met with by the death of a favourite child? The more power of imagination and expression you here employ, the more you increase his despair and affliction.

The shame, confusion, and terror of Verres, no doubt, rose in proportion to the noble eloquence and vehemence of Cicero: so also did his pain and uneasiness. These former passions were too strong for the pleasure arising from the beauties of elocution; and operated, though from the same principle, yet in a contrary manner, to the sympathy, compassion, and indignation of the audience.

Lord Clarendon, when he approaches towards the catastrophe of the royal party, supposes that his narration must then become infinitely disagreeable; and he hurries over the king's death without giving us one circumstance of it. He considers it as too horrid a scene to be contemplated with any satisfaction, or even without the utmost pain and aversion. He himself, as well as the readers of that age, were too deeply concerned in the events, and felt a pain from subjects which an historian and a reader of another age would regard as the most pathetic and most interesting, and, by consequence, the most agreeable.

An action, represented in tragedy, may be too bloody and atrocious. It may excite such movements of horror as will not soften into pleasure; and the greatest energy of expression, bestowed on descriptions of that nature, serves only to augment our uneasiness. Such is that action represented in the *Ambitious Step-mother*, where a venerable old man, raised to the height of fury and despair, rushes against a pillar, and striking his head upon it, besmears it all over with mingled brains and gore. The English theatre abounds too much with such shocking images.

Even the common sentiments of compassion require to be softened by some agreeable affection, in order to give a thorough satisfaction to the audience. The mere suffering of plaintive virtue, under the triumphant tyranny and oppression of vice, forms a disagreeable spectacle, and is carefully avoided by all masters of the drama. In order to dismiss the audience with entire satisfaction and contentment, the virtue must either convert itself into a noble courageous despair, or the vice receive its proper punishment.

Most painters appear in this light to have been very unhappy in their subjects. As they wrought much for churches and convents, they have chiefly represented such horrible subjects as crucifixions and martyr-doms, where nothing appears but tortures, wounds, executions, and passive suffering, without any action or affection. When they turned their pencil from this ghastly mythology, they had commonly recourse to Ovid, whose fictions, though passionate and agreeable, are scarcely natural or probable enough for painting.

The same inversion of that principle which is here insisted on, displays itself in common life, as in the effects of oratory and poetry. Raise so the subordinate passion that it becomes the predominant, it swallows up that affection which it before nourished and increased. Too much jealousy extinguishes love; too much difficulty renders us indifferent; too much sickness and infirmity disgusts a selfish and unkind parent.

What so disagreeable as the dismal, gloomy, disastrous stories, with which melancholy people entertain their companions? The uneasy passion being there raised alone, unaccompanied with any spirit, genius, or eloquence, conveys a pure uneasiness, and is attended with nothing that can soften it into pleasure or satisfaction.

Five

Adam Smith

1723–1790

Adam Smith was born on or around 5 June 1723 at Kirkcaldy in Fife. He attended the Burgh School of Kirkcaldy and in 1737 entered the University of Glasgow, where he studied under Francis Hutcheson. In 1740 he became a Snell Exhibitioner at Balliol College, Oxford, but left in 1746 without taking a degree and returned to Scotland.

From 1748 to 1751 Smith gave courses of public lectures in Edinburgh on rhetoric, history of philosophy, and jurisprudence. Then in 1751 he was appointed Professor of Logic at Glasgow and soon moved to the Chair of Moral Philosophy, which he occupied until 1764. Smith's lectures on moral philosophy at Glasgow provided the basis of his first book, *The Theory of Moral Sentiments* (1759), which brought him immediate fame. By 1774 the work was in its fourth edition. It was greatly enlarged in the sixth and final edition, published in the year of Smith's death. During his lifetime three French and two German translations were published.

Smith resigned his Chair in 1764 to become travelling tutor to the Duke of Buccleuch. He spent the winter of 1765-6 in Paris where he met economists and philosophers including Quesnay, Turgot, Helvétius and D'Holbach. In November 1766 he returned to London with the material for his second and best-known book, *An Inquiry into the Nature and Causes of the Wealth of Nations*, though this was not in fact completed for another ten years. The book was finally published on 9 March 1776, and before the end of the century, two German translations, two French, one Danish, one Dutch, one Italian and one Spanish translation had appeared.

While Smith was preparing the second edition of *The Wealth of Nations*, he was appointed Commissioner of the Customs and Salt Duties for Scotland. This required him to move to Edinburgh, where he spent the rest of his life. In Edinburgh he established a weekly dining club, the Oyster Club, which met on Fridays at a tavern in Grassmarket. Its members included Robert Adam, Adam Ferguson, John Playfair and Dugald Stewart. Smith was also a founder member of the Royal Society of Edinburgh, and from 1787 to 1789 Rector of Glasgow University. During this period, he published four further editions of *The Wealth of Nations* and the fifth and sixth of the *Theory of Moral Sentiments*.

Smith died in Edinburgh on 17 June 1790. His surviving papers were published as *Essays on Philosophical Subjects* in 1795.

The first extract reprinted here is taken from one of these essays, the 'History of Astronomy'. In it Smith distinguishes two separate but easily confused phenomena, surprise and wonder. It is in the second that he identifies the origins of intellectual enquiry which by his account consists essentially in the innate desire of the human mind to explain the unfamiliar in terms of the familiar. The second extract, from the *Theory of Moral Sentiments*, concerns Smith's most famous contribution to moral philosophy – the role of sympathy. Like his teacher Hutcheson, Smith's aim is to replace the egoistic conception of human nature espoused by the English philosophers Hobbes and Mandeville, with an account of the human mind that attributes a vital role to our ability to enter into the feelings and experience of others.

Biographical information: Hiroshi Mizuta, *Thoemmes Dictionary of C18th British Philosophers.*

READING VII

The Origins of Philosophy: Surprise and Wonder[1]

Wonder, Surprise, and Admiration, are words which, though often confounded, denote, in our language, sentiments that are indeed allied, but that are in some respects different also, and distinct from one another. What is new and singular, excites that sentiment which, in strict propriety, is called Wonder; what is unexpected, Surprise; and what is great or beautiful, Admiration.

We wonder at all extraordinary and uncommon objects, at all the rarer phenomena of nature, at meteors, comets, eclipses, at singular plants and animals, and at every thing, in short, with which we have before been either a little or not at all acquainted; and we still wonder, though forewarned of what we are to see.

We are surprised at those things which we have seen often, but which we least of all expected to meet with in the place where we find them; we are surprised at the sudden appearance of a friend, whom we have seen a thousand times, but whom we did not imagine we were to see then.

We admire the beauty of a plain or the greatness of a mountain, though we have seen both often before, and though nothing appears to us in either, but what we had expected with certainty to see.

Whether this criticism upon the precise meaning of these words be just, is of little importance. I imagine it is just, though I acknowledge, that the best writers in our language have not always made use of them

---

[1]   Extracted from *Essays on Philosophical Subjects*, New York: Olms, 1982, pp. 3–20.

according to it . . . All that I contend for is, that the sentiments excited by what is new, by what is unexpected, and by what is great and beautiful, are really different, however the words made use of to express them may sometimes be confounded. Even the admiration which is excited by beauty, is quite different (as will appear more fully hereafter) from that which is inspired by greatness, though we have but one word to denote them.

These sentiments, like all others when inspired by one and the same object, mutually support and enliven one another: an object with which we are quite familiar, and which we see every day, produces, though both great and beautiful, but a small effect upon us; because our admiration is not supported either by Wonder or by Surprise: and if we have heard a very accurate description of a monster, our Wonder will be the less when we see it, because our previous knowledge of it will in a great measure prevent our Surprise.

It is the design of this Essay to consider particularly the nature and causes of each of these sentiments, whose influence is of far wider extent than we should be apt upon a careless view to imagine. I shall begin with Surprise.

I: Of the Effects of Unexpectedness, or of Surprise

When an object of any kind, which has been for some time expected and foreseen, presents itself, whatever be the emotion which it is by nature fitted to excite, the mind must have been prepared for it, and must have in some measure have conceived it beforehand; because the idea of the object having been so long present to it, must have beforehand excited some degree of the same emotion which the object itself would excite: the change, therefore, which its presence produces comes thus to be less considerable, and the emotion or passion which it excites glides gradually and easily into the heart, without violence, pain, or difficulty.

But the contrary of all this happens when the object is unexpected; the passion is then poured in all at once upon the heart, which is thrown, if it is a strong passion, into the most violent and convulsive emotions, such as sometimes cause immediate death; sometimes, by the suddenness of the ecstasy, so entirely disjoint the whole frame of the imagination, that it never after returns to its former tone and composure, but falls either into a frenzy or habitual lunacy; and such as almost always occasions a momentary loss of reason, or of that attention to other things which our situation or our duty requires.

How much we dread the effects of the more violent passions, when they come suddenly upon the mind, appears from those preparations which all men think necessary when going to inform any one of what is capable of exciting them. Who would choose all at once to inform his friend of an extraordinary calamity that had befallen him, without taking care beforehand, by alarming him with an uncertain fear, to announce, if one may say so, his misfortune, and thereby prepare and dispose him for receiving the tidings?

Those panic terrors which sometimes seize armies in the field, or great cities, when an enemy is in the neighbourhood, and which deprive for a time the most determined of all deliberate judgements, are never excited but by the sudden apprehension of unexpected danger. Such violent consternations, which at once confound whole multitudes, benumb their understandings, and agitate their hearts, with all agony of extravagant fear, can never be produced by any foreseen danger, how great soever. Fear, though naturally a very strong passion, never rises to such excesses, unless exasperated both by Wonder, from the uncertain nature of the danger, and by Surprise, from the suddenness of the apprehension.

Surprise, therefore, is not to be regarded as an original emotion of a species distinct from all others. The violent and sudden change produced upon the mind, when an emotion of any kind is brought suddenly upon it, constitutes the whole nature of Surprise.

But when not only a passion and a great passion comes all at once upon the mind, but when it comes upon it while the mind is in the mood most unfit for conceiving it, the Surprise is then the greatest. Surprises of joy when the mind is sunk into grief, or of grief when it is elated with joy, are therefore the most unsupportable. The change is in this case the greatest possible. Not only a strong passion is conceived all at once, but a strong passion the direct opposite of that which was before in possession of the soul. When a load of sorrow comes down upon the heart that is expanded and elated with gaiety and joy, it seems not only to damp and oppress it, but almost to crush and bruise it, as a real weight would crush and bruise the body. On the contrary, when from an unexpected change of fortune, a tide of gladness seems, if I may say so, to spring up all at once within it, when depressed and contracted with grief and sorrow, it feels as if suddenly extended and heaved up with violent and irresistible force, and is torn with pangs of all others most exquisite, and which almost always occasion faintings, deliriums, and sometimes instant death. For it may be worthwhile to observe, that though grief be a more violent passion than joy, as indeed all uneasy sensations seem naturally more pungent than the opposite agreeable ones, yet of the two, surprises of joy are still more insupportable than surprises of grief. We are told that after the battle of Thrasimenus, while a Roman lady, who had been informed that her son was slain in the action, was sitting alone bemoaning her misfortunes, the young man who escaped came suddenly into the room to her, and that she cried out and expired instantly in a transport of joy. Let us suppose the contrary of this to have happened, and that in the midst of domestic festivity and mirth, he had suddenly fallen down dead at her feet, is it likely that the effects would have been equally violent? I imagine not. The heart springs to joy with a sort of natural elasticity, it abandons itself to so agreeable an emotion, as soon as the object is presented; it seems to pant and leap forward to meet it, and the passion in its full force takes at once entire and complete possession of the soul. But it is otherways with grief; the heart recoils from, and resists the first approaches of that disagreeable passion, and it requires some time before the melancholy object can produce its full effect. Grief comes on slowly and gradually, nor ever rises at once to that height of agony to which it increased after a little time. But joy comes rushing upon us all at once like a torrent. The change produced therefore by a Surprise of joy is more sudden, and upon that account more violent and apt to have more fatal effects, than that which is occasioned by a Surprise of grief; there seems to be something in the nature of Surprise, which makes it unite more easily with the brisk and quick motion of joy, than with the slower and heavier movement of grief. Most men who can take the trouble to recollect, will find that they have heard of more people who died or became distracted with sudden joy, than with sudden grief. Yet from the nature of human affairs, the latter must be much more frequent than the former. A man may break his leg, or lose his son, though he has had no warning of either of these events, but he can hardly meet with an extraordinary piece of good fortune, without having had some foresight of what was to happen.

Not only grief and joy but all other passions, are more violent, when opposite extremes succeed each other. Is any resentment so keen as what follows the quarrels of lovers, or any love so passionate as what attends their reconcilement?

Even the objects of the external senses affect us in a more lively manner, when opposite extremes succeed to, or are placed beside each other. Moderate warmth seems intolerable heat if felt after extreme cold. What is bitter will seem more so when tasted after what is very sweet; a dirty white will seem bright and pure when placed by a jet black. The vivacity in short of every sensation, as well as of every sentiment, seems to be greater or less in proportion to the change made by the impression of either upon the situation of the mind or organ; but this change must necessarily be the greatest when opposite sentiments and sensations are contrasted, or succeed immediately to one another. Both sentiments and sensations are then the liveliest; and this superior vivacity proceeds from nothing but their being brought upon the mind or organ when in a state most unfit for conceiving them.

As the opposition of contrasted sentiments heightens their vivacity, so the resemblance of those which immediately succeed each other renders them more faint and languid. A parent who has lost several children immediately after one another, will be less affected with the death on the last than with that of the first, though the loss in itself be, in this case, undoubtedly greater; but his mind being altogether sunk into sorrow, the new misfortune seems to produce no other effect than a continuance of the same melancholy, and is by no means apt to occasion such transports of grief as are ordinarily excited by the first calamity of the kind; he receives it, though with great dejection, yet with some degree of calmness and composure, and without any thing of that anguish and agitation of mind which the novelty of the misfortune is apt to occasion. Those who have been unfortunate through the whole course of their lives are often indeed habitually melancholy, and sometimes peevish and splenetic, yet upon any fresh disappointment, though they are vexed and complain a little, they seldom fly out into any more violent passion, and never fall into those transports of rage and grief which often, upon the like occasions, distract the fortunate and successful.

Upon this are founded, in a great measure, some of the effects of habit and custom. It is well known that custom deadens the vivacity of both pain and pleasure, abates the grief we should feel for the one, and weakens the joy we should derive from the other. The pain is supported without agony, and pleasure enjoyed without rapture: because custom and the frequent repetition of any object comes at last to form and bend the mind or organ to that habitual mood and disposition which fits them to receive its impression, without undergoing any very violent change.

II: Of Wonder, or of the Effects of Novelty

It is evident that the mind takes pleasure in observing the resemblances that are discoverable betwixt different objects. It is by means of such observation that it endeavours to arrange and methodise all its ideas, and to reduce them into proper classes and assortments. Where it can observe but one single quality, that is common to a great variety of otherwise widely different objects, that single circumstance will be sufficient for it to connect them all together, to reduce them to one common class, and to call them by one general name. It is thus that all things endowed with a power of self-motion, beasts, birds, fishes, insects, are classed under the general name of Animal; that these again, along with those which want that power, are arranged under the still more general word Substance: and this is the origin of those assortments of objects and ideas which in the schools are called Genera and Species, and of those abstract and general names, which in all languages are made use of to express them.

The further we advance in knowledge and experience, the greater number of divisions and subdivisions of those Genera and Species we are both inclined and obliged to make. We observe a greater variety of particularities amongst those things which have a gross resemblance; and having made new divisions of them, according to those newly-observed particularities, we are then no longer to be satisfied with being able to refer an object to a remote genus, or very general class of things, to many of which it has but a loose and imperfect resemblance. A person, indeed, unacquainted with botany may expect to satisfy your curiosity, by telling you, that such a vegetable is a weed, or, perhaps in still more general terms, that it is a plant. But a botanist will neither give nor accept of such an answer. He has broke and divided that great class of objects into a number of inferior assortments, according to those varieties which his experience has discovered among them; and he wants to refer each individual plant to some tribe of vegetables, with all of which it may have a more exact resemblance, than with many things comprehended under the extensive genus of plants. A child imagines that it gives a satisfactory answer when it tells you, that an object whose name it knows not is a thing, and fancies that it informs you of something, when it thus ascertains to which of the two most obvious and comprehensive classes of objects a particular impression ought to be referred; to the class of realities or solid substances which it calls *things*, or to that of appearances which it calls *nothings*.

Whatever, in short, occurs to us we are fond of referring to some species or class of things, with all of which it has a nearly exact resemblance; and though we often know more about them than about it, yet we are apt to fancy that by being able to do so, we show ourselves to be better acquainted with it, and to have a more thorough insight into its nature. But when something quite new and singular is presented, we feel ourselves incapable of doing this. The memory cannot, from all its stores, cast up any image that nearly resembles this strange appearance. If by some of its qualities it seems to resemble, and to be connected with a species which we have before been acquainted with, it is by others separated and detached from that, and from all the other assortments of things we have hitherto been able to make. It stands alone and by itself in the imagination, and refuses to be grouped or confounded with any set of objects whatever. The imagination and memory exert themselves to no purpose, and in vain look around all their classes of ideas in order to find one under which it may be arranged. They fluctuate to no purpose from thought to thought, and we remain still uncertain and undetermined where to place it, or what to think of it. It is this fluctuation and vain recollection, together with the emotion or movement of spirits that they excite, which constitute the sentiment properly called *Wonder*, and which occasion that staring, and sometimes that rolling of the eyes, that suspension of the breath, and that swelling of the heart, which we may all observe, both in ourselves and others, when wondering at some new object, and which are the natural symptoms of uncertain and undetermined thought. What sort of thing can that be? What is that like? Are the questions which, upon such an occasion, we are all naturally disposed to ask. If we can recollect many such objects which exactly resemble this new appearance, and which present themselves to the imagination naturally, and as it were of their own accord, our Wonder is entirely at an end. If we can recollect but a few, and which it requires too some trouble to be able to call up, our Wonder is indeed diminished, but not quite destroyed. If we can recollect none, but are quite at a loss, it is the greatest possible.

With what curious attention does a naturalist examine a singular plant, or a singular fossil, that is presented to him? He is at no loss to refer it to the general genus of plants or fossils; but this does not satisfy him, and when he considers all the different tribes or species of either with which he has hitherto been acquainted, they all, he thinks, refuse to admit the new object among them. It stands alone in his imagination, and as it were detached from all the other species of that genus to which it belongs. He labours, however, to connect it with some one or other of them. Sometimes he thinks it may be placed in this, and sometimes in that other assortment; nor is he ever satisfied, till he has fallen upon one which, in most of its qualities, it resembles. When he cannot do this, rather than it should stand quite by itself, he will enlarge the precincts, if I may say so, of some species, in order to make room for it; or he will create a new species on purpose to receive it, and call it a Play of Nature, or give it some other appellation, under which he arranges all the oddities that he knows not what else to do with. But to some class or other of known objects he must refer it, and betwixt it and them he must find out some resemblance or other, before he can get rid of that Wonder, that uncertainty and anxious curiosity excited by its singular appearance, and by its dissimilitude with all the objects he had hitherto observed.

As single and individual objects thus excite our Wonder when, by their uncommon qualities and singular appearance, they make us uncertain to what species of things we ought to refer them, so a succession of objects which follow one another in an uncommon train or order, will produce the same effect, though there be nothing particular in any one of them taken by itself.

When one accustomed object appears after another, which it does not usually follow, it first excites, by its unexpectedness, the sentiment properly called Surprise, and afterwards, by the singularity of the succession, or order of its appearance, the sentiment properly called Wonder. We start and are surprised at seeing it there, and then wonder how it came there. The motion of a small piece of iron along a plain table is in itself no extraordinary object, yet the person who first saw it begin, without any visible impulse, in consequence of the motion of a loadstone at some little distance from it, could not behold it without the most extreme Surprise; and when that momentary emotion was over, he would still wonder how it came to be conjoined to an event with which, according to the ordinary train of things, he could have so little suspected it to have any connection.

When two objects, however unlike, have often been observed to follow each other, and have constantly presented themselves to the senses in that order, they come to be so connected together in the fancy, that the idea of the one seems, of its own accord, to call up and introduce that of the other. If the objects are still observed to succeed each other as before, this connection, or, as it has been called, this association of their ideas, becomes stricter and stricter, and the habit of the imagination to pass from the conception of the one to that of the other, grows more and more riveted and confirmed. As its ideas move more rapidly than external objects, it is continually running before them, and therefore anticipates, before it happens, every event which falls out according to this ordinary course of things. When objects succeed each other in the same train in which the ideas of the imagination have thus been accustomed to move, and in which, though not conducted by that chain of events presented to the senses, they have acquired a tendency to go on of their own accord, such objects appear all closely connected with one another, and the thought glides easily along them, without effort and without interruption. They fall in with the natural career of the imagination; and as the ideas which represented such a train of things would seem all mutually to introduce each other, every last thought to be called up by the foregoing, and to call up the succeeding; so when the objects themselves occur, every last event seems, in the same manner, to be introduced by the foregoing, and to introduce the succeeding. There is no break, no stop, no gap, no interval. The ideas excited by so coherent a chain of things seem, as it were, to float through the mind of their own accord, without obliging it to exert itself, or to make any effort in order to pass from one of them to another.

But if this customary connection be interrupted, if one or more objects appear in an order quite different from that to which the imagination has been accustomed, and for which it is prepared, the contrary of all this happens. We are at first surprised by the unexpectedness of the new appearance, and when that momentary emotion is over, we still wonder how it came to occur in that place. The imagination no longer feels the usual facility of passing from the event which goes before to that which comes after. It is an order or law of succession to which it has not been accustomed, and which it therefore finds some difficulty in following, or in attending to. The fancy is stopped and interrupted in that natural movement or career, according to which it was proceeding. Those two events seem to stand at a distance from each other; it endeavours to bring them together, but they refuse to unite; and it feels, or imagines it feels, something like a gap or interval betwixt them. It naturally hesitates, and, as it were, pauses upon the brink of this interval; it endeavours to find out something which may fill up the gap, which, like a bridge, may so far at least unite those seemingly distant objects, as to render the passage of the thought betwixt them smooth, and natural, and easy. The supposition of a chain of intermediate, though invisible, events, which succeed each other in a train similar to that in which the imagination can fill up this interval is the only bridge which, if one may say so, can smooth its passage from the one object to the other. Thus, when we observe the motion of the iron, in consequence of that of the loadstone, we gaze and hesitate, and feel a want of connection betwixt two events which follow one another in so unusual a train. But when, with Descartes, we imagine certain invisible effluvia to circulate round one of them, and by their repeated impulses to impel the other, both to move toward it, and to follow its motion, we fill up the interval betwixt them, we join them together by a sort of bridge, and thus take off that hesitation and difficulty which the imagination felt in passing from the one to the other. That the iron should move after the loadstone seems, upon this hypothesis, in some measure according to the ordinary course of things. Motion after impulse is an order of succession with which of all things we are the most familiar. Two objects which are so connected seem no longer to be disjoined, and the imagination flows smoothly and easily along them.

Such is the nature of this second species of Wonder, which arises from an unusual succession of things. The stop which is thereby given to the career of the imagination, the difficulty which it finds in passing along such disjointed objects, and the feeling of something like a gap or interval betwixt them, constitute the whole essence of this emotion. Upon the clear discovery of a connecting chain of intermediate events, it vanishes altogether. What obstructed the movement of the imagination is then removed. Who wonders at the machinery of the opera-house who has once been admitted behind the scenes? In the wonders of nature, however, it rarely happens that we can discover so clearly this connecting chain. With regard to a few even of them, indeed, we seem to have been really admitted behind the scenes, and our Wonder accordingly is entirely at an end. Thus the eclipses of the sun and moon, which once, more than all the other appearances in the heavens, excited the terror and amazement of mankind, seem now no longer to be wonderful, since the connecting chain has been found out which joins them to the ordinary course of things. Nay, in those cases in which we have been less successful, even the vague hypotheses of Descartes, and the yet more indetermined notions of Aristotle, have, with their followers, contributed to give some coherence to the appearances of nature, and might diminish, though they could not destroy, their Wonder. If they did not completely fill up the interval betwixt the two disjoined objects, they bestowed upon them, however, some sort of loose connection which they wanted before.

That the imagination feels a real difficulty in passing along two events which follow one another in an uncommon order, may be confirmed by many obvious observations. If it attempts to attend beyond a certain time to a long series of this kind, the continual efforts it is obliged to make, in order to pass from one object to another, and thus follow the progress of the succession, soon fatigue it, and if repeated too often, disorder and disjoint its whole frame. It is thus that too severe an application to study sometimes brings on lunacy and frenzy, in those especially who are somewhat advanced in life, but whole imaginations, from being too late in applying, have not got those habits which dispose them to follow easily the reasonings in the abstract sciences. Every step of a demonstration, which to an old practitioner is quite natural and easy, requires from them the most intense application of thought. Spurred on, however, either by ambition, or by admiration for the subject, they still continue till they become, first confused, then giddy, and at last distracted. Could we conceive a person of the soundest judgment, who had grown up to maturity, and whose imagination had acquired those habits, and that mould, which the constitution of things in this world necessarily impress upon it, to be all at once transported alive to some other planet, where nature was governed by laws quite different from those which take place here; as he would be continually obliged to attend to events, which must to him appear in the highest degree jarring, irregular, and discordant, he would soon feel the same confusion and giddiness begin to come upon him, which would at last end in the same manner, in lunacy and distraction. Neither, to produce this effect, is it necessary that the objects should be either great or interesting, or even uncommon, in themselves. It is sufficient that they follow one another in an uncommon order. Let anyone attempt to look over even a game of cards, and to attend particularly to every single stroke, and if he is unacquainted with the nature and rules of the game; that is, with the laws which regulate the succession of the cards, he will soon feel the same confusion and giddiness begin to come upon him, which, were it to be continued for days and months, would end in the same manner, in lunacy and distraction. But if the mind be thus thrown into the most violent disorder, when it attends to a long series of events which follow one another in an uncommon train, it must feel some degree of the same disorder, when it observes even a single event fall out in this unusual manner: for the violent disorder can arise from nothing but the too frequent repetition of this smaller uneasiness.

That it is the unusualness alone of the succession which occasions this stop and interruption in the progress of the imagination, as well as the notion of an interval betwixt the two immediately succeeding objects, to be filled up by some chain of intermediate events, is not less evident. The same orders of succession, which to one set of men seem quite according to the natural course of things, and such as require no intermediate events to join them, shall to another appear altogether incoherent and disjointed, unless some such events be supposed: and this for no other reason, but because such orders of succession are familiar to the one, and strange to the other. When we enter the work-houses of the most common artisans, such as dyers, brewers, distillers, we observe a number of appearances, which present themselves in an order that seems to us very strange and wonderful. Our thought cannot easily follow it, we feel an interval betwixt every two of them, and require some chain of intermediate events, to fill it up, and link them together. But the artisan himself, who has been for many years familiar with the consequences of all the operations of his art, feels no such interval. They fall in with what custom has made the natural movement of his imagination: they no longer excite his wonder, and if he is not a genius superior to his profession, so as to be capable of making the very easy reflection, that those things, though familiar to him, may be strange to us, he will be disposed rather to laugh at, than sympathise with our Wonder. He cannot conceive what occasion there is for any connecting events to unite those appearances, which seem to him to succeed each other very naturally. It is their nature, he tells us, to follow one another in this order, and that accordingly they always do so. In the same manner bread has, since the world began, been the common nourishment of the human body, and men have long seen it, every day, converted into flesh and bones, substances in all respects so unlike it, that they have seldom had the curiosity to inquire by what process of intermediate events this change is brought about. Because the passage of the thought from the one object to the other is by custom become quite smooth and easy, almost without the supposition of any such process. Philosophers, indeed, who often look for a chain of invisible objects to join together two events that occur in an order familiar to all the world, have endeavoured to find out a chain of this kind betwixt the two events I have just now mentioned; in the same manner as they have endeavoured, by a like intermediate chain, to connect the gravity, the elasticity, and even the cohesion of natural bodies, with some of their other qualities. These, however, are all of them such combinations of events as give no stop to the imaginations of the bulk of mankind, as excite no Wonder, nor any apprehension that there is wanting the strictest connection between them. But as in those sounds, which to the greater part of men seem perfectly agreeable to measure and harmony, the nicer ear of a musician will discover a want, both of the most exact time, and of the most perfect coincidence, so the more practised thought of a philosopher, who has spent his whole life in the study of the connecting principles of nature, will often feel an interval betwixt two objects, which, to more careless observers, seem very strictly conjoined. By long attention to the connections which have ever been presented to his observation, by having often compared them with one another, he has, like the musician, acquired, if one may say so, a nicer ear, and a more delicate feeling with regard to things of this nature. And as to the one, that music seems dissonance which falls short of the most perfect harmony; so to the other, those events seem altogether separated and disjoined, which fall short of the strictest and most perfect connection.

READING VIII
Sympathy[2]

I

ow selfish so ever man may be supposed, there are evidently some principles in his nature, which interest him in the fortune of others, and render their happiness necessary to him, though he derives nothing from it except the pleasure of seeing it. Of this kind is pity or compassion, the emotion which we feel for the misery of others, when we either see it, or are made to conceive it in a very lively manner. That we often derive sorrow from the sorrow of others, is a matter of fact too obvious to require any instances to prove it; for this sentiment, like all the other original passions of human nature, is by no means confined to the virtuous and humane, though they may perhaps feel it with the most exquisite sensibility. The greatest ruffian, the most hardened violator of the laws of society, is not altogether without it.

As we have no immediate experience of what other men feel, we can form no idea of the manner in which they are affected, but by conceiving what we ourselves should feel in the like situation. Though our brother is upon the rack, as long as we ourselves are at our ease, our senses will never inform us of what he suffers. They never did, and never can, carry us beyond our own person, and it is by the imagination only that we can form any conception of what are his sensations. Neither can that faculty help us to this any other way, than by representing to us what would be our own, if we were in his case. It is the impressions of our own senses only, not those of his, which our imaginations copy. By the imagination we place ourselves in his situation, we conceive ourselves enduring all the same torments, we enter as it were into his body, and become in some measure the same person with him, and thence form some idea of his sensations, and even feel something which, though weaker in degree, is not altogether unlike them. His agonies, when they are thus brought home to ourselves, when we have thus adopted and made them our own, begin at last to affect us, and we then tremble and shudder at the thought of what he feels. For as to be in pain or distress of any kind excites the most excessive sorrow, so to conceive or to imagine that we are in it, excites some degree of the same emotion, in proportion to the vivacity or dullness of the conception.

That this is the source of our fellow-feeling for the misery of others, that it is by changing places in fancy with the sufferer, that we come either to conceive or to be affected by what he feels, may be demonstrated by many obvious observations, if it should not be thought sufficiently evident of itself. When we see a stroke aimed and just ready to fall

[2]   Extracted from *The Theory of Moral Sentiments,* ed. Knud Haakonssen, Cambridge: University Press, 2002, pp. 11–32.

upon the leg or arm of another person, we naturally shrink and draw back our own leg or our own arm; and when it does fall, we feel it in some measure, and are hurt by it as well as the sufferer. The mob, when they are gazing at a dancer on the slack rope, naturally writhe and twist and balance their own bodies, as they see him do, and as they feel that they themselves must do if in his situation. Persons of delicate fibres and a weak constitution of body complain, that in looking on the sores and ulcers which are exposed by beggars in the streets, they are apt to feel an itching or uneasy sensation in the correspondent part of their own bodies. The horror which they conceive at the misery of those wretches affects that particular part in themselves more than any other; because that horror arises from conceiving what they themselves would suffer, if they really were the wretches whom they are looking upon, and if that particular part in themselves was actually affected in the same miserable manner. The very force of this conception is sufficient, in their feeble frames, to produce that itching or uneasy sensation complained of. Men of the most robust make, observe that in looking upon sore eyes they often feel a very sensible soreness in their own, which proceeds from the same reason, that organ being in the strongest man more delicate, than any other part of the body is in the weakest.

Neither is it those circumstances only, which create pain or sorrow, that call forth our fellow-feeling. Whatever is the passion which arises from any object in the person principally concerned, an analogous emotion springs up, at the thought of his situation, in the breast of every attentive spectator. Our joy for the deliverance of those heroes of tragedy or romance who interest us, is as sincere as our grief for their distress, and our fellow-feeling with their misery is not more real than that with their happiness. We enter into their gratitude towards those faithful friends who did not desert them in their difficulties, and we heartily go along with their resentment against those perfidious traitors who injured, abandoned, or deceived them. In every passion of which the mind of man is susceptible, the emotions of the bystander always correspond to what, by bringing the case home to himself, he imagines should be the sentiments of the sufferer.

Pity and compassion are words appropriated to signify our fellow-feeling with the sorrow of others. Sympathy, though its meaning was, perhaps, originally the same, may now, however, without much impropriety, be made use of to denote our fellow-feeling with any passion whatever.

Upon some occasions sympathy may seem to arise merely from the view of a certain emotion in another person. The passions, upon some occasions, may seem to be transfused from one man to another, instantaneously, and antecedent to any knowledge of what excited them in the person principally concerned. Grief and joy, for example, strongly expressed in the look and gestures of any one, at once affect the spectator with some degree of a like painful or agreeable emotion. A smiling face is, to everybody that sees it, a cheerful object, as a sorrowful countenance, on the other hand, is a melancholy one.

This, however, does not hold universally, or with regard to every passion. There are some passions of which the expressions excite no sort of sympathy, but before we are acquainted with what gave occasion to them, serve rather to disgust and provoke us against them. The furious behaviour of an angry man is more likely to exasperate us against himself than against his enemies. As we are unacquainted with his provocation, we cannot bring his case home to ourselves, nor conceive anything like the passions which it excites. But we plainly see what is the situation of those with whom he is angry, and to what violence they may be exposed from so enraged an adversary. We readily, therefore, sympathize with their fear or resentment, and are immediately disposed to take part against the man from whom they appear to be in so much danger.

If the very appearances of grief and joy inspire us with some degree of the like emotions, it is because they suggest to us the general idea of some good or bad fortune that has befallen the person in whom we observe them: and in these passions this is sufficient to have some little influence upon us. The effects of grief and joy terminate in the person who feels those emotions, of which the expressions do not, like those of resentment, suggest to us the idea of any other person for whom we are concerned, and whose interests are opposite to his. The general idea of good or bad fortune, therefore, creates some concern for the person who has met with it, but the general idea of provocation excites no sympathy with the anger of the man who has received it. Nature, it seems, teaches us to be more averse to enter into this passion, and, till informed of its cause, to be disposed rather to take part against it.

Even our sympathy with the grief or joy of another, before we are informed of the cause of either, is always extremely imperfect. General lamentations, which express nothing but the anguish of the sufferer, create rather a curiosity to inquire into his situation, along with some disposition to sympathize with him, than any actual sympathy that is very sensible. The first question which we ask is, What has befallen you? Till this be answered, though we are uneasy both from the vague idea of his misfortune, and still more from torturing ourselves with conjectures about what it may be, yet our fellow-feeling is not very considerable.

Sympathy, therefore, does not arise so much from the view of the passion, as from that of the situation which excites it. We sometimes feel for another, a passion of which he himself seems to be altogether incapable; because when we put ourselves in his case, that passion arises in our breast from the imagination, though it does not in his from the reality. We blush for the impudence and rudeness of another, though he himself appears to have no sense of the impropriety of his own behaviour; because we cannot help feeling with what confusion we ourselves should be covered, had we behaved in so absurd a manner.

Of all the calamities to which the condition of mortality exposes mankind, the loss of reason appears, to those who have the least spark of humanity, by far the most dreadful, and they behold that last stage of human wretchedness with deeper commiseration than any other. But the poor wretch, who is in it, laughs and sings perhaps, and is altogether insensible of his own misery. The anguish which humanity feels, therefore, at the sight of such an object, cannot be the reflection of any sentiment of the sufferer. The compassion of the spectator must arise altogether from the consideration of what he himself would feel if he was reduced to the same unhappy situation, and, what perhaps is impossible, was at the same time able to regard it with his present reason and judgement.

What are the pangs of a mother, when she hears the moanings of her infant that during the agony of disease cannot express what it feels? In her idea of what it suffers, she joins, to its real helplessness, her own consciousness of that helplessness, and her own terrors for the unknown consequences of its disorder; and out of all these, forms, for her own sorrow, the most complete image of misery and distress. The infant, however, feels only the uneasiness of the present instant, which can never be great. With regard to the future, it is perfectly secure, and in its thoughtlessness and want of foresight, possesses an antidote against fear and anxiety, the great tormentors of the human breast, from which reason and philosophy will, in vain, attempt to defend it, when it grows up to a man.

We sympathize even with the dead, and overlooking what is of real importance in their situation, that awful futurity which awaits them, we are chiefly affected by those circumstances which strike our senses, but can have no influence upon their happiness. It is miserable, we think, to be deprived of the light of the sun; to be shut out from life and conversation; to be laid in the cold grave, a prey to corruption and the reptiles of the earth; to be no more thought of in this world, but to be obliterated, in a little time, from the affections, and almost from the memory, of their dearest friends and relations. Surely, we imagine, we can never feel too much for those who have suffered so dreadful a calamity. The tribute of our fellow-feeling seems doubly due to them now, when they are in danger of being forgot by everybody, and, by the vain honours which we pay to their memory, we endeavour, for our own misery, artificially to keep alive our melancholy remembrance of their misfortune. That our sympathy can afford them no consolation seems to be an addition to their calamity; and to think that all we can do is unavailing, and that, what alleviates all other distress, the regret, the love, and the lamentations of their friends, can yield no comfort to them, serves only to exasperate our sense of their misery. The happiness of the dead, however, most assuredly, is affected by none of these circumstances; nor is it the thought of these things which can ever disturb the profound security of their repose. The idea of that dreary and endless melancholy, which the fancy naturally ascribes to their condition, arises altogether from our joining to the change which has been produced upon them, our own consciousness of that change, from our putting ourselves in their situation, and from our lodging, if I may be allowed to say so, our own living souls in their inanimated bodies, and thence conceiving what would be our emotions in this case. It is from this very illusion of the imagination, that the foresight of our own dissolution is so terrible to us, and that the idea of those circumstances, which undoubtedly can give us no pain when we are dead, makes us miserable while we are alive. And from thence arises one of the most important principles in human nature, the dread of death, the great poison to the happiness, but the great restraint upon the injustice of mankind, which, while it afflicts and mortifies the individual, guards and protects the society.

II: Of the Pleasure of Mutual Sympathy

But whatever may be the cause of sympathy, or however it may be excited, nothing pleases us more than to observe in other men a fellow-feeling with all the emotions of our own breast; nor are we ever so much shocked as by the appearance of the contrary. Those who are fond of deducing all our sentiments from certain refinements of self-love, think themselves at no loss to account, according to their own principles, both for this pleasure and this pain. Man, say they, conscious of his own weakness, and of the need which he has for the assistance of others, rejoices whenever he observes that they adopt his own passions, because he is then assured of that assistance, and grieves whenever he observes the contrary, because he is then assured of their opposition. But both the pleasure and the pain are always felt so instantaneously, and often upon such frivolous occasions, that it seems evident that neither of them can be derived from any such self-interested consideration. A man is mortified when, after having endeavoured to divert the company, he looks round and sees that nobody laughs at his jests but himself. On the contrary, the mirth of the company is highly agreeable to him, and he regards this correspondence of their sentiments with his own as the greatest applause.

Neither does his pleasure seem to arise altogether from the additional vivacity which his mirth may receive from sympathy with theirs, nor his pain from the disappointment he meets with when he misses this pleasure, though both the one and the other, no doubt, do in some measure. When we have read a book or poem so often that we can no longer find any amusement in reading it by ourselves, we can still take pleasure in reading it to a companion. To him it has all the graces of novelty; we enter into the surprise and admiration which it naturally excites in him, but which it is no longer capable of exciting in us; we consider all the ideas which it presents rather in the light in which they appear to him, than in that in which they appear to ourselves, and we are amused by sympathy with his amusement which thus enlivens our own. On the contrary, we should be vexed if he did not seem to be entertained with it, and we could no longer take any pleasure in reading it to him. It is the same case here. The mirth of the company, no doubt, enlivens our own mirth, and their silence, no doubt, disappoints us. But though this may contribute both to the pleasure which we derive from the one, and to the pain which we feel from the other, it is by no means the sole cause of either; and this correspondence of the sentiments of others with our own appears to be a cause of pleasure, and the want of it a cause of pain, which cannot be accounted for in this manner. The sympathy, which my friends express with my joy, might, indeed, give me pleasure by enlivening that joy: but that which they express with my grief could give me none, if it served only to enliven that grief. Sympathy, however, enlivens joy and alleviates grief. It enlivens joy by presenting another source of satisfaction; and it alleviates grief by insinuating into the heart almost the only agreeable sensation which it is at that time capable of receiving.

It is to be observed accordingly, that we are still more anxious to communicate to our friends our disagreeable than our agreeable passions, that we derive still more satisfaction from their sympathy with the former than from that with the latter, and that we are still more shocked by the want of it.

How are the unfortunate relieved when they have found out a person to whom they can communicate the cause of their sorrow? Upon his sympathy they seem to disburthen themselves of a part of their distress: he is not improperly said to share it with them. He not only feels a sorrow of the same kind with that which they feel, but as if he had derived a part of it to himself, what he feels seems to alleviate the weight of what they feel. Yet by relating their misfortunes they in some measure renew their grief. They awaken in their memory the remembrance of those circumstances which occasioned their affliction. Their tears accordingly flow faster than before, and they are apt to abandon themselves to all the weakness of sorrow. They take pleasure, however, in all this, and, it is evident, are sensibly relieved by it, because the sweetness of his sympathy more than compensates the bitterness of that sorrow, which, in order to excite this sympathy, they had thus enlivened and renewed. The cruellest insult, on the contrary, which can be offered to the unfortunate, is to appear to make light of their calamities. To seem not to be affected with the joy of our companions is but want of politeness; but not to wear a serious countenance when they tell us their afflictions, is real and gross inhumanity.

Love is an agreeable, resentment a disagreeable passion, and accordingly we are not half so anxious that our friends should adopt our friendships, as that they should enter into our resentments. We can forgive them though they seem to be little affected with the favours which we may have received, but lose all patience if they seem indifferent about the injuries which may have been done to us: nor are we half so angry with them for not entering into our gratitude, as for not sympathizing with our resentment. They can easily avoid being friends to our friends, but can hardly avoid being enemies to those with whom we are at variance. We seldom resent their being at enmity with the first, though upon that account we may sometimes affect to make an awkward quarrel with them; but we quarrel with them in good earnest if they live in friendship with the last. The agreeable passions of love and joy can satisfy and support the heart without any auxiliary pleasure. The bitter and painful emotions of grief and resentment more strongly require the healing consolation of sympathy.

As the person who is principally interested in any event is pleased with our sympathy, and hurt by the want of it, so we, too, seem to be pleased when we are able to sympathize with him, and to be hurt when we are unable to do so. We run not only to congratulate the successful, but to condole with the afflicted; and the pleasure which we find in the conversation of one whom in all the passions of his heart we can entirely sympathize with, seems to do more than compensate the painfulness of that sorrow with which the view of his situation affects us. On the contrary, it is always disagreeable to feel that we cannot sympathize with him, and instead of being pleased with this exemption from sympathetic pain, it hurts us to find that we cannot share his uneasiness. If we hear a person loudly lamenting his misfortunes, which however, upon bringing the case home to ourselves, we feel, can produce no such violent effect upon us, we are shocked at his grief, and, because we cannot enter into it, call it pusillanimity and weakness. It gives us the spleen, on the other hand, to see another too happy or too much elevated, as we call it, with any little piece of good fortune. We are disobliged even with his joy, and, because we cannot go along with it, call it levity and folly. We are even put out of humour if our companion laughs louder or longer at a joke than we think it deserves, that is, than we feel that we ourselves could laugh at it.

III: Of the Manner in which We Judge of the Propriety or Impropriety of the Affections of Other Men, by Their Concord or Dissonance with Our Own

When the original passions of the person principally concerned are in perfect concord with the sympathetic emotions of the spectator, they necessarily appear to this last just and proper, and suitable to their objects; and, on the contrary, when, upon bringing the case home to himself, he finds that they do not coincide with what he feels, they necessarily appear to him unjust and improper, and unsuitable to the causes which excite them. To approve of the passions of another, therefore, as suitable to their objects, is the same thing as to observe that we entirely sympathize with them, and not to approve of them as such, is the same thing as to observe that we do not entirely sympathize with them. The man who resents the injuries that have been done to me, and observes that I resent them precisely as he does, necessarily approves of my resentment. The man whose sympathy keeps time to my grief, cannot but admit the reasonableness of my sorrow. He who admires the same poem, or the same picture, and admires them exactly as I do, must surely allow the justness of my admiration. He who laughs at the same joke, and laughs along with me, cannot well deny the propriety of my laughter. On the contrary, the person who, upon these different occasions, either feels no such emotion as that which I feel, or feels none that bears any proportion to mine, cannot avoid disapproving my sentiments on account of their dissonance with his own. If my animosity goes beyond what the indignation of my friend can correspond to, if my grief exceeds what his most tender compassion can go along with; if my admiration is either too high or too low to tally with his own, if I laugh loud and heartily when he only smiles, or, on the contrary, only smile when he laughs loud and heartily – in all these cases, as soon as he comes from considering the object, to observe how I am affected by it, according as there is more or less disproportion between his sentiments and mine, I must incur a greater or less degree of his disapprobation, and upon all occasions his own sentiments are the standards and measures by which he judges of mine.

To approve of another man's opinions is to adopt those opinions, and to adopt them is to approve of them. If the same arguments which convince you convince me likewise, I necessarily approve of your conviction; and if they do not, I necessarily disapprove of it: neither can I possibly conceive that I should do the one without the other. To approve or disapprove, therefore, of the opinions of others is acknowledged, by everybody, to mean no more than to observe their agreement or disagreement with our own. But this is equally the case with regard to our approbation or disapprobation of the sentiments or passions of others.

There are, indeed, some cases in which we seem to approve without any sympathy or correspondence of sentiments, and in which, consequently, the sentiment of approbation would seem to be different from the perception of this coincidence. A little attention, however, will convince us that even in these cases our approbation is ultimately founded upon a sympathy or correspondence of this kind. I shall give an instance in things of a very frivolous nature, because in them the judgements of mankind are less apt to be perverted by wrong systems. We may often approve of a jest, and think the laughter of the company quite just and proper, though we ourselves do not laugh, because perhaps, we are in a grave humour, or happen to have our attention engaged with other objects. We have learned, however, from experience, what sort of pleasantry is upon most occasions capable of making us laugh, and we observe that this is one of that kind. We approve, therefore, of the laughter of the company, and feel that it is natural and suitable to its object, because, though in our present mood we cannot easily enter into it, we are sensible that upon most occasions we should very heartily join in it.

The same thing often happens with regard to all the other passions. A stranger passes by us in the street with all the marks of the deepest affliction, and we are immediately told that he has just received the news of the death of his father. It is impossible that, in this case, we should not approve of his grief. Yet it may often happen, without any defect of humanity on our part, that, so far from entering into the violence of his sorrow, we should scarce conceive the first movements of concern upon his account. Both he and his father, perhaps, are entirely unknown to us, or we happen to be employed about other things, and do not take time to picture out in our imagination the different circumstances of distress which must occur to him. We have learned, however, from experience, that such a misfortune naturally excites such a degree of sorrow, and we know that if we took time to consider his situation, fully and in all its parts, we should, without doubt, most sincerely sympathize with him. It is upon the consciousness of this conditional sympathy, that our approbation of his sorrow is founded, even in those cases in which that sympathy does not actually take place; and the general rules derived from our preceding experience of what our sentiments would commonly correspond with, correct upon this, as upon many other occasions, the impropriety of our present emotions.

The sentiment or affection of the heart from which any action proceeds, and upon which its whole virtue or vice must ultimately depend, may be considered under two different aspects, or in two different relations; first, in relation to the cause which excites it, or the motive which gives occasion to it, and secondly, in relation to the end which it proposes, or the effect which it tends to produce.

In the suitableness or unsuitableness, in the proportion or disproportion which the affection seems to bear to the cause or object which excites it, consists the propriety or impropriety, the decency or ungracefulness of the consequent action.

In the beneficial or hurtful nature of the effects which the affection aims at, or tends to produce, consists the merit or demerit of the action, the qualities by which it is entitled to reward, or is deserving of punishment.

Philosophers have, of late years, considered chiefly the tendency of affections, and have given little attention to the relation which they stand in to the cause which excites them. In common life, however, when we judge of any person's conduct, and of the sentiments which directed it, we constantly consider them under both these aspects. When we blame in another man the excesses of love, of grief, of resentment, we not only consider the ruinous effects which they tend to produce, but the little occasion which was given for them. The merit of his favourite, we say, is not so great, his misfortune is not so dreadful, his provocation is not so extraordinary, as to justify so violent a passion. We should have indulged, we say, perhaps have approved of the violence of his emotion, had the cause been in any respect proportioned to it.

When we judge in this manner of any affection, as proportioned or disproportioned to the cause which excites it, it is scarce possible that we should make use of any other rule or canon but the correspondent affection in ourselves. If, upon bringing the case home to our own breast, we find that the sentiments which it gives occasion to, coincide and tally with our own, we necessarily approve of them as proportioned and suitable to their objects; if otherwise, we necessarily disapprove of them, as extravagant and out of proportion.

Every faculty in one man is the measure by which he judges of the like faculty in another. I judge of your sight by my sight, of your ear by my ear, of your reason by my reason, of your resentment by my resentment, of your love by my love. I neither have, nor can have, any other way of judging about them.

IV: The Same Subject Continued

We may judge of the propriety or impropriety of the sentiments of another person by their correspondence or disagreement with our own, upon two different occasions; either, first, when the objects which excite them are considered without any peculiar relation, either to ourselves or to the person whose sentiments we judge of; or, secondly, when they are considered as peculiarly affecting one or other of us.

I.   With regard to those objects which are considered without any peculiar relation either to ourselves or to the person whose sentiments we judge of, wherever his sentiments entirely correspond with our own, we ascribe to him the qualities of taste and good judgement. The beauty of a plain, the greatness of a mountain, the ornaments of a building, the expression of a picture, the composition of a discourse, the conduct of a third person, the proportions of different quantities and numbers, the various appearances which the great machine of the universe is perpetually exhibiting, with the secret wheels and springs which produce them; all the general subjects of science and taste, are what we and our companion regard as having no peculiar relation to either of us. We both look at them from the same point of view, and we have no occasion for sympathy, or for that imaginary change of situation from which it arises, in order to produce, with regard to these, the most perfect harmony of sentiments and affections. If, notwithstanding, we are often differently affected, it arises either from the different degrees of attention, which our different habits of life allow us to give easily to the several parts of those complex objects, or from the different degrees of natural acuteness in the faculty of the mind to which they are addressed.

When the sentiments of our companion coincide with our own in things of this kind, which are obvious and easy, and in which, perhaps, we never found a single person who differed from us, though we, no doubt, must approve them, yet he seems to deserve no praise or admiration on account of them. But when they not only coincide with our own, but lead and direct our own, when in forming them he appears to have attended to many things which we had overlooked, and to have adjusted them to all the various circumstances of their objects, we not only approve of them, but wonder and are surprised at their uncommon and unexpected acuteness and comprehensiveness, and he appears to deserve a very high degree of admiration and applause. For approbation heightened by wonder and surprise, constitutes the sentiment which is properly called admiration, and of which applause is the natural expression. The decision of the man who judges that exquisite beauty is preferable to the grossest deformity, or that twice two are equal to four, must certainly be approved of by all the world, but will not, surely, be much admired. It is the acute and delicate discernment of the man of taste, who distinguishes the minute, and scarce perceptible differences of beauty and deformity; it is the comprehensive accuracy of the experienced mathematician, who unravels, with ease, the most intricate and perplexed proportions; it is the great leader in science and taste, the man who directs and conducts our own sentiments, the extent and superior justness of whose talents astonish us with wonder and surprise, who excites our admiration, and seems to deserve our applause: and upon this foundation is grounded the greater part of the praise which is bestowed upon what are called the intellectual virtues.

The utility of those qualities, it may be thought, is what first recommends them to us, and, no doubt, the consideration of this, when we come to attend to it, gives them a new value. Originally, however, we approve of another man's judgement, not as something useful, but as right, as accurate, as agreeable to truth and reality: and it is evident we attribute those qualities to it for no other reason but because we find that it agrees with our own. Taste, in the same manner, is originally approved off, not as useful, but as just, as delicate, and as precisely suited to its object. The idea of the utility of all qualities of this kind, is plainly an after-thought, and not what first recommends them to our approbation.

II.   With regard to those objects, which affect in particular manner either ourselves or the person whose sentiments we judge of, it is at once more difficult to preserve this harmony and correspondence, and at the same time, vastly more important. My companion does not naturally look upon the misfortune that has befallen me, or the injury that has been done me, from the same point of view in which I consider them. They affect me much more nearly. We do not view them from the same station, as we do a picture, or a poem, or a system of philosophy, and are, therefore, apt to be very differently affected by them. But I can much more easily overlook the want of this correspondence of sentiments with regard to such indifferent objects as concern neither me nor my companion, than with regard to what interests me so much as the misfortune

that has befallen me, or the injury that has been done me. Though you
despise that picture, or that poem, or even that system of philosophy,
which I admire, there is little danger of our quarrelling upon that
account. Neither of us can reasonably be much interested about them.
They ought all of them to be matters of great indifference to us both, so
that, though our opinions may be opposite, our affections may still be
very nearly the same. But it is quite otherwise with regard to those
objects by which either you or I are particularly affected. Though your
judgements in matters of speculation, though your sentiments in matters of taste, are quite opposite to mine, I can easily overlook this opposition, and if I have any degree of temper, I may still find some
entertainment in your conversation, even upon those very subjects. But
if you have either no fellow-feeling for the misfortunes I have met with,
or none that bears any proportion to the grief which distracts me; or if
you have either no indignation at the injuries I have suffered, or none
that bears any proportion to the resentment which transports me, we can
no longer converse upon these subjects. We become intolerable to one
another. I can neither support your company, nor you mine. You are
confounded at my violence and passion, and I am enraged at your cold
insensibility and want of feeling.

In all such cases, that there may be some correspondence of sentiments between the spectator and the person principally concerned, the
spectator must, first of all, endeavour, as much as he can, to put himself
in the situation of the other, and to bring home to himself every little circumstance of distress which can possibly occur to the sufferer. He must
adopt the whole case of his companion with all its minutest incidents;
and strive to render as perfect as possible, that imaginary change of situation upon which his sympathy is founded.

After all this, however, the emotions of the spectator will still be very
apt to fall short of the violence of what is felt by the sufferer. Mankind,
though naturally sympathetic, never conceive, for what has befallen
another, that degree of passion which naturally animates the person
principally concerned. That imaginary change of situation, upon which
their sympathy is founded, is but momentary. The thought of their own
safety, the thought that they themselves are not really the sufferers, continually intrudes itself upon them; and though it does not hinder them
from conceiving a passion somewhat analogous to what is felt by the
sufferer, hinders them from conceiving anything that approaches to the
same degree of violence. The person principally concerned is sensible of
this, and at the same time passionately desires a more complete sympathy. He longs for that relief which nothing can afford him but the entire
concord of the affections of the spectators with his own. To see the emotions of their hearts, in every respect, beat time to his own, in the violent
and disagreeable passions, constitutes his sole consolation. But he can
only hope to obtain this by lowering his passion to that pitch, in which
the spectators are capable of going along with him. He must flatten, if I

may be allowed to say so, the sharpness of its natural tone, in order to reduce it to harmony and concord with the emotions of those who are about him. What they feel, will, indeed, always be, in some respects, different from what he feels, and compassion can never be exactly the same with original sorrow; because the secret consciousness that the change of situations, from which the sympathetic sentiment arises, is but imaginary, not only lowers it in degree, but, in some measure, varies it in kind, and gives it a quite different modification. These two sentiments, however, may, it is evident, have such a correspondence with one another, as is sufficient for the harmony of society. Though they will never be unisons, they may be concords, and this is all that is wanted or required.

In order to produce this concord, as nature teaches the spectators to assume the circumstances of the person principally concerned, so she teaches this last in some measure to assume those of the spectators. As they are continually placing themselves in his situation, and thence conceiving emotions similar to what he feels, so he is as constantly placing himself in theirs, and thence conceiving some degree of that coolness about his own fortune, with which he is sensible that they will view it. As they are constantly considering what they themselves would feel, if they actually were the sufferers, so he is as constantly led to imagine in what manner he would be affected if he was only one of the spectators of his own situation. As their sympathy makes them look at it, in some measure, with his eyes, so his sympathy makes him look at it, in some measure, with theirs, especially when in their presence and acting under their observation: and as the reflected passion, which he thus conceives, is much weaker than the original one, it necessarily abates the violence of what he felt before he came into their presence, before he began to recollect in what manner they would be affected by it, and to view his situation in this candid and impartial light.

The mind, therefore, is rarely so disturbed, but that the company of a friend will restore it to some degree of tranquillity and sedateness. The breast is, in some measure, calmed and composed the moment we come into his presence. We are immediately put in mind of the light in which he will view our situation, and we begin to view it ourselves in the same light; for the effect of sympathy is instantaneous. We expect less sympathy from a common acquaintance than from a friend: we cannot open to the former all those little circumstances which we can unfold to the latter: we assume, therefore, more tranquillity before him, and endeavour to fix our thoughts upon those general outlines of our situation which he is willing to consider. We expect still less sympathy from an assembly of strangers, and we assume, therefore, more tranquillity before them, and always endeavour to bring down our passion to that pitch, which the particular company we are in may be expected to go along with. Nor is this only an assumed appearance: for if we are at all masters of ourselves, the presence of a mere acquaintance will really compose us, still

more than that of a friend; and that of an assembly of strangers still more
than that of an acquaintance.

Society and conversation, therefore, are the most powerful remedies
for restoring the mind to its tranquillity, if, at anytime, it has unfortunately lost it; as well as the best preservatives of that equal and happy
temper, which is so necessary to self-satisfaction and enjoyment. Men of
retirement and speculation, who are apt to sit brooding at home over
either grief or resentment, though they may often have more humanity,
more generosity, and a nicer sense of honour, yet seldom possess that
equality of temper which is so common among men of the world.

V: Of the Amiable and Respectable Virtues

Upon these two different efforts, upon that of the spectator to enter into
the sentiments of the person principally concerned, and upon that of the
person principally concerned, to bring down his emotions to what the
spectator can go along with, are founded two different sets of virtues.
The soft, the gentle, the amiable virtues, the virtues of candid condescen-
sion and indulgent humanity, are founded upon the one: the great, the
awful and respectable, the virtues of self-denial, of self-government, of
that command of the passions which subjects all the movements of our
nature to what our own dignity and honour, and the propriety of our
own conduct require, take their origin from the other.

How amiable does he appear to be, whose sympathetic heart seems to
re-echo all the sentiments of those with whom he converses, who grieves
for their calamities, who resents their injuries, and who rejoices at their
good fortune! When we bring home to ourselves the situation of his
companions, we enter into their gratitude, and feel what consolation
they must derive from the tender sympathy of so affectionate a friend.
And for a contrary reason, how disagreeable does he appear to be,
whose hard and obdurate heart feels for himself only, but is altogether
insensible to the happiness or misery of others! We enter, in this case too,
into the pain which his presence must give to every mortal with whom
he converses, to those especially with whom we are most apt to sympathize, the unfortunate and the injured.

On the other hand, what notable propriety and grace do we feel in the
conduct of those who, in their own case, exert that recollection and
self-command which constitute the dignity of every passion, and which
bring it down to what others can enter into! We are disgusted with that
clamorous grief, which, without any delicacy, calls upon our compassion with sighs and tears and importunate lamentations. But we reverence that reserved, that silent and majestic sorrow, which discovers
itself only in the swelling of the eyes, in the quivering of the lips and
cheeks, and in the distant, but affecting, coldness of the whole behaviour. It imposes the like silence upon us. We regard it with respectful
attention, and watch with anxious concern over our whole behaviour,

lest by any impropriety we should disturb that concerted tranquillity, which it requires so great an effort to support.

The insolence and brutality of anger, in the same manner, when we indulge its fury without check or restraint, is, of all objects, the most detestable. But we admire that noble and generous resentment which governs its pursuit of the greatest injuries, not by the rage which they are apt to excite in the breast of the sufferer, but by the indignation which they naturally call forth in that of the impartial spectator; which allows no word, no gesture, to escape it beyond what this more equitable sentiment would dictate; which never, even in thought, attempts any greater vengeance, nor desires to inflict any greater punishment, than what every indifferent person would rejoice to see executed.

And hence it is, that to feel much for others and little for ourselves, that to restrain our selfish, and to indulge our benevolent affections, constitutes the perfection of human nature; and can alone produce among mankind that harmony of sentiments and passions in which consists their whole grace and propriety. As to love our neighbour as we love ourselves is the great law of Christianity, so it is the great precept of nature to love ourselves only as we love our neighbour, or what comes to the same thing, as our neighbour is capable of loving us.

As taste and good judgement, when they are considered as qualities which deserve praise and admiration, are supposed to imply a delicacy of sentiment and an acuteness of understanding not commonly to be met with, so the virtues of sensibility and self-command are not apprehended to consist in the ordinary, but in the uncommon degrees of those qualities. The amiable virtue of humanity requires, surely, a sensibility, much beyond what is possessed by the rude vulgar of mankind. The great and exalted virtue of magnanimity undoubtedly demands much more than that degree of self-command, which the weakest of mortals is capable of exerting. As in the common degree of the intellectual qualities, there is no abilities, so in the common degree of the moral, there is no virtue. Virtue is excellence, something uncommonly great and beautiful, which rises far above what is vulgar and ordinary. The amiable virtues consist in that degree of sensibility which surprises by its exquisite and unexpected delicacy and tenderness. The awful and respectable, in that degree of self-command which astonishes by its amazing superiority over the most ungovernable passions of human nature.

There is, in this respect, a considerable difference between virtue and mere propriety, between those qualities and actions which deserve to be admired and celebrated, and those which simply deserve to be approved of. Upon many occasions, to act with the most perfect propriety requires no more than that common and ordinary degree of sensibility or self-command which the most worthless of mankind are possessed of, and sometimes even that degree is not necessary. Thus, to give a very low instance, to eat when we are hungry, is certainly, upon ordinary occasions, perfectly right and proper, and cannot miss being approved of as such by everybody. Nothing, however, could be more absurd than to say it was virtuous.

On the contrary, there may frequently be a considerable degree of virtue in those actions which fall short of the most perfect propriety, because they may still approach nearer to perfection than could well be expected upon occasions in which it was so extremely difficult to attain it: and this is very often the case upon those occasions which require the greatest exertions of self-command. There are some situations which bear so hard upon human nature, that the greatest degree of self-government, which can belong to so imperfect a creature as man, is not able to stifle altogether the voice of human weakness, or reduce the violence of the passions to that pitch of moderation in which the impartial spectator can entirely enter into them. Though in those cases, therefore, the behaviour of the sufferer fall short of the most perfect propriety, it may still deserve some applause, and even in a certain sense, may be denominated virtuous. It may still manifest an effort of generosity and magnanimity of which the greater part of men are incapable; and though it fails of absolute perfection, it may be a much nearer approximation towards perfection, than what, upon such trying occasions, is commonly either to be found or to be expected.

In cases of this kind, when we are determining the degree of blame or applause which seems due to any action, we very frequently make use of two different standards. The first is the idea of complete propriety and perfection, which, in those difficult situations, no human conduct ever did, or ever can come up to, and in comparison with which the actions of all men must forever appear blameable and imperfect. The second is the idea of that degree of proximity or distance from this complete perfection, which the actions of the greater part of men commonly arrive at. Whatever goes beyond this degree, how far so ever it may be removed from absolute perfection, seems to deserve applause; and whatever falls short of it, to deserve blame.

It is in the same manner that we judge of the productions of all the arts which address themselves to the imagination. When a critic examines the work of any of the great masters in poetry or painting, he may sometimes examine it by an idea of perfection, in his own mind, which neither that nor any other human work will ever come up to, and as long as he compares it with this standard, he can see nothing in it but faults and imperfections. But when he comes to consider the rank which it ought to hold among other works of the same kind, he necessarily compares it with a very different standard, the common degree of excellence which is usually attained in this particular art; and when he judges of it by this new measure, it may often appear to deserve the highest applause, upon account of its approaching much nearer to perfection than the greater part of those works which can be brought into competition with it.

Six

Thomas Reid

1710–1796

Thomas Reid was born on 26 April 1710, the son of the Presbyterian minister of Strachan in Kincardineshire, Scotland. He attended Kincardine
parish school and Aberdeen Grammar School, and in 1722 entered
Marischal College, Aberdeen, where he followed the four-year general
arts course before going on to study divinity. He completed his theological training in 1731, and was admitted to the ministry of the Church of
Scotland. After a brief spell as presbytery clerk, he was employed by
Marischal College as librarian from 1733–6. Following a tour of England,
Reid became minister of New Machar in 1737, a position in the gift of the
other Aberdonian college, King's.

Reid's first publication was, 'An Essay on Quantity; Occasioned by
Reading a Treatise in which Simple and Compound Ratios are Applied
to Virtue and Merit'. Written while Minister of New Machar and presented to the Royal Society in 1748, it is a criticism of Hutcheson's *Inquiry
into the Original of Our Ideas of Beauty and Virtue*. This led to his being
appointed regent at King's College in 1751, a position that required him
to teach the whole of the arts curriculum except Greek. He played an
active part in the administration of King's and was one of the founders of
and leading lights in the Aberdeen Philosophical Society, better known as
the Wise Club. In 1764 he published his first major work *An Inquiry into the
Human Mind, on the Principles of Common Sense* (1764).

In 1764 Reid was appointed to the Chair of Moral Philosophy at Glasgow in succession to Adam Smith. During the following years, he developed the philosophy of Common Sense systematically and in great
detail. He was also active in university government, represented Glasgow University in the General Assembly of the Church of Scotland, and
was a keen member of the Glasgow College Literary Society, to which he
presented papers and debating questions on a very wide variety of scientific, philosophical, political and economic topics. Reid retired from
teaching in 1780. In 1785 he published the *Essays on the Intellectual Powers
of Man* and in 1788 *Essays on the Active Powers of Man*. He died on 7 October 1796.

Reid's philosophy had significant influence in continental Europe and North America, where 'common sense' philosophy had a considerable impact on college education for several decades. It is as founder of this 'School of Common Sense' that Reid became best known, though the expression was subsequently misunderstood by his proponents almost as much as his detractors. (Immanuel Kant called the appeal to 'common sense', 'the last refuge of the stalest windbag'!) However, Reid's principal aim was not to establish a 'School' but to put the philosophical investigation of the human mind on a firmer foundation. In the extracts printed here he argues that it is a certain sort of cleverness, rather than the lack of it, that fills philosophy 'with error and false theory', a tendency to 'disdain the mean offices of digging for a foundation and removing rubbish'. Accordingly, he takes a more modest approach to the subject, and begins with a close analysis of a central concept, 'sense'. It is from this analysis that his account of a common or shared 'sense' arises. Reid then sets out the principles of reason that any satisfactory inquiry must observe.

Reid's style of writing reflects his style of thought, and is remarkable for a striking clarity that few philosophers achieve.

Biographical information: Knud Haakonssen, *Thoemmes Dictionary of C18th British Philosophers*.

READING IX
Inquiring into the Human Mind[1]

I: The Importance of the Subject, and the Means of Prosecuting it

The fabric of the human mind is curious and wonderful, as well as that of the human body. The faculties of the one are with no less wisdom adapted to their several ends, than the organs of the other. Nay, it is reasonable to think, that as the mind is a nobler work, and of a higher order than the body, even more of the wisdom and skill of the divine Architect has been employed in its structure. It is therefore a subject highly worthy of inquiry on its own account, but still more worthy on account of the extensive influence which the knowledge of it has over every other branch of science.

In the arts and sciences which have least connection with the mind, its faculties are the engines which we must employ; and the better we understand their nature and use, their defects and disorders, the more skilfully we shall apply them, and with the greater success. But in the noblest arts, the mind is also the subject upon which we operate. The painter, the poet, the actor, the orator, the moralist, and the statesman,

---

[1]   Extracted from *An Inquiry into the Human Mind on the Principles of Common Sense*, ed. Derek R. Brookes, Edinburgh: University Press, 1997, pp. 11–24.

attempt to operate upon the mind in different ways, and for different ends; and they succeed according as they touch properly the strings of the human frame. Nor can their several arts ever stand on a solid foundation, or rise to the dignity of science, until they are built on the principles of the human constitution.

Wise men now agree, or ought to agree in this, that there is but one way to the knowledge of nature's works, the way of observation and experiment. By our constitution, we have a strong propensity to trace particular facts and observations to general rules, and to apply such general rules to account for other effects, or to direct us in the production of them. This procedure of the understanding is familiar to every human creature in the common affairs of life, and it is the only one by which any real discovery in philosophy can be made.

The man who first discovered that cold freezes water, and that heat turns it into vapour, proceeded on the same general principles, and in the same method, by which Newton discovered the law of gravitation and the properties of light. His *regulæ philosophandi* [Rules of Philosophizing] are maxims of common sense, and are practised every day in common life; and he who philosophises by other rules, either concerning the material system, or concerning the mind, mistakes his aim.

Conjectures and theories are the creatures of men, and will always be found very unlike the creatures of God. If we would know the works of God, we must consult themselves with attention and humility, without daring to add any thing of ours to what they declare. A just interpretation of nature is the only sound and orthodox philosophy: whatever we add of our own, is apocryphal, and of no authority.

All our curious theories of the formation of the earth, of the generation of animals, of the origin of natural and moral evil, so far as they go beyond a just induction from facts, are vanity and folly, no less than the vortices of Descartes, or the Archæus of Paracelsus. Perhaps the philosophy of the mind has been no less adulterated by theories, than that of the material system. The theory of ideas is indeed very ancient, and has been very universally received; but as neither of these titles can give it authenticity, they ought not to screen it from a free and candid examination; especially in this age, when it has produced a system of scepticism, that seems to triumph over all science, and even over the dictates of common sense.

All that we know of the body, is owing to anatomical dissection and observation, and it must be by an anatomy of the mind that we can discover its powers and principles.

II: The Impediments to our Knowledge of the Mind

But it must be acknowledged, that this kind of anatomy is much more difficult than the other, and therefore it need not seem strange, that mankind have made less progress in it. To attend accurately to the operations of our minds, and make them an object of thought, is no easy matter even to the contemplative, and to the bulk of mankind is next to impossible.

An anatomist who has happy opportunities, may have access to examine with his own eyes, and with equal accuracy, bodies of all different ages, sexes, and conditions; so that what is defective, obscure, or preternatural in one, may be discerned clearly, and in its most perfect state in another. But the anatomist of the mind cannot have the same advantage. It is his own mind only that he can examine, with any degree of accuracy and distinctness. This is the only subject he can look into. He may, from outward signs, collect the operations of other minds, but these signs are for the most part ambiguous, and must be interpreted by what he perceives within himself.

So that if a philosopher could delineate to us, distinctly and methodically, all the operations of the thinking principle within him, which no man was ever able to do, this would be only the anatomy of one particular subject; which would be both deficient and erroneous, if applied to human nature in general. For a little reflection may satisfy us, that the difference of minds is greater than that of any other beings, which we consider as of the same species.

Of the various powers and faculties we possess, there are some which nature seems both to have planted and reared, so as to have left nothing to human industry. Such are the powers which we have in common with the brutes, and which are necessary to the preservation of the individual, or the continuance of the kind. There are other powers, of which nature has only planted the seeds in our minds, but has left the rearing of them to human culture. It is by the proper culture of these, that we are capable of all those improvements in intellectuals, in taste, and in morals, which exalt and dignify human nature; while, on the other hand, the neglect or perversion of them makes its degeneracy and corruption.

The two-legged animal that eats of nature's dainties, what his taste or appetite craves, and satisfies his thirst at the crystal fountain, who propagates his kind as occasion and lust prompt, repels injuries, and takes alternate labour and repose, is, like a tree in the forest, purely of nature's growth. But this same savage has within him the seeds of the logician, the man of taste and breeding, the orator, the statesman, the man of virtue, and the saint; which seeds, though planted in his mind by nature, yet, through want of culture and exercise, must lie for ever buried, and be hardly perceivable by himself or by others.

The lowest degree of social life will bring to light some of those principles which lay hid in the savage state; and according to his training, and company, and manner of life, some of them, either by their native vigour, or by the force of culture, will thrive and grow up to great perfection, others will be strangely perverted from their natural form, and others checked, or perhaps quite eradicated.

This makes human nature so various and multiform in the individuals that partake of it, that, in point of morals, and intellectual endowments, it fills up all that gap which we conceive to be between brutes and devils below, and the celestial orders above; and such a prodigious diversity of minds must make it extremely difficult to discover the common principles of the species.

The language of philosophers, with regard to the original faculties of the mind, is so adapted to the prevailing system, that it cannot fit any other; like a coat that fits the man for whom it was made, and shows him to advantage, which yet will sit very awkward upon one of a different make, although perhaps as handsome and as well proportioned. It is hardly possible to make any innovation in our philosophy concerning the mind and its operations, without using new words and phrases, or giving a different meaning to those that are received; a liberty which, even when necessary, creates prejudice and misconstruction, and which must wait the sanction of time to authorise it. For innovations in language, like those in religion and government, are always suspected and disliked by the many, till use has made them familiar, and prescription has given them a title.

If the original perceptions and notions of the mind were to make their appearance single and unmixed, as we first received them from the hand of nature, one accustomed to reflection would have less difficulty in tracing them; but before we are capable of reflection, they are so mixed, compounded, and decompounded, by habits, associations, and abstractions, that it is hard to know what they were originally. The mind may in this respect be compared to an apothecary or a chemist, whose materials indeed are furnished by nature; but for the purposes of his art, he mixes, compounds, dissolves, evaporates, and sublimes them, till they put on a quite different appearance; so that it is very difficult to know what they were at first, and much more to bring them back to their original and natural form. And this work of mind is not carried on by deliberate acts of mature reason, which we might recollect, but by means of instincts, habits, associations, and other principles, which operate before we come to the use of reason; so that it is extremely difficult for the mind to return upon its own footsteps, and trace back those operations which have employed it since it first began to think and to act.

Could we obtain a distinct and full history of all that has passed in the mind of a child, from the beginning of life and sensation, till it grows up to the use of reason; how its infant faculties began to work, and how they brought forth and ripened all the various notions, opinions, and sentiments, which we find in ourselves when we come to be capable of reflection, this would be a treasure of natural history, which would probably give more light into the human faculties, than all the systems of philosophers about them since the beginning of the world. But it is in vain to wish for what nature has not put within the reach of our power. Reflection, the only instrument by which we can discern the powers of the mind, comes too late to observe the progress of nature, in raising them from their infancy to perfection.

It must therefore require great caution, and great application of mind, for a man that is grown up in all the prejudices of education, fashion, and philosophy, to unravel his notions and opinions, till he finds out the simple and original principles of his constitution, of which no account can be given but the will of our Maker. This may be truly called an *analysis* of the human faculties, and till this is performed, it is in vain we expect any just *system* of the mind, that is, an enumeration of the original powers and laws of our constitution, and an explication from them of the various phænomena of human nature.

Success in an inquiry of this kind, it is not in human power to command; but perhaps it is possible, by caution and humility, to avoid error and delusion. The labyrinth may be too intricate, and the thread too fine, to be traced through all its windings; but if we stop where we can trace it no farther, and secure the ground we have gained, there is no harm done; a quicker eye may in time trace it farther.

It is genius, and not the want of it, that adulterates philosophy, and fills it with error and false theory. A creative imagination disdains the mean offices of digging for a foundation, of removing rubbish, and carrying materials: leaving these servile employments to the drudges in science, it plans a design, and raises a fabric. Invention supplies materials where they are wanting, and fancy adds colouring, and every befitting ornament. The work pleases the eye, and wants nothing but solidity and a good foundation. It seems even to vie with the works of nature, till some succeeding architect blows it into rubbish, and builds as goodly a fabric of his own in its place. Happily for the present age, the castle- builders employ themselves more in romance than in philosophy. That is undoubtedly their province, and in those regions the offspring of fancy is legitimate, but in philosophy it is all spurious.

III: The Present State of this Part of Philosophy. Of Descartes, Malebranche, and Locke

That our philosophy concerning the mind and its faculties, is but in a very low state, may be reasonably conjectured, even by those who never have narrowly examined it. Are there any principles with regard to the mind, settled with that perspicuity and evidence, which attends the principles of mechanics, astronomy, and optics? These are really sciences, built upon laws of nature which universally obtain. What is discovered in them, is no longer a matter of dispute: future ages may add to it, but till the course of nature be changed, what is already established can never be overturned. But when we turn our attention inward, and consider the phænomena of human thoughts, opinions, and perceptions, and endeavour to trace them to the general laws and the first principles of our constitution, we are immediately involved in darkness and perplexity. And if common sense, or the principles of education, happen not to be stubborn, it is odds but we end in absolute scepticism.

Descartes finding nothing established in this part of philosophy, in order to lay the foundation of it deep, resolved not to believe his own existence till he should be able to give a good reason for it. He was, perhaps, the first that took up such a resolution: but if he could indeed have effected his purpose, and really become diffident of his existence, his case would have been deplorable, and without any remedy from reason or philosophy. A man that disbelieves his own existence, is surely as unfit to be reasoned with, as a man that believes he is made of glass. There may be disorders in the human frame that may produce such extravagancies, but they will never be cured by reasoning. Descartes indeed would make us believe, that he got out of this delirium by this logical argument, *Cogito ergo sum* [I think, therefore I am]. But it is evident he was in his senses all the time, and never seriously doubted of his existence. For he takes it for granted in this argument, and proves nothing at all. I am thinking, says he, therefore I am: and is it not as good reasoning to say, I am sleeping, therefore I am? or, I am doing nothing, therefore I am? If a body moves, it must exist, no doubt; but if it is at rest, it must exist likewise.

Perhaps Descartes meant not to assume his own existence in this enthymeme, but the existence of thought; and to infer from that the existence of a mind, or subject of thought. But why did he not prove the existence of his thought? Consciousness, it may be said, vouches that. But who is voucher for consciousness? Can any man prove that his consciousness may not deceive him? No man can: nor can we give a better reason for trusting to it, than that every man, while his mind is sound, is determined, by the constitution of his nature, to give implicit belief to it, and to laugh at, or pity the man who doubts its testimony. And is not every man, in his wits, as much determined to take his existence upon trust as his consciousness?

The other proposition assumed in this argument that thought cannot be without a mind or subject – is liable to the same objection, not that it wants evidence, but that its evidence is no clearer, nor more immediate, than that of the proposition to be proved by it. And taking all these propositions together, 'I think', 'I am conscious', 'Every thing that thinks, exists', 'I exist', would not every sober man form the same opinion of the man who seriously doubted any one of them? And if he was his friend, would he not hope for his cure from physic and good regimen, rather than from metaphysic and logic?

But supposing it proved, that my thought and my consciousness must have a subject, and consequently that I exist, how do I know that all that train and succession of thoughts which I remember, belong to one subject, and that the I of this moment, is the very individual I of yesterday, and of times past?

Descartes did not think proper to start this doubt, but Locke had done it; and, in order to resolve it, gravely determines, that personal identity consists in consciousness; that is, if you are conscious that you did such a thing a twelve-month ago, this consciousness makes you to be the very person that did it. Now, consciousness of what is past, can signify nothing else but the remembrance that I did it. So that Locke's principle must be, that identity consists in remembrance, and consequently a man must lose his personal identity with regard to every thing he forgets.

Nor are these the only instances whereby our philosophy concerning the mind appears to be very fruitful in creating doubts, but very unhappy in resolving them.

Descartes, Malebranche, and Locke, have all employed their genius and skill, to prove the existence of a material world, and with very bad success. Poor untaught mortals believe undoubtedly, that there is a sun, moon, and stars, an earth, which we inhabit, country, friends, and relations, which we enjoy, land, houses, and movables, which we possess. But philosophers, pitying the credulity of the vulgar, resolve to have no faith but what is founded upon reason. They apply to philosophy to furnish them with reasons for the belief of those things which all mankind have believed, without being able to give any reason for it. And surely one would expect, that, in matters of such importance, the proof would not be difficult: but it is the most difficult thing in the world. For these three great men, with the best good will, have not been able, from all the treasures of philosophy, to draw one argument, that is fit to convince a man that can reason, of the existence of any one thing without him. Admired Philosophy! daughter of light! parent of wisdom and knowledge! if thou art she! surely thou hast not yet arisen upon the human mind, nor blessed us with more of thy rays, than are sufficient to shed a darkness visible upon the human faculties, and to disturb that repose and security which happier mortals enjoy, who never approached thine altar, nor felt thine influence! But if indeed thou hast not power to dispel those clouds and phantoms which thou hast discovered or created, withdraw this penurious and malignant ray; I despise Philosophy, and renounce its guidance: let my soul dwell with Common Sense.

IV: Apology For Those Philosophers

But instead of despising the dawn of light, we ought rather to hope for its increase: instead of blaming the philosophers I have mentioned, for the defects and blemishes of their system, we ought rather to honour their memories, as the first discoverers of a region in philosophy formerly unknown; and however lame and imperfect the system may be, they have opened the way to future discoveries, and are justly entitled to a great share in the merit of them. They have removed an infinite deal of dust and rubbish, collected in the ages of scholastic sophistry, which had obstructed the way. They have put us in the right road, that of experience and accurate reflection. They have taught us to avoid the snares of ambiguous and ill-defined words, and have spoken and thought upon this subject with a distinctness and perspicuity formerly unknown. They have made many openings that may lead to the discovery of truths which they did not reach, or to the detection of errors in which they were involuntarily entangled.

It may be observed, that the defects and blemishes in the received philosophy concerning the mind, which have most exposed it to the contempt and ridicule of sensible men, have chiefly been owing to this: That the votaries of this Philosophy, from a natural prejudice in her favour, have endeavoured to extend her jurisdiction beyond its just limits, and to call to her bar the dictates of Common Sense. But these decline this jurisdiction; they disdain the trial of reasoning, and disown its authority; they neither claim its aid, nor dread its attacks.

In this unequal contest betwixt Common Sense and Philosophy, the latter will always come off both with dishonour and loss; nor can she ever thrive till this rivalship is dropped, these encroachments given up, and a cordial friendship restored: for, in reality, Common Sense holds nothing of Philosophy, nor needs her aid. But, on the other hand, Philosophy (if I may be permitted to change the metaphor) has no other root but the principles of Common Sense; it grows out of them, and draws its nourishment from them: severed from this root, its honours wither, its sap is dried up, it dies and rots.

The philosophers of the last age, whom I have mentioned, did not attend to the preserving this union and subordination so carefully as the honour and interest of philosophy required: but those of the present have waged open war with Common Sense, and hope to make a complete conquest of it by the subtleties of Philosophy; an attempt no less audacious and vain, than that of the giants to dethrone almighty Jove.

V: Of Bishop Berkeley; the Treatise of Human Nature; and of Scepticism

The present age, I apprehend, has not produced two more acute or more practised in this part of philosophy, than the Bishop of Cloyne [George Berkeley], and the author of the *Treatise of human nature* [David Hume]. The first was no friend to scepticism, but had that warm concern for religious and moral principles which became his order: yet the result of his inquiry was, a serious conviction, that there is no such thing as a material world, nothing in nature but spirits and ideas, and that the belief of material substances, and of abstract ideas, are the chief causes of all our errors in philosophy, and of all infidelity and heresy in religion. His arguments are founded upon the principles which were formerly laid down by Descartes, Malebranche, and Locke, and which have been very generally received.

And the opinion of the ablest judges seems to be, that they neither have been, nor can be confuted; and that he has proved by unanswerable arguments what no man in his senses can believe.

The second proceeds upon the same principles, but carries them to their full length; and as the Bishop undid the whole material world, this author, upon the same grounds, undoes the world of spirits, and leaves nothing in nature but ideas and impressions, without any subject on which they may be impressed.

It seems to be a peculiar strain of humour in this author, to set out in his introduction, by promising, with a grave face, no less than a complete system of the sciences, upon a foundation entirely new, to wit, that of human nature, when the intention of the whole work is to show, that there is neither human nature nor science, in the world. It may perhaps be unreasonable to complain of this conduct in an author, who neither believes his own existence, nor that of his reader, and therefore could not mean to disappoint him, or to laugh at his credulity. Yet I cannot imagine, that the author of the *Treatise of human nature* is so sceptical as to plead this apology. He believed, against his principles, that he should be read, and that he should retain his personal identity, till he reaped the honour and reputation justly due to his metaphysical acumen. Indeed he ingenuously acknowledges, that it was only in solitude and retirement that he could yield any assent to his own philosophy; society, like day-light, dispelled the darkness and the fogs of scepticism, and made him yield to the dominion of Common Sense. Nor did I ever hear him charged with doing any thing, even in solitude, that argued such a degree of scepticism as his principles maintain. Surely if his friends apprehended this, they would have the charity never to leave him alone.

Pyrrho the Elean, the father of this philosophy, seems to have carried it to a greater perfection than any of his successors: for if we may believe Antigonus the Carystian, quoted by Diogenes Laertius, his life corresponded to his doctrine. And therefore, if a cart run against him, or a dog attacked him, or if he came upon a precipice, he would not stir a foot to avoid the danger, giving no credit to his senses. But his attendants, who, happily, for him were not so great sceptics, took care to keep him out of harm's way, so that he lived till he was ninety years of age. Nor is it to be doubted, but this author's friends would have been equally careful to keep him from harm, if ever his principles had taken too strong a hold of him.

It is probable the *Treatise of human nature* was not written in company; yet it contains manifest indications, that the author every now and then relapsed into the faith of the vulgar, and could hardly, for half a dozen pages, keep up the sceptical character.

In like manner, the great Pyrrho himself forgot his principles on some occasions; and is said once to have been in such a passion with his cook, who probably had not roasted his dinner to his mind, that with the spit in his hand, and the meat upon it, he pursued him even into the market-place.

It is a bold philosophy that rejects, without ceremony, principles which irresistibly govern the belief and the conduct of all mankind in the common concerns of life; and to which the philosopher himself must yield, after he imagines he has confuted them. Such principles are older, and of more authority, than Philosophy: she rests upon them as her basis, not they upon her. If she could overturn them, she must be buried in their ruins; but all the engines of philosophical subtlety are too weak for this purpose; and the attempt is no less ridiculous, than if a mechanic should contrive an *axis in peritrochio* to remove the earth out of its place; or if a mathematician should pretend to demonstrate, that things equal to the same thing are not equal to one another.

Zeno endeavoured to demonstrate the impossibility of motion; Hobbes, that there was no difference between right and wrong; and this author, that no credit is to be given to our senses, to our memory, or even to demonstration. Such philosophy is justly ridiculous, even to those who cannot detect the fallacy of it. It can have no other tendency, than to show the acuteness of the sophist, at the expense of disgracing reason and human nature, and making mankind Yahoos.

VI: Of the Treatise of Human Nature

There are other prejudices against this system of human nature, which, even upon a general view, may make one diffident of it.

Descartes, Hobbes, and this author, have each of them given us a system of human nature, an undertaking too vast for any one man, how great so ever his genius and abilities may be. There must surely be reason to apprehend, that many parts of human nature never came under their observation, and that others have been stretched and distorted, to fill up blanks, and complete the system. Christopher Columbus, or Sebastian Cabot, might almost as reasonably have undertaken to give us a complete map of America.

There is a certain character and style in Nature's works, which is never attained in the most perfect imitation of them. This seems to be wanting in the systems of human nature I have mentioned, and particularly in the last. One may see a puppet make variety of motions and gesticulations, which strike much at first view; but when it is accurately observed, and taken to pieces, our admiration ceases; we comprehend the whole art of the maker. How unlike is it to that which it represents! what a poor piece of work compared with the body of a man, whose structure the more we know, the more wonders we discover in it, and more sensible we are of our ignorance! Is the mechanism of the mind so easily comprehended, when that of the body is so difficult? Yet, by this system, three laws of association, joined to a few original feelings, explain the whole mechanism of sense, imagination, memory, belief, and of all the actions and passions of the mind. Is this the man that Nature made? I suspect it is not so easy to look behind the scenes in Nature's work. This is a puppet surely, contrived by too bold an apprentice of Nature, to mimic her work. It shows tolerably by candlelight, but brought into clear day, and taken to pieces, it will appear to be a man made with mortar and a trowel. The more we know of other parts of nature, the more we like and approve them. The little I know of the planetary system, of the earth which we inhabit, of minerals, vegetables, and animals; of my own body, and of the laws which obtain in these parts of nature, opens to my mind grand and beautiful scenes, and contributes equally to my happiness and power. But when I look within, and consider the mind itself, which makes me capable of all these prospects and enjoyments, if it is indeed what the *Treatise of human nature* makes it, I find I have been only in an enchanted castle, imposed upon by spectres and apparitions. I blush inwardly to think how I have been deluded; I am ashamed of my frame, and can hardly forbear expostulating with my destiny: Is this thy pastime, O Nature, to put such tricks upon a silly creature, and then to take off the mask, and show him how he has been befooled? If this is the philosophy of human nature, my soul enter thou not into her secrets. It is surely the forbidden tree of knowledge; I no sooner taste of it, than I perceive myself naked, and stripped of all things, yea even of my very self. I see myself, and the whole frame of nature, shrink into fleeting ideas, which, like Epicurus's atoms, dance about in emptiness.

VII: The System of All These Authors is the Same, and Leads to Scepticism

But what if these profound disquisitions into the first principles of human nature, do naturally and necessarily plunge a man into this abyss of scepticism? May we not reasonably judge so from what has happened? Descartes no sooner began to dig in this mine, than scepticism was ready to break in upon him. He did what he could to shut it out. Malebranche and Locke, who dug deeper, found the difficulty of keeping out this enemy still to increase; but they laboured honestly in the design. Then Berkeley, who carried on the work, despairing of securing all, bethought himself of an expedient: By giving up the material world, which he thought might be spared without loss, and even with advantage, he hoped by an impregnable partition to secure the world of spirits. But, alas! The *Treatise of human nature* wantonly sapped the foundation of this partition, and drowned all in one universal deluge.

These facts, which are undeniable, do indeed give reason to apprehend, that Descartes's system of the human understanding, which I shall beg leave to call *the ideal system*, and which, with some improvements made by later writers, is now generally received, has some original defect; that this scepticism is inlaid in it, and reared along with it; and, therefore, that we must lay it open to the foundation, and examine the materials, before we can expect to raise to any solid and useful fabric of knowledge on this subject.

VIII: We Ought not to Despair of a Better

But is this to be despaired of, because Descartes and his followers have failed? By no means. This pusillanimity would be injurious to ourselves, and injurious to truth. Useful discoveries are sometimes indeed the effect of superior genius, but more frequently they are the birth of time and of accidents. A traveller of good judgement may mistake his way, and be unawares led into a wrong track; and while the road is fair before him, he may go on without suspicion, and be followed by others; but when it ends in a coal-pit, it requires no great judgement to know that he has gone wrong, nor perhaps to find out what misled him.

In the mean time, the unprosperous state of this part of philosophy has produced an effect, somewhat discouraging indeed to any attempt of this nature, but an effect which might be expected, and which time only and better success can remedy. Sensible men, who never will be sceptics in matters of common life, are apt to treat with sovereign contempt every thing that has been said, or is to be said, upon this subject. It is metaphysic, say they: Who minds it? Let scholastic sophisters entangle themselves in their own cobwebs; I am resolved to take my own existence, and the existence of other things, upon trust; and to believe that snow is cold, and honey sweet, whatever they may say to the contrary. He must either be a fool, or want to make a fool of me, that would reason me out of my reason and senses.

I confess I know not what a sceptic can answer to this, nor by what good argument he can plead even for a hearing; for either his reasoning is sophistry, and so deserves contempt; or there is no truth in the human faculties, and then why should we reason?

If therefore a man find himself entangled in these metaphysical toils, and can find no other way to escape, let him bravely cut the knot which he cannot loose, curse metaphysic, and dissuade every man from meddling with it. For if I have been led into bogs and quagmires by following an *ignis fatuus* [will o' the wisp], what can I do better, than to warn others to beware of it? If Philosophy contradicts herself, befools her votaries, and deprives them of every object worthy to be pursued or enjoyed, let her be sent back to the infernal regions from which she must have had her original.

But is it absolutely certain that this fair lady is of the party? Is it not possible she may have been misrepresented? Have not men of genius in former ages often made their own dreams to pass for her oracles? Ought she then to be condemned without any farther hearing? This would be unreasonable. I have found her in all other matters an agreeable companion, a faithful counsellor, a friend to Common Sense, and to the happiness of mankind. This justly entitles her to my correspondence and confidence, till I find infallible proofs of her infidelity.

READING X:
Common Sense[2]

he word *sense*, in common language, seems to have a different meaning from that which it has in the writings of Philosophers; and those different meanings are apt to be confounded, and to occasion embarrassment and error.

Not to go back to ancient philosophy upon this point, modern Philosophers consider sense as a power that has nothing to do with judgement. Sense they consider as the power by which we receive certain ideas or impressions from objects; and judgement as the power by which we compare those ideas, and perceive their necessary agreements and disagreements.

The external senses give us the idea of colour, figure, sound, and other qualities of body, primary or secondary. Mr Locke gave the name of an internal sense to consciousness, because by it we have the ideas of thought, memory, reasoning, and other operations of our own minds. Dr Hutcheson of Glasgow, conceiving that we have simple and original ideas which cannot be imputed either to the external senses, or to consciousness, introduced other internal senses; such as the sense of harmony, the sense of beauty, and the moral sense. Ancient Philosophers also spoke of internal senses, of which memory was accounted one.

But all these senses, whether external or internal, have been represented by Philosophers, as the means of furnishing our minds with ideas, without including any kind of judgement. Dr Hutcheson defines a sense to be a determination of the mind to receive any idea from the presence of an object independent on our will.

> By this term (sense) Philosophers in general have denominated those faculties, in consequence of which we are liable to feelings relative to ourselves only, and from which they have not pretended to draw any conclusions concerning the nature of things; whereas truth is not relative, but absolute and real (Joseph Priestly).

On the contrary, in common language, sense always implies judgement. A man of sense is a man of judgement. Good sense is good judgement. Nonsense is what is evidently contrary to right judgement. Common sense is that degree of judgement which is common to men with whom we can converse and transact business.

Seeing and hearing by Philosophers are called senses, because we have ideas by them; by the vulgar they are called senses, because we judge by them. We judge of colours by the eye; of sounds by the ear; of beauty and deformity by taste; of right and wrong in conduct by our moral sense or conscience.

---

[2]   Extracted from *Essays on the Intellectual Powers of Man*, Edinburgh University Press, Edinburgh, 2002, pp. 423–34.

Sometimes Philosophers, who represent it as the sole province of sense to furnish us with ideas, fall unawares into the popular opinion, that they are judging faculties. Thus Locke, book 4. chap. 11.

> And of this, (that the quality or accident of colour doth really exist, and hath a being without me,) the greatest assurance I can possibly have, and to which my faculties can attain, is the testimony of my eyes, which are the proper and sole judges of this thing.

This popular meaning of the word *sense* is not peculiar to the English language. The corresponding words in Greek, Latin, and I believe in all the European languages, have the same latitude. The Latin words, *sentire, sententia, sensa, sensus,* from the last of which the English word *sense* is borrowed, express judgement or opinion, and are applied indifferently to objects of external sense, of taste, of morals, and of the understanding.

I cannot pretend to assign the reason why a word, which is no term of art, which is familiar in common conversation, should have so different a meaning in philosophical writings. I shall only observe, that the philosophical meaning corresponds perfectly with the account which Mr Locke and other modern Philosophers give of judgement. For if the sole province of the senses, external and internal, be to furnish the mind with the ideas about which we judge and reason, it seems to be a natural consequence, that the sole province of judgement should be to compare those ideas, and perceive their necessary relations.

These two opinions seem to be so connected, that one may have been the cause of the other. I apprehend, however, that if both be true, there is no room left for any knowledge or judgement, either of the real existence of contingent things, or of their contingent relations.

To return to the popular meaning of the word sense. I believe it would be much more difficult to find good authors who never use it in that meaning, than to find such as do.

We may take Mr Pope as good authority for the meaning of an English word. He uses it often, and in his Epistle to the Earl of Burlington, has made a little descant upon it.

> Oft have you hinted to your brother Peer,
> A certain truth, which many buy too dear;
> Something there is more needful than expence,
> And something previous ev'n to taste, — 'tis sense.
> Good sense, which only is the gift of Heaven;
> And though no science, fairly worth the seven;
> A light, which in yourself you must perceive,
> Jones and Le Nôtre have it no to give.[3]

---

[3]   Alexander Pope, *An epistle to the Right Honourable Richard Earl of Burlington* . . . (London, 1731), lines 39-46. ('Inigo Jones, the celebrated architect; and M. Le Notre, the designer of the best gardens in France' — Pope).

This inward light or sense is given by Heaven to different persons in different degrees. There is a certain degree of it which is necessary to our being subjects of law and government, capable of managing our own affairs, and answerable for our conduct towards others: This is called common sense, because it is common to all men with whom we can transact business, or call to account for their conduct.

The laws of all civilised nations distinguish those who have this gift of Heaven, from those who have it not. The last may have rights which ought not to be violated, but having no understanding in themselves to direct their actions, the laws appoint them to be guided by the understanding of others. It is easily discerned by its effects in men's actions, in their speeches, and even in their looks; and when it is made a question, whether a man has this natural gift or not, a judge or a jury, upon a short conversation with him, can, for the most part, determine the question with great assurance.

The same degree of understanding which makes a man capable of acting with common prudence in the conduct of life, makes him capable of discovering what is true and what is false in matters that are self-evident, and which he distinctly apprehends.

All knowledge, and all science, must be built upon principles that are self-evident; and of such principles, every man who has common sense is a competent judge, when he conceives them distinctly. Hence it is, that disputes very often terminate in an appeal to common sense.

While the parties agree in the first principle on which their arguments are grounded, there is room for reasoning; but when one denies what to the other appears too evident to need, or to admit of proof, reasoning seems to be at an end; an appeal is made to common sense, and each party is left to enjoy his own opinion.

There seems to be no remedy for this, nor any way left to discuss such appeals, unless the decisions of common sense can be brought into a code, in which all reasonable men shall acquiesce. This indeed, if it be possible, would be very desirable, and would supply a desideratum in logic; and why should it be thought impossible that reasonable men should agree in things that are self-evident?

All that is intended in this chapter, is to explain the meaning of common sense, that it may not be treated, as it has been by some, as a new principle, or as a word without any meaning. I have endeavoured to show, that sense, in its most common, and therefore its most proper meaning, signifies judgement, though Philosophers often use it in another meaning. From this it is natural to think, that common sense should mean common judgement; and so it really does.

What the precise limits are which divide common judgement from what is beyond it on the one hand, and from what falls short of it on the other, may be difficult to determine; and men may agree in the meaning of the word who have different opinions about those limits, or who even never thought of fixing them. This is as intelligible as, that all Englishmen should mean the same thing by the county of York, though perhaps not a hundredth part of them can point out its precise limits.

Indeed, it seems to me, that common sense is as unambiguous a word, and as well understood as the county of York. We find it in innumerable places in good writers; we hear it on innumerable occasions in conversation; and, as far as I am able to judge, always in the same meaning. And this is probably the reason why it is so seldom defined or explained.

Dr Johnson, in the authorities he gives, to show that the word *sense* signifies understanding, soundness of faculties, strength of natural reason, quotes Dr Bentley for what may be called a definition of common sense, though probably not intended for that purpose, but mentioned accidentally: 'God hath endowed mankind with power and abilities, which we call natural light and reason, and common sense'.[4]

It is true, that common sense is a popular, and not a scholastic word, and by most of those who have treated systematically of the powers of the understanding, it is only occasionally mentioned, as it is by other writers. But I recollect two philosophical writers, who are exceptions to this remark. One is Buffier, who treated largely of common sense, as a principle of knowledge, above fifty years ago. The other is Bishop Berkeley, who, I think, has laid as much stress upon common sense, in opposition to the doctrines of Philosophers, as any Philosopher that has come after him . . .

Men rarely ask what common sense is; because every man believes himself possessed of it, and would take it for an imputation upon his understanding to be thought unacquainted with it. Yet I remember two very eminent authors who have put this question; and it is not improper to hear their sentiments upon a subject so frequently mentioned, and so rarely canvassed.

It is well known, that Lord Shaftesbury gave to one of his Treatises the title of *Sensus Communis; an Essay on the freedom of wit and humour, in a letter to a friend* [London, 1709] in which he puts his friend in mind of a free conversation with some of their friends on the subjects of morality and religion. Amidst the different opinions started and maintained with great life and ingenuity, one or other would every now and then take the liberty to appeal to common sense. Every one allowed the appeal; no one would offer to call the authority of the court in question, till a gentleman, whose good understanding was never yet brought in doubt, desired the company very gravely that they would tell him what common sense was.

> If, said he, by the word *sense*, we were to understand opinion and judgement, and by the word *common*, the generality, or any considerable part of mankind, it would be hard to discover where the subject of common sense could lie; for that which was according to the sense of one part of mankind, was against the

[4]   Samuel Johnson, *A Dictionary of the English Language* (London, 1755), 'SENSE'.

sense of another: And if the majority were to determine common sense, it would change as often as men changed [Shaftesbury, p. 29].

That in religion, common sense was as hard to determine as *catholic* or *orthodox*. What to one was absurdity, to another was demonstration.

In policy, if plain British or Dutch sense were right, Turkish and French must certainly be wrong. And as mere nonsense, as passive obedience seemed, we found it to be the common sense of a great party amongst ourselves, a greater party in Europe, and perhaps the greatest part of all the world besides. As for morals, the difference was still wider; for even the Philosophers could never agree in one and the same system. And some even of our most admired modern Philosophers had fairly told us,' that virtue and vice had no other law or measure than mere fashion and vogue' [Shaftesbury, pp. 30–2].

This is the substance of the gentleman's speech, which, I apprehend, explains the meaning of the word perfectly, and contains all that has been said, or can be said against the authority of common sense, and the propriety of appeals to it.

As there is no mention of any answer immediately made to this speech, we might be apt to conclude, that the noble author adopted the sentiments of the intelligent gentleman, whose speech he recites. But the contrary is manifest, from the title of *Sensus Communis* given to his Essay, from his frequent use of the word, and from the whole tenor of the Essay.

The author appears to have a double intention in that Essay, corresponding to the double title prefixed to it. One intention is, to justify the use of wit, humour, and ridicule, in discussing among friends the gravest subjects. 'I can very well suppose, says he, men may be frightened out of their wits; but I have no apprehension they should be laughed out of them. I can hardly imagine, that, in a pleasant way, they should ever be talked out of their love for society, or reasoned out of humanity and common sense' [Shaftesbury, p. 54].

The other intention, signified by the title *Sensus Communis*, is carried on hand in hand with the first, and is to show, that common sense is not so vague and uncertain a thing as it is represented to be in the sceptical speech before recited. 'I will try', says he, 'what certain knowledge or assurance of things may be recovered in that very way, (to wit, of humour), by which all certainty, you thought, was lost, and an endless scepticism introduced'.

He gives some criticisms upon the word *sensus communis* in Juvenal, Horace, Seneca; and after showing, in a facetious way throughout the Treatise, that the fundamental principles of morals, of politics, of criticism, and of every branch of knowledge, are the dictates of common sense, he sums up the whole in these words: 'That some moral and philosophical truths there are so evident in themselves, that it would be easier to imagine half mankind run mad, and joined precisely in the same species of folly, than to admit any thing as truth, which should be advanced against such natural knowledge, fundamental reason, and common sense'.[5] And on taking leave, he adds: 'And now, my friend, should you find I had moralised in any tolerable manner, according to common sense, and without canting, I should be satisfied with my performance'.[6]

Another eminent writer who has put the question what common sense is, is Fenelon, the famous Archbishop of Cambray.

That ingenious and pious author, having had an early prepossession in favour of the Cartesian philosophy, made an attempt to establish, on a sure foundation, the metaphysical arguments which Descartes had invented to prove the being of the Deity. For this purpose, he begins with the Cartesian doubt. He proceeds to find out the truth of his own existence, and then to examine wherein the evidence and certainty of this and other such primary truths consisted. This, according to Cartesian principles, he places in the clearness and distinctness of the ideas. On the contrary, he places the absurdity of the contrary propositions, in their being repugnant to his clear and distinct ideas.

To illustrate this, he gives various examples of questions manifestly absurd and ridiculous, which every man of common understanding would at first sight perceive to be so, and then goes on to this purpose.

> What is it that makes these questions ridiculous? Wherein does this ridicule precisely consist? It will perhaps be replied, that it consists in this, that they shock common sense. But what is this same common sense? It is not the first notions that all men have equally of the same things. This common sense, which is always and in all places the same; which prevents enquiry; which makes enquiry in some cases ridiculous; which, instead of enquiring, makes man laugh whether he will or not; which puts it out of a man's power to doubt; this sense, which only waits to be consulted; which shows itself at the first glance, and immediately discovers the evidence or the absurdity of a question; is not this the same that I call my ideas?
>
> Behold then those ideas or general notions, which it is not in my power either to contradict or examine, and by which I examine and decide in every case, insomuch that I laugh instead of answering, as often as any thing is proposed to me, which is evidently contrary to what these immutable ideas represent.[7]

From the account I have given of the meaning of this term, it is easy to judge both of the proper use and of the abuse of it.

It is absurd to conceive that there can be any opposition between reason and common sense. It is indeed the first-born of reason, and as they are commonly joined together in speech and in writing, they are inseparable in their nature.

[5]   Shaftesbury, *Sensus Communis*, p. 117.
[6]   Shaftesbury, *Sensus Communis*, p.119.
[7]   Françoise de Fénelon, *Demonstration de l'existence de Dieu* (1713), translated as *A Demonstration of the Existence and Attributes of God*, 2nd edn (London, 1720), pp. 238–9.

We ascribe to reason two offices, or two degrees. The first is to judge of things self-evident; the second to draw conclusions that are not self-evident from those that are. The first of these is the province, and the sole province of common sense; and therefore it coincides with reason in its whole extent, and is only another name for one branch or one degree of reason. Perhaps it may be said, Why then should you give it a particular name, since it is acknowledged to be only a degree of reason? It would be a sufficient answer to this, Why do you abolish a name which is to be found in the language of all civilized nations, and has acquired a right by prescription? Such an attempt is equally foolish and ineffectual. Every wise man will be apt to think, that a name which is found in all languages as far back as we can trace them, is not without some use.

But there is an obvious reason why this degree of reason should have a name appropriated to it; and that is, that in the greatest part of mankind no other degree of reason is to be found. It is this degree that entitles them to the denomination of reasonable creatures. It is this degree of reason, and this only, that makes a man capable of managing his own affairs, and answerable for his conduct towards others. There is therefore the best reason why it should have a name appropriated to it.

These two degrees of reason differ in other respects, which would be sufficient to entitle them to distinct names.

The first is purely the gift of Heaven. And where Heaven has not given it, no education can supply the want. The second is learned by practice and rules when the first is not wanting. A man who has common sense may be taught to reason. But if he has not that gift, no teaching will make him able either to judge of first principles or to reason from them.

I have only this farther to observe, that the province of common sense is more extensive in refutation than in confirmation. A conclusion drawn by a train of just reasoning from true principles cannot possibly contradict any decision of common sense, because truth will always be consistent with itself. Neither can such a conclusion receive any confirmation from common sense, because it is not within its jurisdiction.

But it is possible, that, by setting out from false principles, or by an error in reasoning, a man may be led to a conclusion that contradicts the decisions of common sense. In this case, the conclusion is within the jurisdiction of common sense, though the reasoning on which it was grounded be not; and a man of common sense may fairly reject the conclusion, without being able to show the error of the reasoning that led to it.

Thus, if a Mathematician, by a process of intricate demonstration, in which some false step was made, should be brought to this conclusion, that two quantities, which are both equal to a third, are not equal to each other, a man of common sense, without pretending to be a judge of the demonstration, is well entitled to reject the conclusion, and to pronounce it absurd.

READING XI:
The Principles of Reason[8]

One of the most important distinctions of our judgement is, that some of them are intuitive, others grounded on argument.

It is not in our power to judge as we will. The judgment is carried along necessarily by the evidence, real or seeming, which appears to us at the time. But in propositions that are submitted to our judgment, there is this great difference; some are of such a nature that a man of ripe understanding may apprehend them distinctly, and perfectly understand their meaning without finding himself under any necessity of believing them to be true or false, probable or improbable. The judgment remains in suspense, until it is inclined to one side or another by reasons or arguments.

But there are other propositions which are no sooner understood than they are believed. The judgment follows the apprehension of them necessarily, and both are equally the work of nature, and the result of our original powers. There is no searching for evidence, no weighing of arguments; the proposition is not deduced or inferred from another; it has the light of truth in itself, and has no occasion to borrow it from another.

Propositions of the last kind, when they are used in matters of science, have commonly been called *axioms*; and on whatever occasion they are used, are called *first principles, principles of common sense, common notions, self-evident truths.* ...

What has been said, I think, is sufficient to distinguish first principles, or intuitive judgments, from those which may be ascribed to the power of reasoning; nor is it a just objection against this distinction, that there may be some judgments concerning which we may be dubious to which class they ought to be referred. There is a real distinction between persons within the house, and those that are without; yet it may be dubious to which the man belongs that stands upon the threshold.

The power of reasoning, that is of drawing a conclusion from a chain of premises, may with some propriety be called an art. 'All reasoning', says Mr Locke, 'is search and casting about, and requires pains and application' [Locke, *Essay*, I.ii.10, p. 52]. It resembles the power of walking, which is acquired by use and exercise. Nature prompts to it, and has given the power of acquiring it; but must be aided by frequent exercise before we are able to walk. After repeated efforts, much stumbling, and many falls, we learn to walk; and it is in a similar manner that we learn to reason.

But the power of judging in self-evident propositions, which are clearly understood, may be compared to the power of swallowing our

[8] Extracted from *Essays on the Intellectual Powers of Man*, Edinburgh University Press, Edinburgh, 2002, pp. 452–67.

food. It is purely natural, and therefore common to the learned, and the unlearned; to the trained, and the untrained. It requires ripeness of understanding, and freedom from prejudice, but nothing else.

I take it for granted, that there are self-evident principles. Nobody, I think, denies it. And if any man were so sceptical as to deny that there is any proposition that is self-evident, I see not how it would be possible to convince him by reasoning.

But yet there seems to be great difference of opinions among Philosophers about first principles. What one takes to be self-evident, another labours to prove by arguments, and a third denies altogether.

Thus, before the time of Descartes, it was taken for a first principle, that there is a sun and a moon, an earth and sea, which really exist, whether we think of them or not. Descartes thought that the existence of those things ought to be proved by argument; and in this he has been followed by Malebranche, Arnauld, and Locke. They have all laboured to prove, by very weak reasoning, the existence of external objects of sense; and Berkeley and Hume, sensible of the weakness of their arguments, have been led to deny their existence altogether.

The ancient Philosophers granted, that all knowledge must be grounded on first principles, and that there is no reasoning without them. The Peripatetic philosophy was redundant rather than deficient in first principles. Perhaps the abuse of them in that ancient system may have brought them into discredit in modern times; for as the best things may be abused, so that abuse is apt to give a disgust to the thing itself; and as one extreme often leads into the opposite, this seems to have been the case in respect paid to first principles in ancient and in modern times.

Descartes thought one principle, expressed in one word *cogito*, a sufficient foundation for his whole system, and asked no more.

Mr Locke seems to think first principles of very small use. Knowledge consisting, according to him, in the perception of the agreement or disagreement of our ideas, when we have clear ideas, and are able to compare them together, we may always fabricate first principles as often as we have occasion for them. Such differences we find among Philosophers about first principles.

It is likewise a question of some moment, whether the differences among men about first principles can be brought to any issue? When, in disputes, one man maintains that to be a first principle, which another denies, commonly both parties appeal to common sense, and so the matter rests. Now, is there no way of discussing this appeal? Is there no mark or criterion, whereby first principles that are truly such, may be distinguished from those that assume the character without a just title? I shall humbly offer in the following propositions what appears to me to be agreeable to truth in these matters, always ready to change my opinion upon conviction.

1. *First*, I hold it to be certain, and even demonstrable, That all knowledge got by reasoning must be built upon first principles.

This is as certain as that every house must have a foundation. The power of reasoning, in this respect, resembles the mechanical powers or engines; it must have a fixed point to rest upon, otherwise it spends its force in the air, and produces no effect.

When we examine, in the way of analysis, the evidence of any proposition, either we find it self-evident, or it rests upon one or more propositions that support it. The same thing may be said of the propositions that support it; and of those that support them, as far back as we can go. But we cannot go back in this track to infinity. Where then must this analysis stop? It is evident that it must stop only when we come to propositions, which support all that are built upon them, but are themselves supported by none, that is, to self-evident propositions.

Let us again consider a synthetical proof of any kind, where we begin with the premises, and pursue a train of consequences, until we come to the last conclusion, or thing to be proved. Here we must begin, either with self-evident propositions, or with such as have been already proved. When the last is the case, the proof of the propositions, thus assumed, is a part of our proof; and the proof is deficient without it. Suppose then the deficiency supplied, and the proof completed, is it not evident that it must set out with self-evident propositions, and that the whole evidence must rest upon them? So that it appears to be demonstrable that, without first principles, analytical reasoning could have no end, and synthetical reasoning could have no beginning; and that every conclusion got by reasoning must rest with its whole weight upon first principles, as the building does upon its foundation.

2. A *second* proposition is, That some first principles yield conclusions that are certain, others such as are probable, in various degrees, from the highest probability to the lowest.

In just reasoning, the strength or weakness of the conclusion will always correspond to that of the principles on which it is grounded.

In a matter of testimony, it is self-evident, that the testimony of two is better than that of one, supposing them equal in character, and in their means of knowledge; yet the simple testimony may be true, and that which is preferred to it may be false.

When an experiment has succeeded in several trials, and the circumstances have been marked with care, there is a self-evident probability of its succeeding in a new trial; but there is no certainty. The probability, in some cases, is much greater than in others, because, in some cases, it is much easier to observe all the circumstances that may have influence upon the event than in others. And it is possible, that, after many experiments made with care, our expectation may be frustrated in a succeeding one, by the variation of some circumstance that has not, or perhaps could not be observed.

Sir Isaac Newton has laid it down as a first principle in natural philosophy, that a property which has been found in all bodies upon which we have had access to make experiments, and which has always been found in its quantity to be in exact proportion to the quantity of matter in every body, is to be held as an universal property of matter.

This principle, as far as I know, has never been called in question. The evidence we have, that all matter is divisible, moveable, solid, and inert, is resolvable into this principle, and if it be not true, we cannot have any rational conviction that all matter has those properties. From the same principle that great man has shown, that we have reason to conclude, that all bodies gravitate towards each other.

This principle, however, has not that kind of evidence which mathematical axioms have. It is not a necessary truth whose contrary is impossible; nor did Sir Isaac ever conceive it to be such. And if it should ever be found, by just experiments, that there is any part in the composition of some bodies which has not gravity, the fact, if duly ascertained, must be admitted as an exception to the general law of gravitation.

In games of chance, it is a first principle, that every side of a die has an equal chance to be turned up; and that, in a lottery, every ticket has an equal chance of being drawn out. From such first principles as these, which are the best we can have in such matters, we may deduce, by demonstrative reasoning, the precise degree of probability of every event in such games.

But the principles of all this accurate and profound reasoning can never yield a certain conclusion, it being impossible to supply a defect in the first principles by any accuracy in the reasoning that is grounded upon them. As water, by its gravity, can rise no higher in its course than the fountain, however artfully it be conducted; so no conclusion of reasoning can have a greater degree of evidence than the first principles from which it is drawn.

From these instances, it is evident, that as there are some first principles that yield conclusions of absolute certainty; so there are others that can only yield probable conclusions; and that the lowest degree of probability must be grounded on first principles as well as absolute certainty.

3. A *third* proposition is, that it would contribute greatly to the stability of human knowledge, and consequently to the improvement of it, if the first principles upon which the various parts of it are grounded were pointed out and ascertained.

We have ground to think so, both from facts, and from the nature of the thing.

There are two branches of human knowledge in which this method has been followed, to wit, mathematics and natural philosophy, in mathematics, as far back as we have books. It is in this science only, that, for more than two thousand years since it began to be cultivated, we find no sects, no contrary systems, and hardly any disputes; or, if there have been disputes, they have ended as soon as the animosity of parties subsided, and have never been again revived. The science, once firmly established upon the foundation of a few axioms and definitions, as upon a rock, has grown from age to age, so as to become the loftiest and the most solid fabric that human reason can boast.

Natural philosophy, till less than two hundred years ago, remained in the same fluctuating state with the other sciences. Every new system, pulled up the old by the roots. The system-builders, indeed, were always willing to accept of the aid of first principles, when they were of their side; but finding them insufficient to support the fabric which their imagination had raised, they were only brought in as auxiliaries, and so intermixed with conjectures, and with lame inductions, that their systems were like Nebuchadnezzar's image, whose feet were partly of iron and partly of clay.

Lord Bacon first delineated the only solid foundation on which natural philosophy can be built, and Sir Isaac Newton reduced the principles laid down by Bacon into three or four axioms, which he calls *regulæ philosophandi*. From these, together with the phenomena observed by the senses, which he likewise lays down as first principles, he deduces, by strict reasoning, the propositions contained in the third book of his *Principia*, and in his *Optics*, and by this means has raised a fabric in those two branches of natural philosophy, which is not liable to be shaken by doubtful disputation, but stands immoveable upon the basis of self-evident principles.

This fabric has been carried on by the accession of new discoveries; but is no more subject to revolutions.

The disputes about *materia prima* [primary matter], substantial forms, Nature's abhorring a vacuum, and bodies having no gravitation in their proper place, are now no more. The builders in this work are not put to the necessity of holding a weapon in one hand while they build with the other; their whole employment is to carry on the work.

Yet it seems to be very probable, that if natural philosophy had not been reared upon this solid foundation of self-evident principles, it would have been to this day a field of battle, wherein every inch of ground would have been disputed, and nothing fixed and determined.

I acknowledge that mathematics and natural philosophy, especially the former, have this advantage of most other sciences, that it is less difficult to form distinct and determinate conceptions of the objects about which they are employed; but as this difficulty is not insuperable, it afford a good reason, indeed, why other sciences should have a longer infancy, but no reason at all why they may not at last arrive at maturity, by the same steps as those of quicker growth.

The facts I have mentioned may therefore lead us to conclude, that if in other branches of philosophy the first principles were laid down, as has been done in mathematics and natural philosophy, and the subsequent conclusions grounded upon them, this would make it much more easy to distinguish what is solid and well supported from the vain fictions of human fancy.

But laying aside facts, the nature of the thing leads to the same conclusion.

For when any system is grounded upon first principles, and deduced regularly from them, we have a thread to lead us through the labyrinth. The judgement has a distinct and determinate object. The heterogeneous parts being separated, can be examined each by itself.

The whole system is reduced to axioms, definitions, and deductions. These are materials of a very different nature, and to be measured by a very different standard; and it is much more easy to judge of each, taken by itself, than to judge of a mass wherein they are kneaded together without distinction. Let us consider how we judge of each of them.

First, as to definitions, the matter is very easy. They relate only to words, and differences about them may produce different ways of speaking, but can never produce different ways of thinking, while every man keeps to his own definitions.

But as there is not a more plentiful source of fallacies in reasoning than mens using the same word sometimes in one sense and at other times in another, the best means of preventing such fallacies, or of detecting them when they are committed, is definitions of words as accurate as can be given.

Secondly, as to deductions drawn from principles granted on both sides, I do not see how they can long be a matter of dispute among men who are not blinded by prejudice or partiality. For the rules of reasoning by which inferences may be drawn from premises have been for two thousand years fixed with great unanimity. No man pretends to dispute the rules of reasoning laid down by Aristotle, and repeated by every writer in dialectics.

And we may observe by the way, that the reason why logicians have been so unanimous in determining the rules of reasoning, from Aristotle down to this day, seems to be, that they were by that great genius raised, in a scientific manner, from a few definitions and axioms. It may farther be observed, that when men differ about a deduction, whether it follows from certain premises, this I think is always owing to their differing about some first principle. I shall explain this by an example.

Suppose that, from a thing having begun to exist, one man infers that it must have had a cause; another man does not admit the inference. Here it is evident, that the first takes it for a self-evident principle, that every thing which begins to exist must have a cause. The other does not allow this to be self-evident. Let them settle this point, and the dispute will be at an end.

Thus I think it appears, that in matters of science, if the terms be properly explained, the first principles upon which the reasoning is grounded be laid down and exposed to examination, and the conclusions regularly deduced from them, it might be expected, that men of candour and capacity, who love truth, and have patience to examine things coolly, might come to unanimity with regard to the force of the deductions, and that their differences might be reduced to those they may have about first principles.

4. A *fourth* proposition is, that Nature has not left us destitute of means whereby the candid and honest part of mankind may be brought to unanimity when they happen to differ about first principles.

When men differ about things that are taken to be first principles or self-evident truths, reasoning seems to be at an end. Each party appeals to common sense. When one man's common sense gives one determination, another man's a contrary determination, there seems to be no remedy but to leave every man to enjoy his own opinion. This is a common observation, and I believe a just one, if it be rightly understood.

It is in vain to reason with a man who denies the first principles on which the reasoning is grounded. Thus, it would be in vain to attempt the proof of a proposition in Euclid to a man who denies the axioms. Indeed, we ought never to reason with men who deny first principles from obstinacy and unwillingness to yield to reason.

But is it not possible, that men who really love truth, and are open to conviction, may differ about first principles?

I think it is possible, and that it cannot, without great want of charity, be denied to be possible.

When this happens, every man who believes that there is a real distinction between truth and error, and that the faculties which God has given us are not in their nature fallacious, must be convinced that there is a defect, or a perversion of judgment on the one side or the other.

A man of candour and humility will, in such a case, very naturally suspect his own judgment, so far as to be desirous to enter into a serious examination, even of what he has long held as a first principle. He will think it not impossible, that although his heart be upright, his judgment may have been perverted, by education, by authority, by party zeal, or by some other of the common causes of error, from the influence of which neither parts nor integrity exempt the human understanding.

In such a state of mind, so amiable, and so becoming every good man, has Nature left him destitute of any rational means by which he may be enabled, either to correct his judgment if it be wrong, or to confirm it if it be right?

I hope it is not so. I hope that, by the means which Nature has furnished, controversies about first principles may be brought to an issue, and that the real lovers of truth may come to unanimity with regard to them.

It is true, that, in other controversies, the process by which the truth of a proposition is discovered, or its falsehood detected, is, by showing its necessary connection with first principles, or its repugnancy to them. It is true, likewise, that when the controversy is, whether a proposition be itself a first principle, this process cannot be applied. The truth, therefore, in controversies of this kind, labours under a peculiar disadvantage. But it has advantages of another kind to compensate this.

1. For, in the *first* place, in such controversies, every man is a competent judge; and therefore it is difficult to impose upon mankind.

To judge of first principles, requires no more than a sound mind free from prejudice, and a distinct conception of the question. The learned and the unlearned, the philosopher and the day-labourer, are upon a level, and will pass the same judgment, when they are not misled by some bias, or taught to renounce their understanding from some mistaken religious principle.

In matters beyond the reach of common understanding, the many are led by the few, and willingly yield to their authority. But, in matters of common sense, the few must yield to the many, when local and temporary prejudices are removed. No man is now moved by the subtle arguments of Zeno against motion, though perhaps he knows not how to answer them.

The ancient sceptical system furnishes a remarkable instance of this truth. That system, of which Pyrrho was reputed the father, was carried down, through a succession of ages, by very able and acute philosophers, who taught men to believe nothing at all, and esteemed it the highest pitch of human wisdom to withhold assent from every proposition whatsoever. It was supported with very great subtlety and learning, as we see from the writings of Sextus Empiricus, the only author of that sect whose writings have come down to our age. The assault of the Sceptics against all science seems to have been managed with more art and address than the defence of the Dogmatists.

Yet, as this system was an insult upon the common sense of mankind, it died away of itself; and it would be in vain to attempt to revive it. The modern scepticism is very different from the ancient, otherwise it would not have been allowed a hearing; and, when it has lost the grace of novelty, it will die away also, though it should never be refuted.

The modern scepticism, I mean that of Mr Hume, is built upon principles which were very generally maintained by philosophers, though they did not see that they led to scepticism. Mr Hume, by tracing, with great acuteness and ingenuity, the consequences of principles commonly received, has shown that they overturn all knowledge, and at last overturn themselves, and leave the mind in perfect suspense.

2. *Secondly,* We may observe, that opinions which contradict first principles are distinguished from other errors by this; that they are not only false, but absurd. And, to discountenance absurdity, Nature hath given us a particular emotion, to wit, that of ridicule, which seems intended for this very purpose of putting out of countenance what is absurd, either in opinion or practice.

This weapon, when properly applied, cuts with as keen an edge as argument. Nature hath furnished us with the first to expose absurdity, as with the last to refute error. Both are well fitted for their several offices, and are equally friendly to truth when properly used.

Both may be abused to serve the cause of error. But the same degree of judgment, which serves to detect the abuse of argument in false reasoning, serves to detect the abuse of ridicule when it is wrong directed.

Some have from nature a happier talent for ridicule than others, and the same thing holds with regard to the talent of reasoning. Indeed, I conceive there is hardly any absurdity, which, when touched with the pencil of a Lucian, a Swift, or a Voltaire, would not be put out of countenance, when there is not some religious panic, or very powerful prejudice, to blind the understanding.

But it must be acknowledged, that the emotion of ridicule, even when most natural, may be stifled by an emotion of a contrary nature, and cannot operate till that is removed.

Thus, if the notion of sanctity is annexed to an object, it is no longer a laughable matter, and this visor must be pulled off before it appears ridiculous. Hence we see, that notions which appear most ridiculous to all who consider them coolly and indifferently, have no such appearance to those who never thought of them, but under the impression of religious awe and dread.

Even where religion is not concerned, the novelty of an opinion to those who are too fond of novelties, the gravity and solemnity with which it is introduced, the opinion we have entertained of the author, its apparent connection with principles already embraced, or subserviency to interest which we have at heart, and, above all, its being fixed in our minds at that time of life when we receive implicitly what we are taught, may cover its absurdity, and fascinate the understanding for a time.

But if ever we are able to view it naked, and stripped of those adventitious circumstances from which it borrowed its importance and authority, the natural emotion of ridicule will exert its force. An absurdity can be entertained by men of sense no longer than it wears a mask. When any man is found who has the skill or the boldness to pull off the mask, it can no longer bear the light; it slinks into dark corners for a while, and then is no more heard of, but as an object of ridicule.

Thus I conceive, that first principles, which are really the dictates of common sense, and directly opposed to absurdities in opinion, will always, from the constitution of human nature, support themselves, and gain rather than lose ground among mankind.

3. *Thirdly*, It may be observed, that although it is contrary to the nature of first principles to admit of direct or *apodictical* proof; yet there are certain ways of reasoning even about them, by which those that are just and solid may be confirmed, and those that are false may be detected. It may here be proper to mention some of the topics from which we may reason in matters of this kind.

First, It is a good argument *ad hominem*, if it can be shown, that a first principle which a man rejects, stands upon the same footing with others which he admits: For, when this is the case, he must be guilty of an inconsistency who holds the one and rejects the other.

Thus the faculties of consciousness, of memory, of external sense, and of reason, are all equally the gifts of Nature, No good reason can be assigned for receiving the testimony of one of them, which is not of equal force with regard to the others. The greatest Sceptics admit the testimony of consciousness, and allow, that what it testifies is to be held as a first principle. If therefore they reject the immediate testimony of sense, or of memory, they are guilty of an inconsistency.

Secondly, A first principle may admit of proof *ad absurdum*.

In this kind of proof, which is very common in mathematics, we suppose the contradictory proposition to be true. We trace the consequences of that supposition in a train of reasoning; and if we find any of its necessary consequences to be manifestly absurd, we conclude the supposition from which it followed to be false; and therefore its contradictory to be true.

There is hardly any proposition, especially of those that may claim the character of first principles, that stands alone and unconnected. It draws many other along with it in a chain that cannot be broken. He that takes it up must bear the burden of all its consequences; and if that is too heavy for him to bear, he must not pretend to take it up.

Thirdly, I conceive, that the consent of ages and nations, of the learned and unlearned, ought to have great authority with regard to first principles, where every man is a competent judge.

Our ordinary conduct in life is built upon first principles, as well as our speculations in philosophy; and every motive to action supposes some belief. When we find a general agreement among men, in principles that concern human life, this must have great authority with every sober mind that loves truth.

It is pleasant to observe the fruitless pains which Bishop Berkeley takes to show, that his system of the non-existence of a material world did not contradict the sentiments of the vulgar, but those only of the philosophers. With good reason he dreaded more to oppose the authority of vulgar opinion in a matter of this kind, than all the schools of philosophers.

Here perhaps it will be said, What has authority to do in matters of opinion? Is truth to be determined by most votes? Or is authority to be again raised out of its grave to tyrannise over mankind? I am aware that, in this age, an advocate for authority has a very unfavourable plea; but I wish to give no more to authority than is its due.

Most justly do we honour the names of those benefactors to mankind who have contributed more or less to break the yoke of that authority which deprives men of the natural, the unalienable right of judging for themselves; but while we indulge a just animosity against this authority, and against all who would subject us to its tyranny, let us remember how common the folly is, of going from one faulty extreme into the opposite. Authority, though a very tyrannical mistress to private judgment, may yet, on some occasions, be a useful handmaid; this is all she is entitled to, and this is all I plead in her behalf.

The justice of this plea will appear by putting a case in a science, in which, of all sciences, authority is acknowledged to have least weight. Suppose a mathematician has made a discovery in that science which he thinks important; that he has put his demonstration in just order; and, after examining it with an attentive eye, has found no flaw in it. I would ask, Will there not be still in his breast some dissidence, some jealousy lest the ardour of invention may have made him overlook some false step? This must be granted.

He commits his demonstration to the examination of a mathematical friend, whom he esteems a competent judge, and waits with impatience the issue of his judgment. Here I would ask again, Whether the verdict of his friend, according as it is favourable or unfavourable, will not greatly increase or diminish his confidence in his own judgment? Most certainly it will, and it ought.

If the judgment of his friend agree with his own, especially if it be confirmed by two or three able judges, he rests secure of his discovery without farther examination; but if it be unfavourable, he is brought back into a kind of suspense, until the part that is suspected undergoes a new and a more rigorous examination.

I hope what is supposed in this case is agreeable to nature, and to the experience of candid and modest men on such occasions; yet here we see a man's judgment, even in a mathematical demonstration, conscious of some feebleness in itself, seeking the aid of authority to support it, greatly strengthened by that authority, and hardly able to stand erect against it, without some new aid.

Society in judgment, of those who are esteemed fair and competent judges, has effects very similar to those of civil society; it gives strength and courage to every individual; it removes that timidity which is as naturally the companion of solitary judgment, as of a solitary man in the state of nature. Let us judge for ourselves therefore, but let us not disdain to take that aid from the authority of other competent judges, which a mathematician thinks necessary to take in that science, which of all sciences has least to do with authority.

In a matter of common sense, every man is no less competent judge than a mathematician is in a mathematical demonstration, and there must be a great presumption that the judgment of mankind, in such a matter, is the natural issue of those faculties which God has given them. Such a judgment can be erroneous only when there is some cause of the error, as general as the error is. When this can be shown to be the case, I acknowledge it ought to have its due weight. But to suppose a general deviation from truth among mankind in things self-evident, of which no cause can be assigned, is highly unreasonable.

Perhaps it may be thought impossible to collect the general opinion of men upon any point whatsoever, and therefore, that this authority can serve us in no stead in examining first principles. But I apprehend, that in many cases this is neither impossible nor difficult.

Who can doubt whether men have universally believed the existence of a material world? Who can doubt whether men have universally believed, that every change that happens in nature must have a cause? Who can doubt whether men have universally believed, that there is a right and a wrong in human conduct; some things that merit blame, and others that are entitled to approbation?

The universality of these opinions, and of many such that might be named, is sufficiently evident from the whole tenor of human conduct, as far as our acquaintance reaches, and from the history of all ages and nations of which we have any records.

There are other opinions that appear to be universal, from what is common in the structure of all languages. Language is the express image and picture of human thoughts; and from the picture we may draw some certain conclusions concerning the original. We find in all languages the same parts of speech; we find nouns, substantive and adjective; verbs, active and passive, in their various tenses, numbers, and moods. Some rules of syntax are the same in all languages.

Now what is common in the structure of languages, indicates a uniformity of opinion in those things upon which that structure is grounded. The distinction between substances, and the qualities belonging to them, between thought, and the being that thinks, between thought and the objects of thought, is to be found in the structure of all languages. And therefore, systems of philosophy, which abolish those distinctions, wage war with the common sense of mankind.

We are apt to imagine, that those who formed languages were no metaphysicians, but the first principles of all sciences are the dictates of common sense, and lie open to all men; and every man who has considered the structure of language in a philosophical light, will find infallible proofs that those who have framed it, and those who use it with understanding, have the power of making accurate distinctions, and of forming general conceptions, as well as philosophers. Nature has given those powers to all men, and they can use them when their occasions require it; but they leave it to the philosophers to give names to them, and to descant upon their nature. In like manner, Nature has given eyes to all men, and they can make good use of them; but the structure of the eye, and the theory of vision, is the business of philosophers.

Fourthly, Opinions that appear so early in the minds of men, that they cannot be the effect of education, or of false reasoning, have a good claim to be considered as first principles. Thus the belief we have, that the persons about us are living and intelligent beings, is a belief for which perhaps we can give some reason, when we are able to reason, but we had this belief before we could reason, and before we could learn it by instruction. It seems therefore to be an immediate effect of our constitution.

The *last* topic I shall mention is, when an opinion is so necessary in the conduct of life that without the belief of it, a man must be led into a thousand absurdities in practice. Such an opinion, when we can give no other reason for it, may safely be taken for a first principle.

Thus I have endeavoured to show, that although first principles are not capable of direct proof, yet differences, that may happen with regard to them among men of candour, are not without remedy; that Nature has not left us destitute of means by which we may discover errors of this kind; and that there are ways of reasoning, with regard to first principles, by which those that are truly such may be distinguished from vulgar errors or prejudices.

Seven

Dugald Stewart

1753–1828

Dugald Stewart was born in Edinburgh on 22 November 1753 and died there on 11 June 1828. He was a student of Adam Ferguson in Edinburgh and also spent the year 1771–2 listening to Thomas Reid in Glasgow. From 1775 to 1785 he was Professor of Mathematics at Edinburgh, first conjoint with then in succession to his father, Matthew Stewart. Having substituted also in the moral philosophy chair in 1778–9, when Ferguson was in America negotiating for the British government, Stewart succeeded him in 1785. He lectured with such effect that by the time of his retirement from teaching in 1810, he had acquired a distinguished reputation in Europe and North America.

Stewart was an immensely erudite, eclectic philosopher who drew on modern English and French philosophy as well as the domestic Scots tradition. But his early encounter with Reid, who remained a friend and mentor until his death in 1796, had the greatest intellectual influence on him, and he remained an exponent of common sense philosophy, though not an uncritical one.

Stewart had a huge impact on the intellectual climate of his time, partly through his lectures, partly through his writings. He attracted students from England, Europe and America, as well as domestic students, in numbers that had never been seen before. His philosophical approach to contemporary problems was an important factor in the creation of the *Edinburgh Review* and made it into the most powerful Whig force in the country. His French followers made his philosophy the more or less official basis for Restoration France's troubled settlement with the Revolution, while in America, Reid and Stewart dominated the philosophical curriculum for much of the nineteenth century. The diffusion of political economy as a university subject owed much to Stewart's lectures; his ideas of mathematics and methodology remained influential for a long time; his contributions to linguistic theory can still be regarded as a turning point in the history of the subject.   At the time of his death Stewart's prestige was such he was lamented as 'the pride and ornament of Scotland' and a monument erected to him on the Calton Hill in Edinburgh.

This reputation was a result of his inspiring lectures and extensive writings on moral philosophy and the philosophy of mind. Taken together they exemplify his continuation of the Scottish tradition of philosophy in which original investigation and education go hand in hand. 'Surely', he writes in the first extract printed here, 'the great aim of an enlightened and benevolent philosophy, is not to rear a small number of individuals, who may be regarded as prodigies ... but to diffuse as widely as possible a degree of cultivation'.

Biographical information: Knud Haakonssen, *Thoemmes Dictionary of C18th British Philosophers*

READING XII
The Usefulness of the Philosophy of Mind[1]

It has often been remarked, that there is a mutual connexion between the different arts and sciences, and that the improvements which are made in one branch of human knowledge, frequently throw light on others, to which it has apparently a very remote relation. The modern discoveries in astronomy and in pure mathematics, have contributed to bring the art of navigation to a degree of perfection formerly unknown. The rapid progress which has been lately made in astronomy, anatomy, and botany, has been chiefly owing to the aid which these sciences have received from the art of the optician.

Although, however, the different departments of science and of art mutually reflect light on each other, it is not always necessary either for the philosopher or the artist to aim at the acquisition of general knowledge. Both of them may safely take many principles for granted, without being able to demonstrate their truth. A seaman, though ignorant of mathematics, may apply, with correctness and dexterity, the rules for finding the longitude; an astronomer or a botanist, though ignorant of optics, may avail himself of the use of the telescope or the microscope.

These observations are daily exemplified in the case of the artist, who has seldom either inclination or leisure to speculate concerning the principles of his art. It is rarely, however, we meet with a man of science who has confined his studies wholly to one branch of knowledge. That curiosity, which he has been accustomed to indulge in the course of his favourite pursuit will naturally extend itself to every remarkable object which falls under his observation; and can scarcely fail to be a source of perpetual dissatisfaction to his mind, till it has been so far gratified as to enable him to explain all the various phenomena which his professional habits are every day presenting to his view.

As every particular science is in this manner connected with others, to which it naturally directs the attention, so all the pursuits of life, whether

---

[1]   Extracted from *The Collected Works of Dugald Stewart*, vol. II, Bristol: Thommes Press, 1994, pp. 57–73

they terminate in speculation or action, are connected with that general science which has the human mind for its object. The powers of the understanding are instruments which all men employ, and his curiosity must be small indeed, who passes through life in a total ignorance of faculties which his wants and necessities force him habitually to exercise, and which so remarkably distinguish man from the lower animals. The active principles of our nature, which, by their various modifications and combinations, give rise to all the moral differences among men, are fitted in a still higher degree, if possible, to interest those who are either disposed to reflect on their own characters, or to observe with attention the characters of others. The phenomena resulting from these faculties and principles of the mind, are every moment soliciting our notice; and open to our examination a field of discovery as inexhaustible as the phenomena of the material world, and exhibiting not less striking marks of divine wisdom.

While all the sciences, and all the pursuits of life, have this common tendency to lead our inquiries to the philosophy of human nature, this last branch of knowledge borrows its principles from no other science whatever. Hence there is something in the study of it which is peculiarly gratifying to a reflecting and inquisitive mind, and something in the conclusions to which it leads, on which the mind rests with peculiar satisfaction. Till once our opinions are in some degree fixed with respect to it, we abandon ourselves with reluctance to particular scientific investigations; and, on the other hand, a general knowledge of such of its principles as are most fitted to excite the curiosity, not only prepares us for engaging in other pursuits with more liberal and comprehensive views, but leaves us at liberty to prosecute them with a more undivided and concentrated attention.

It is not, however, merely as a subject of speculative curiosity that the principles of the human mind deserve a careful examination. The advantages to be expected from a successful analysis of it are various, and some of them of such importance, as to render it astonishing that, amidst all the success with which the subordinate sciences have been cultivated, this, which comprehends the principles of all of them, should be still suffered to remain in its infancy.

I shall endeavour to illustrate a few of these advantages, beginning with what appears to me to be the most important of any — the light which a philosophical analysis of the principles of the mind would necessarily throw on the subjects of intellectual and moral education.

The most essential objects of education are the two following: First, to cultivate all the various principles of our nature, both speculative and active, in such a manner as to bring them to the greatest perfection of which they are susceptible; and, secondly, by watching over the impressions and associations which the mind receives in early life, to secure it against the influence of prevailing errors, and, as far as possible, to engage its prepossessions on the side of truth. It is only upon a philosophical analysis of the mind, that a systematical plan can be founded for the accomplishment of either of these purposes.

There are few individuals whose education has been conducted in every respect with attention and judgment. Almost every man of reflection is conscious, when he arrives at maturity, of many defects in his mental powers, and of many inconvenient habits, which might have been prevented or remedied in his infancy or youth. Such a consciousness is the first step towards improvement; and the person who feels it, if he is possessed of resolution and steadiness, will not scruple to begin, even in advanced years, a new course of education for himself. The degree of reflection and observation, indeed, which is necessary for this purpose, cannot be expected from any one at a very early period of life, as these are the last powers of the mind which unfold themselves; but it is never too late to think of the improvement of our faculties; and much progress may be made in the art of applying them successfully to their proper objects, or in obviating the inconveniences resulting from their imperfection, not only in manhood, but in old age.

It is not, however, to the mistakes of our early instructors that all our intellectual defects are to be ascribed. There is no profession or pursuit which has not habits peculiar to itself, and which does not leave some powers of the mind dormant, while it exercises and improves the rest. If we wish, therefore, to cultivate the mind to the extent of its capacity, we must not rest satisfied with that employment which its faculties receive from our particular situation in life. It is not in the awkward and professional form of a mechanic, who has strengthened particular muscles of his body by the habits of his trade, that we are to look for the perfection of our animal nature: neither is it among men of confined pursuits, whether speculative or active, that we are to expect to find the human mind in its highest state of cultivation. A variety of exercises is necessary to preserve the animal frame in vigour and beauty; and a variety of those occupations which literature and science afford, added to a promiscuous intercourse with the world, in the habits of conversation and business, is no less necessary for the improvement of the understanding. I acknowledge, that there are some professions, in which a man of very confined acquisitions may arrive at the first eminence; and in which he will perhaps be the more likely to excel, the more he has concentrated the whole force of his mind to one particular object. But such a person, however distinguished in his own sphere, is educated merely to be a literary artisan; and neither attains the perfection nor the happiness of his nature. 'That education only can be considered as complete and generous, which', in the language of Milton, 'fits a man to perform justly, skilfully, and magnanimously, all the offices, both private and public, of peace and war'.

I hope it will not be supposed, from the foregoing observations, that they are meant to recommend an indiscriminate attention to all the objects of speculation and of action. Nothing can be more evident than the necessity of limiting the field of our exertion, if we wish to benefit society by our labours. But it is perfectly consistent with the most intense application to our favourite pursuit, to cultivate that general acquaintance with letters and with the world, which may be sufficient to enlarge the mind, and to preserve it from any danger of contracting the pedantry of a particular profession. In many cases (as we already remarked) the sciences reflect light on each other, and the general acquisitions which we have made in other pursuits, may furnish us with useful helps for the farther prosecution of our own. But even in those instances in which the case is otherwise, and in which these liberal accomplishments must be purchased by the sacrifice of a part of our professional eminence, the acquisition of them will amply repay any loss we may sustain. It ought not to be the leading object of any one, to become an eminent metaphysician, mathematician, or poet, but to render himself happy as an individual, and an agreeable, a respectable, and a useful member of society. A man who loses his sight improves the sensibility of his touch: but who would consent, for such a recompense, to part with the pleasures which he receives from the eye?

It is almost unnecessary for me to remark, how much individuals would be assisted in the proper and liberal culture of the mind, if they were previously led to take a comprehensive survey of human nature in all its parts; of its various faculties, and powers, and sources of enjoyment, and of the effects which are produced on these principles by particular situations. It is such a knowledge alone of the capacities of the mind, that can enable a person to judge of his own acquisitions, and to employ the most effectual means for supplying his defects, and removing his inconvenient habits. Without some degree of it, every man is in danger of contracting bad habits before he is aware, and of suffering some of his powers to go to decay for want of proper exercise.

If the business of early education were more thoroughly and more generally understood, it would be less necessary for individuals, when they arrive at maturity, to form plans of improvement for themselves. But education never can be systematically directed to its proper objects, till we have obtained, not only an accurate analysis of the general principles of our nature, and an account of the most important laws which regulate their operation, but an explanation of the various modifications and combinations of these principles, which produce that diversity of talents, genius, and character, we observe among men. To instruct youth in the languages and in the sciences, is comparatively of little importance, if we are inattentive to the habits they acquire, and are not careful in giving, to all their different faculties, and all their different principles of action, a proper degree of employment. Abstracting entirely from the culture of their moral powers, how extensive and difficult is the business of conducting their intellectual improvement! To watch over the associations which they form in their tender years; to give them early habits of mental activity; to rouse their curiosity, and to direct it to proper objects;

to exercise their ingenuity and invention; to cultivate in their minds a turn for speculation, and at the same time preserve their attention alive to the objects around them; to awaken their sensibilities to the beauties of nature, and to inspire them with a relish for intellectual enjoyment; — these form but a part of the business of education. And yet the execution even of this part requires an acquaintance with the general principles of our nature, which seldom falls to the share of those to whom the instruction of youth is commonly entrusted.

Nor will such a theoretical knowledge of the human mind, as I have now described, be always sufficient in practice. An uncommon degree of sagacity is frequently requisite, in order to accommodate general rules to particular tempers and characters. In whatever way we choose to account for it, whether by original organization, or by the operation of moral causes in very early infancy, no fact can be more undeniable, than that there are important differences discernible in the minds of children, previous to that period at which, in general, their intellectual education commences. There is, too, a certain hereditary character (whether resulting from physical constitution, or caught from imitation and the influence of situation) which appears remarkably in particular families. One race, for a succession of generations, is distinguished by a genius for the abstract sciences, while it is deficient in vivacity, in imagination, and in taste: another is no less distinguished for wit, and gaiety, and fancy; while it appears incapable of patient attention, or of profound research. The system of education which is proper to be adopted in particular cases, ought, undoubtedly, to have some reference to these circumstances: and to be calculated, as much as possible, to develop and to cherish those intellectual and active principles, in which a natural deficiency is most to be apprehended. Montesquieu, and other speculative politicians, have insisted much on the reference which education and laws should have to climate. I shall not take upon me to say, how far their conclusions on this subject are just; but I am fully persuaded, that there is a foundation in philosophy, and good sense, for accommodating, at a very early period of life, the education of individuals to those particular turns of mind, to which, from hereditary propensities, or from moral situation, they may be presumed to have a natural tendency.

There are few subjects more hackneyed than that of education; and yet there is none, upon which the opinions of the world are still more divided. Nor is this surprising; for most of those who have speculated concerning it, have confined their attention chiefly to incidental question about the comparative advantages of public or private instruction, or the utility of particular languages or sciences, without attempting a previous examination of those faculties and principles of the mind, which it is the great object of education to improve. Many excellent detached observations, indeed, both on the intellectual and moral powers, are to be collected from the writings of ancient and modern authors; but I do not know, that in any language an attempt has been made to ana-

lyse and illustrate the principles of human nature, in order to lay a philosophical foundation for their proper culture.

I have even heard some very ingenious and intelligent men dispute
the propriety of so systematical a plan of instruction. The most successful and splendid exertions, both in the sciences and arts (it has been frequently remarked), have been made by individuals, in whose minds the
seeds of genius were allowed to shoot up, wild and free, while, from the
most careful and skilful tuition, seldom any thing results above medioc-
rity. I shall not, at present, enter into any discussions with respect to the
certainty of the fact on which this opinion is founded. Supposing the fact
to be completely established, it must still be remembered, that originality of genius does not always imply vigour and comprehensiveness, and
liberality of mind; and that it is desirable only, in so far as it is compatible
with these more valuable qualities. I already hinted, that there are some
pursuits, in which, as they require the exertion only of a small number of
our faculties, an individual, who has a natural turn for them, will be
more likely to distinguish himself, by being suffered to follow his original bias, than if his attention were distracted by a more liberal course of
study. But wherever such men are to be found, they must be considered,
on the most favourable supposition, as having sacrificed, to a certain
degree, the perfection and the happiness of their nature, to the amusement or instruction of others. It is, too, in times of general darkness and
barbarism, that what is commonly called originality of genius most frequently appears: and surely the great aim of an enlightened and benevolent philosophy, is not to rear a small number of individuals, who may
be regarded as prodigies in an ignorant and admiring age, but to diffuse,
as widely as possible, that degree of cultivation which may enable the
bulk of a people to possess all the intellectual and moral improvement of
which their nature is susceptible. 'Original genius', says Voltaire, 'occurs but seldom in a nation where the literary taste is formed. The number of cultivated minds which there abound, like the trees in a thick and
flourishing forest, prevent any single individual from rearing his head
far above the rest. Where trade is in few hands, we meet with a small
number of overgrown fortunes in the midst of a general poverty: in proportion as it extends, opulence becomes general, and great fortunes rare.
It is, precisely, because there is at present much light and much cultivation in France, that we are led to complain of the want of superior
genius'.

To what purpose, indeed, it may be said, all this labour? Is not the
importance of everything to man, to be ultimately estimated by its tendency to promote his happiness? And is not our daily experience sufficient to convince us, that this is, in general, by no means proportioned to
the culture which his nature has received? — Nay, is there not some
ground for suspecting, that the lower orders of men enjoy, on the whole,
a more enviable condition than their more enlightened and refined
superiors?

The truth, I apprehend, is, that happiness, in so far as it arises from the mind itself, will be always proportioned to the degree of perfection which its powers have attained, but that, in cultivating these powers, with a view to this most important of all objects, it is essentially necessary that such a degree of attention be bestowed on all of them, as may preserve them in that state of relative strength, which appears to be agreeable to the intentions of nature. In consequence of an exclusive attention to the culture of the imagination, the taste, the reasoning faculty, or any of the active principles, it is possible that the pleasures of human life may be diminished, or its pains increased; but the inconveniences which are experienced in such cases, are not to be ascribed to education, but to a partial and injudicious education. In such cases, it is possible that the poet, the metaphysician, or the man of taste and refinement, may appear to disadvantage, when compared with the vulgar; for such is the benevolent appointment of Providence with respect to the lower orders, that, although not one principle of their nature be completely unfolded, the whole of these principles preserve among themselves that balance which is favourable to the tranquillity of their minds, and to a prudent and steady conduct in the limited sphere which is assigned to them, far more completely than in those of their superiors, whose education has been conducted on an erroneous or imperfect system: but all this, far from weakening the force of the foregoing observations, only serves to demonstrate how impossible it always will be to form a rational plan for the improvement of the mind, without an accurate and comprehensive knowledge of the principles of the human constitution.

The remarks which have been already made, are sufficient to illustrate the dangerous consequences which are likely to result from a partial and injudicious cultivation of the mind; and, at the same time, to point out the utility of the intellectual philosophy, in enabling us to preserve a proper balance among all its various faculties, principles of action, and capacities of enjoyment. Many additional observations might be offered, on the tendency which an accurate analysis of its powers might probably have, to suggest rules for their farther improvement, and for a more successful application of them to their proper purposes; but this subject I shall not prosecute at present, as the illustration of it is one of the leading objects of the following work. That the memory, the imagination, or the reasoning faculty, are to be instantly strengthened in consequence of our speculations concerning their nature, it would be absurd to suppose; but it is surely far from being unreasonable to think, that an acquaintance with the laws which regulate these powers, may suggest some useful rules for their gradual cultivation; for remedying their defects, in the case of individuals, and even for extending those limits which nature seems, at first view, to have assigned them.

To how great a degree of perfection the intellectual and moral nature of man is capable of being raised by cultivation, it is difficult to conceive.

The effects of early, continued, and systematical education, in the case of those children who are trained, for the sake of gain, to feats of strength and agility, justify, perhaps, the most sanguine views which it is possible for a philosopher to form, with respect to the improvement of the species.

I now proceed to consider, how far the philosophy of mind may be useful in accomplishing the second object of education; by assisting us in the management of early impressions and associations.

By far the greater part of the opinions on which we act in life are not the result of our own investigations, but are adopted implicitly, in infancy and youth, upon the authority of others. Even the great principles of morality, although implanted in every heart, are commonly aided and cherished, at least to a certain degree, by the care of our instructors. All this is undoubtedly agreeable to the intentions of nature; and, indeed, were the case otherwise, society could not subsist, for nothing can be more evident than that the bulk of mankind, condemned as they are to laborious occupations, which are incompatible with intellectual improvement, are perfectly incapable of forming their own opinions on some of the most important subjects that can employ the human mind. It is evident, at the same time, that as no system of education is perfect, a variety of prejudices must, in this way, take an early hold of our belief, so as to acquire over it an influence not inferior to that of the most incontrovertible truths. When a child hears either a speculative absurdity or an erroneous principle of action, recommended and enforced daily, by the same voice which first conveyed to it those simple and sublime lessons of morality and religion which are congenial to its nature, is it to be wondered at, that, in future life, it should find it so difficult to eradicate prejudices which have twined their roots with all the essential principles of the human frame? If such, however be the obvious intentions of nature, with respect to those orders of men who are employed in bodily labour, it is equally clear that she meant to impose it as a double obligation on those who receive the advantages of a liberal education, to examine, with the most scrupulous care, the foundation of all those received opinions, which have any connexion with morality, or with human happiness. If the multitude must be led, it is of consequence, surely, that it should be led by enlightened conductors; by men who are able to distinguish truth from error; and to draw the line between those prejudices which are innocent or salutary (if indeed there are any prejudices which are really salutary), and those which are hostile to the interests of virtue and of mankind.

In such a state of society as that in which we live, the prejudices of a moral, a political, and a religious nature, which we imbibe in early life, are so various, and at the same time so intimately blended with the belief we entertain of the most sacred and important truths, that a great part of the life of a philosopher must necessarily be devoted, not so much to the acquisition of new knowledge, as to unlearn the errors to which he had been taught to give an implicit assent before the dawn of reason and reflection. And unless he submit in this manner to bring all his opinions to the test of a severe examination, his ingenuity and his learning, instead of enlightening the world, will only enable him to give an additional currency, and an additional authority, to established errors. To attempt such a struggle against early prejudices, is indeed the professed aim of all philosophers, but how few are to be found who have force of mind sufficient for accomplishing their object; and who, in freeing themselves from one set or errors, do not allow themselves to be carried away with another?

Nor is it merely in order to free the mind from the influence of error, that it is useful to examine the foundation of established opinions. It is such an examination alone, that, in an inquisitive age like the present, can secure a philosopher from the danger of unlimited scepticism. To this extreme, indeed, the complexion of the times is more likely to give him a tendency than to implicit credulity. In the former ages of ignorance and superstition, the intimate association which had been formed, in the prevailing systems of education, between truth and error, had given to the latter an ascendant over the minds of men, which it could never have acquired, if divested of such an alliance. The case has, of late years, been most remarkably reversed: the common sense of mankind, in consequence of the growth of a more liberal spirit of inquiry, has revolted against many of those absurdities which had so long held human reason in captivity; and it was, perhaps, more than could reasonably have been expected, that, in the first moments of their emancipation, philosophers should have stopped short, at the precise boundary, which cooler reflection and more moderate views would have prescribed. The fact is, that they have passed far beyond it; and that, in their zeal to destroy prejudices, they have attempted to tear up by the roots many of the best and happiest and most essential principles of our nature. Having remarked the powerful influence of education over the mind, they have concluded that man is wholly a factitious being; not recollecting that this very susceptibility of education presupposes certain original principles, which are common to the whole species; and that as error can only take a permanent hold of a candid mind by being grafted on truths, which it is unwilling or unable to eradicate, even the influence, which false and absurd opinions occasionally acquire over the belief, instead of being an argument for universal scepticism, is the most decisive argument against it; inasmuch as it shows, that there are some truths so incorporated and identified with our nature, that they can reconcile us even to the absurdities and contradictions with which we suppose them to be inseparably connected. The sceptical philosophers, for example, of the present age, have frequently attempted to hold up to ridicule those contemptible and puerile superstitions which have disgraced the creeds of some of the most enlightened nations, and which have not only commanded the assent, but the reverence of men of the

most accomplished understandings. But these histories of human imbe-
cility are, in truth, the strongest testimonies which can be produced, to
prove how wonderful is the influence of the fundamental principles of
morality over the belief, when they are able to sanctify, in the apprehensions of mankind, every extravagant opinion, and every unmeaning ceremony, which early education has taught us to associate with them.

That implicit credulity is a mark of a feeble mind will not be disputed;
but it may not perhaps be as generally acknowledged, that the case is the
same with unlimited scepticism. On the contrary, we are sometimes apt
to ascribe this disposition to a more than ordinary vigour of intellect.
Such a prejudice was by no means unnatural to that period in the history
of modern Europe, when reason first began to throw off the yoke of
authority, and when it unquestionably required a superiority of understanding, as well as of intrepidity, for an individual to resist the contagion of prevailing superstition. But in the present age, in which the
tendency of fashionable opinions is directly opposite to those of the vulgar, the philosophical creed, or the philosophical scepticism of by far the
greater number of those who value themselves on an emancipation from
popular errors, arises from the very same weakness with the credulity of
the multitude: nor is it going too far to say, with Rousseau, that 'He who,
in the end of the eighteenth century, has brought himself to abandon all
his early principles without discrimination, would probably have been a
bigot in the days of the League'. In the midst of these contrary impulses
of fashionable and of vulgar prejudices, he alone evinces the superiority
and the strength of his mind who is able to disentangle truth from error,
and to oppose the clear conclusions of his own unbiased faculties to the
united clamours of superstition and of false philosophy. Such are the
men whom nature marks out to be the lights of the world, to fix the
wavering opinions of the multitude, and to impress their own characters
on that of their age.

For securing the mind completely from the weaknesses I have now
been describing, and enabling it to maintain a steady course of inquiry
between implicit credulity and unlimited scepticism, the most important of all qualities is a sincere and devoted attachment to truth, which
seldom fails to be accompanied with a manly confidence in the clear conclusions of human reason. It is such a confidence, united (as it generally
is) with personal intrepidity, which forms what the French writers call
force of character, one of the rarest endowments, it must be confessed, of
our species, but which, of all endowments, is the most essential for ren-
dering a philosopher happy in himself, and a blessing to mankind.

From the observations which have been made, it sufficiently appears,
that, in order to secure the mind, on the one hand, from the influence of
prejudice, and on the other, from a tendency to unlimited scepticism, it is
necessary that it should be able to distinguish the original and universal
principles and laws of human nature, from the adventitious effects of
local situation. But if, in the case of an individual who has received an

imperfect or erroneous education, such a knowledge puts it in his power to correct, to a certain degree, his own bad habits, and to surmount his own speculative errors, it enables him to be useful, in a much higher degree, to those whose education he has an opportunity of superintending from early infancy. Such, and so permanent, is the effect of first impressions on the character, that although a philosopher may succeed, by perseverance, in freeing his reason from the prejudices with which it was entangled, they will still retain some hold of his imagination and his affections; and, therefore, however enlightened his understanding may be in his hours of speculation, his philosophical opinions will frequently lose their influence over his mind, in those very situations in which their practical assistance is most required — when his temper is soured by misfortune, or when he engages in the pursuits of life, and exposes himself to the contagion of popular errors. His opinions are supported merely by speculative arguments, and, instead of being connected with any of the active principles of his nature, are counteracted and thwarted by some of the most powerful of them. How different would the case be, if education were conducted from the beginning with attention and judgment? Were the same pains taken to impress truth on the mind in early infancy, that is often taken to inculcate error, the great principles of our conduct would not only be juster than they are, but, in consequence of the aid which they would receive from the imagination and the heart, trained to conspire with them in the same direction, they would render us happier in ourselves, and would influence our practice more powerfully and more habitually. There is surely nothing in error which is more congenial to the mind than truth. On the contrary, when exhibited separately and alone to the understanding, it shocks our reason and provokes our ridicule; and it is only (as I had occasion already to remark) by an alliance with truths which we find it difficult to renounce, that it can obtain our assent, or command our reverence. What advantages, then, might be derived from a proper attention to early impressions and associations, in giving support to those principles which are connected with human happiness? The long reign of error in the world, and the influence it maintains, even in an age of liberal inquiry, far from being favourable to the supposition that human reason is destined to be forever the sport of prejudice and absurdity, demonstrates the tendency which there is to permanence in established opinions, and in established institutions, and promises an eternal stability to true philosophy, when it shall once be employed to support it, by a more perfect system of education.

READING XIII
The Origin of Knowledge

he philosophers who endeavoured to explain the operations of the human mind by the theory of ideas, and who took for granted, that in every exertion of thought there exists in the mind some object distinct from the thinking substance, were naturally led to inquire whence these ideas derive their origin; in particular, whether they are conveyed to the mind from without by means of the senses, or form part of its original furniture?

With respect to this question, the opinions of the ancients were various; but as the influence of these opinions on the prevailing systems of the present age is not very considerable, it is not necessary, for any of the purposes I have in view in this work, to consider them particularly. The moderns, too, have been much divided on the subject, some holding, with Descartes, that the mind is furnished with certain innate ideas, others, with Mr. Locke, that all our ideas may be traced from sensation and reflection, and many (especially among the later metaphysicians in France), that they may be all traced from sensation alone.

Of these theories, that of Mr. Locke deserves more particularly our attention, as it has served as the basis of most of the metaphysical systems which have appeared since his time, and as the difference between it and the theory which derives all our ideas from sensation alone, is rather apparent than real.

In order to convey a just notion of Mr. Locke's doctrine concerning the origin of our ideas, it is necessary to remark, that he refers to sensation all the ideas which we are supposed to receive by the external senses, our ideas, for example, of colours, of sounds, of hardness, of extension, of motion, and, in short, of all the qualities and modes of matter: to reflection, the ideas of our own mental operations which we derive from consciousness, our ideas, for example, of memory, of imagination, of volition, of pleasure, and of pain. These two sources, according to him, furnish us with all our simple ideas, and the only power which the mind possesses over them, is to perform certain operations, in the way of composition, abstraction, generalization, etc., on the materials which it thus collects in the course of its experience. The laudable desire of Mr. Locke to introduce precision and perspicuity into metaphysical speculations, and his anxiety to guard the mind against error in general, naturally prepossessed him in favour of a doctrine which, when compared with those of his predecessors, was intelligible and simple, and which, by suggesting a method, apparently easy and palpable, of analysing our knowledge into its elementary principles, seemed to furnish an antidote against those prejudices which had been favoured by the hypothesis of innate ideas. It is now a considerable time since this fundamental principle of Mr. Locke's system began to lose its authority in England; and the sceptical conclusions which it had been employed to support by some later writers, furnished its opponents with very plausible arguments against it. The late learned Mr. Harris, in particular, frequently mentions this doctrine of Mr. Locke, and always in terms of high indignation. 'Mark', says he, in one passage, 'the order of things, according to the account of our later metaphysicians. First comes that huge body, the sensible world. Then this, and its attributes, beget sensible ideas. Then, out of sensible ideas, by a kind of lopping and pruning, are made ideas intelligible, whether specific or general. Thus, should they admit that mind was coeval with body, yet till the body gave it ideas, and awakened its dormant powers, it could at best have been nothing more than a sort of dead capacity, for innate ideas it could not possibly have any'. And, in another passage: 'For my own part, when I read the detail about sensation and reflection, and am taught the process at large how my ideas are all generated, I seem to view the human soul in the light of a crucible, where truths are produced by a kind of logical chemistry'.

If Dr. Reid's reasonings on the subject of ideas be admitted, all these speculations with respect to their origin fall to the ground, and the question to which they relate is reduced merely to a question of fact concerning the occasions on which the mind is first led to form those simple notions into which our thoughts may be analysed, and which may be considered as the principles or elements of human knowledge. With respect to many of these notions, this inquiry involves no difficulty. No one, for example, can be at a loss to ascertain the occasions on which the notions of colours and sounds are first formed by the mind, for these notions are confined to individuals who are possessed of particular senses, and cannot, by any combination of words, be conveyed to those who never enjoyed the use of them. The history of our notions of extension and figure, (which may be suggested to the mind by the exercise either of sight or of touch,) is not altogether so obvious, and accordingly, it has been the subject of various controversies. To trace the origin of these, and of our other simple notions with respect to the qualities of matter, or, in other words, to describe the occasions on which, by the laws of our nature, they are suggested to the mind, is one of the leading objects of Dr. Reid's inquiry, in his analysis of our external senses, in which he carefully avoids every hypothesis with respect to the inexplicable phenomena of perception and of thought, and confines himself scrupulously to a literal statement of facts. Similar inquiries to these may be proposed, concerning the occasions on which we form the notions of *time*, of *motion*, of *number*, of *causation*, and an infinite variety of others. Thus, it has been observed by different authors, that every perception of change suggests to the mind the notion of a *cause*, without which that change could not have happened. Dr. Reid remarks that, without the faculty of memory, our perceptive powers could never have led us to form the idea of *motion*. I shall afterwards show, in the sequel of this work, that without the same faculty of memory we never could have formed the notion of *time*; and that without the faculty of abstraction, we could not have formed the notion of *number*. Such inquiries with respect to the origin of our knowledge are curious and important, and if conducted with judgment, they may lead to the most certain conclusions, as they aim at nothing more than to ascertain facts, which, although not obvious to superficial observers, may yet be discovered by patient investigation.

From the remarks which have been just made on our notions of time, of motion, and of number, it is evident that the inquiry concerning the origin of human knowledge cannot possibly be discussed at the commencement of such a work as this; but that it must be resumed in different parts of it, as those faculties of the mind come under our view, with which the formation of our different simple notions is connected.

With respect to the general question, Whether all our knowledge may be ultimately traced from our sensations? I shall only observe at present, that the opinion we form concerning it, is of much less consequence than is commonly supposed. That the mind cannot, without the grossest absurdity, be considered in the light of a receptacle which is gradually furnished from without, by materials introduced by the channel of the senses; nor in that of a *tabula rasa*, upon which copies or resemblances of things external are imprinted, I have already shown at sufficient length. Although, therefore, we should acquiesce in the conclusion, that without our organs of sense, the mind must have remained destitute of knowledge, this concession could have no tendency whatever to favour the principles of materialism, as it implies nothing more than that the impressions made on our senses by external objects, furnish the occasions on which the mind, by the laws of its constitution, is led to perceive the qualities of the material world, and to exert all the different modifications of thought of which it is capable.

From the very slight view of the subject, however, which has been already given, it is sufficiently evident, that this doctrine which refers the origin of all our knowledge to the occasions furnished by sense, must be received with many limitations. That those ideas, which Mr. Locke calls ideas of reflection (or, in other words, those notions which we form of the subjects of our own consciousness), are not suggested to the mind immediately by the sensations arising from the use of our organs of perception, is granted on all hands; and, therefore, the amount of the doctrine now mentioned, is nothing more than this: that the first occasions on which our various intellectual faculties are exercised, are furnished by the impressions made on our organs of sense; and consequently, that without these impressions, it would have been impossible for us to arrive at the knowledge of our faculties. Agreeable to this explanation of the doctrine, it may undoubtedly be said with plausibility (and, I am inclined to believe, with truth), that the occasions on which all our notions are formed, are furnished either immediately or ultimately by sense. But, if I am not much mistaken, this is not the meaning which is commonly annexed to the doctrine, either by its advocates or their opponents. One thing at least is obvious, that in this sense it does not lead to those consequences which have interested one party of philosophers in its defence, and another in its refutation.

There is another very important consideration which deserves our attention in this argument: that, even on the supposition that certain impressions on our organs of sense are necessary to awaken the mind to a consciousness of its own existence, and to give rise to the exercise of its various faculties, yet all this might have happened, without our having any knowledge of the qualities, or even of the existence, of the material world. To facilitate the admission of this proposition, let us suppose a being formed in every other respect like man, but possessed of no senses, excepting those of hearing and smelling. I make choice of these two senses, because it is obvious, that by means of them alone we never could have arrived at the knowledge of the primary qualities of matter, or even of the existence of things external. All that we could possibly have inferred from our occasional sensations of smell and sound, would have been, that there existed some unknown cause by which they were produced.

Let us suppose then, a particular sensation to be excited in the mind of such a being. The moment this happens, he must necessarily acquire the knowledge of two facts at once: that of the existence of *the sensation*, and that of *his own existence*, as a sentient being. After the sensation is at an end, he can *remember* he felt it; he can *conceive* that he feels it again. If he has felt a variety of different sensations, he can compare them together in respect of the pleasure or the pain they have afforded him, and will naturally *desire* the return of the agreeable sensations, and be *afraid* of those which were painful. If the sensations of smell and sound are both excited in his mind at the same time, he can *attend* to either of them he chooses, and withdraw his attention from the other; or he can withdraw his *attention* from both, and fix it on some sensation he has felt formerly. In this manner he might be led, merely by sensations existing in his mind, and conveying to him no information concerning matter, to exercise many of his most important faculties; and amidst all these different modifications and operations of his mind, he would feel, with irresistible conviction, that they all belong to one and the same sentient and intelligent being; or, in other words, that they are all modifications and operations of himself. I say nothing at present of the various simple notions (or simple ideas, as they are commonly called) which would arise in his mind; for example, the ideas of *number*, of *duration*, of *cause* and *effect*, of *personal identity*, all of which, though perfectly unlike his sensations, could not fail to be suggested by means of them. Such a being, then, might know all that we know of mind at present; and as his language would be appropriated to mind solely, and not borrowed by analogy from material phenomena, he would even possess important advantages over us in conducting the study of pneumatology.

From these observations it sufficiently appears what is the real amount of the celebrated doctrine, which refers the origin of all our knowledge to our sensations; and that, even granting it to be true, (which for my own part I am disposed to do, in the sense in which I have now explained it,) it would by no means follow from it, that our notions of the operations of mind, nor even many of those notions which are commonly suggested to us, *in the first instance*, by the perception of external objects, are *necessarily subsequent* to our knowledge of the qualities, or even of the existence of matter.

The remarks which I have offered on this doctrine will not appear superfluous to those who recollect that, although it has for many years past been a subject of controversy in England, it continues still to be implicitly adopted by the best philosophical writers in France; and that it has been employed by some of them to support the system of materialism, and by others to show, that the intellectual distinctions between man and brutes arise entirely from the differences in their animal organization, and in their powers of external perception.

Eight

Thomas Brown

1778–1820

Thomas Brown was born in Kirkmabreck, Kirkcudbrightshire on 9 January 1778 and died in London on 2 April 1820. He entered the University of Edinburgh in 1792, and having read the first volume of Dugald Stewart's *Elements of the Philosophy of the Human Mind* during the summer vacation of 1793, attended Stewart's lectures the following winter.

Under Stewart's influence Brown acquired a deep interest in philosophy and literature, but he opted for a career in medicine, graduating MD in 1803, before going into practice. Five years later, however, when Stewart fell ill, Brown assisted in the teaching of moral philosophy at Edinburgh, and in 1810 was appointed to the Chair of Moral Philosophy, being technically Stewart's colleague but effectively his successor, and gaining, like Stewart, a reputation for brilliant and inspiring teaching.

Brown published his first work, *Observations on the Zoonomia of Erasmus Darwin, M.D.*, at the extraordinarily young age of 20. This work sets out his understanding of philosophical method, but his *An Inquiry into the Relation of Cause and Effect*, which appeared in 1818 was much better known. Brown's *Lectures on the Philosophy of the Human Mind* were published posthumously in 1820, following his sudden death at the age of 42. This book proved a very popular work, so much so that it ran to twenty editions, the last being published as much as forty years after its first publication.

Throughout his writings, Brown argues against the notion that there are in nature, or anywhere else, efficient causes hidden from view. In the *Inquiry* he concurs with Hume in arguing that neither reason nor experience can ground the belief in the uniformity of nature that makes induction possible. To this extent Brown was unusual in being a philosopher clearly in the Scottish tradition who argued with rather than against Hume, though his admiration for Hume was not uncritical.

Brown's works were harshly criticised by Stewart as 'radically deficient', and by William Hamilton as riddled with 'radical inconsistencies' and 'frequent misrepresentations of other philosophers'. On the other hand, he had a considerable influence on later Scottish philosophers, notably Alexander Bain, Professor of Logic at Aberdeen from 1860-80, and a founding figure in modern psychology. Another admirer was John Stuart Mill who declared that 'no better introduction to Positivism than the early part of his *Lectures* has yet been produced'. But despite this endorsement, Brown's works were never republished and are now scarcely known, George Davie's *The Scotch Metaphysics* (London, 2001) being the only recent book to offer an extended discussion of his views.

The extract reprinted here conveys both the elegance and subtlety of Brown's philosophical style. It also expresses a view of Hume reflected in Scottish philosophers as far apart in time as Reid and Taylor — that Hume was "an exact and perspicuous metaphysical writer" whose importance lay chiefly in the negative criticism of established views rather than any positive alternative he had to offer.

Biographical information: James Harris, *Thoemmes Dictionary of C19th British Philosophers*

READING XIV
Hume as a Philosopher[1]

I may, perhaps, be indulged in a few remarks, on the character of Mr Hume's mode of writing, on the abstruse subjects to which some of his Essays on the philosophy of mind relate, not with a view to the consequences, or the truth or error, of the opinions delivered in those Essays, but simply with regard to their degree of clearness and precision, as expository of doctrines whether true or false.

That he was an acute thinker, on those subjects to which the vague name of Metaphysics is commonly given, there was, probably, no one, even of his least candid antagonists, who would have ventured to deny. That he was also an exact and perspicuous metaphysical writer, has been generally admitted, but it has been admitted, chiefly as a consequence of the former praise, or from the remembrance of powers of style, which, in many other respects, he unquestionably possessed. We think of him, perhaps, as an historian, while we are praising him as a metaphysician; or, in praising him as a metaphysician, we think of qualities, necessary indeed for the detection of error, but different from those which the development of the system of truths of an abstruse and complicated science peculiarly requires.

In the philosophy of mind, where the objects are all dim and fleeting, it is the more necessary to remedy as much as possible, by regular progressive inquiry, and methodological arrangement, and precision of terms, the uncertainty that otherwise might flow from the shadowy nature of the inquiry itself. The speculations of Mr Hume, however, as I conceive, are far from being marked with this sort of accuracy. The truths, which

---

[1]   Extracted from *Inquiry into the Relation of Cause and Effect*, Edinburgh: Constable, 1818, pp. 327–38

his acuteness is quick to find and to present to us, flit before our eyes in gleamy coruscation, rather than fling on the truths which follow them that harmonizing lustre which makes each in progressive illumination more radiant by the brightness that preceded it, and more fit, therefore, to reflect new radiance on the brightness which is to follow. The genius of his metaphysical style — discursive and rapid, and sometimes in consequence of that very rapidity of transition slow in its general results, from the necessity of recurring to points of inquiry that had been negligently abandoned — is not of the kind that seems best fitted for close and continuous investigation: and though, in the separate views which he gives us of a subject, we are often struck with the singular acuteness of his discernment, and as frequently charmed with an ease of language, which, without the levity of conversation, has many of its playful graces, still, when we consider him as the expositor of a theory, we are not less frequently sensible of a want of rigid order and precision, for which subtlety of thought and occasional graces of the happiest diction are not adequate to atone.

It is when we wish to unfold a system of truths, that we are most careful to exhibit them progressively, in luminous order: for, in the exposure of false opinions, the error, whatever it may be, which we wish to render manifest, may often be exhibited as successfully, by varied views of it in its different aspects, as by the closest analytical investigation. The want of strict continuous method, in some of the theoretical parts of Mr Hume's metaphysical essays — in which we discover more easily what he wishes us not to believe, than what he wishes us positively to believe, or in which at least, the limits of the doubtful and the true are not very precisely defined to our conception — may thus, perhaps, in part be traced to the habits of refined scepticism, in which it seems to have been the early and lasting passion of Mr Hume's mind to indulge. It was more in the detection of fallacies in the common systems of belief, than in the discovery of truths, which might be added to them, that he loved to exercise his metaphysical ingenuity; or, rather, the detections of fallacies was that species of discovery of truth, in which he chiefly delighted. There is, indeed, a calm yet ever-wakeful scepticism of an inquisitive mind, which has nothing in it that is unfavourable, either to closeness of reasoning in the discovery of truth, or to exactness of theoretical arrangement in the communication of it to others. Such a spirit is even so essential to every sort of intellectual inquiry, that the absence of it in any one may be considered as a sufficient proof that he has not the genius of a metaphysician: for the science of metaphysics, as it regards the mind, is, in its most important respects, a science of analysis; and we carry on our analysis, only when we suspect that what is regarded by others as an ultimate principle, admits of still finer evolution into principles still more elementary. It is not, therefore, by such doubts as have only further inquiry in view, that the intellectual character is in any danger of being vitiated: but there is a very great difference between the scepticism

Scottish Philosophy

which examines every principle, only to be sure that inquiry has not terminated too soon, and that which examines them, only to discover and proclaim whatever apparent inconsistencies may be found in them. Astonishment, indeed, is thus produced; and it must be confessed, that there is a sort of triumphant delight in the production of astonishment, which it is not easy to resist, especially at that early period of life[2], when the love of fame is little more than the love of instant wonder and admiration. But he who indulges in the pleasure, and seeks, with a sportful vanity of acuteness, to dazzle and perplex, rather than to enlighten, will find, that though he may have improved his quickness of discernment, by exercises of nice and unprofitable subtlety, he has improved it at the expense of those powers of patient investigation, which give to dialectic subtlety it chief value.

The perpetual consideration of the insufficiency of all inquiry, as deduced from inconsistencies which may seem to be involved in some of our principles of belief, is more encouraging to indolence than to perseverance. By representing to us error, as the necessary termination of every speculative pursuit, it seems, at every moment, to warn us not to proceed so far, and tends, therefore, to seduce the faculties into a luxurious slothfulness of occupation, which prefers a rapid succession of brilliant paradoxes, to truths of more extensive and lasting utility, but of more laborious search.

To show, that it is not from any logical inference, or direct induction, we have derived many of those opinions which, by the very constitution of our nature, it is impossible for us not to hold, and which have been formed without any thought of their origin, requires indeed superior perspicacity, but does not require any process of long continued reasoning. The very habit of ratiocination is thus apt to yield to a love of briefer exercises of discursive subtlety, and this tendency, when the scepticism relates to moral and religious subjects, is still increased by the popular odium attached to infidelity, in those great articles of general belief — an odium, which may naturally be supposed to induce the necessity, in many cases, of exhibiting subjects only by glimpses, and of hinting, rather than fully developing and enforcing a proof.

A mind that has been long habituated to this rapid and lively species of remark, and that has learned to consider all inquiries as of doubtful evidence, and their results therefore as all equally or nearly equally satisfactory or unsatisfactory, does not readily submit to the regularity of slow disquisition. It may exhibit excellencies, for which we may be led immediately to term it, with the justest commendation, acute, or subtle, or ingenious: but it will not be in many cases that there will be reason to ascribe to it that peculiar quality of intellect, which sees through a long train of thought a distant conclusion, and, separating at every stage the

---

[2]   We are told by Mr Hume, that his Treatise on Human Nature was projected by him before he had left College.

essential from the accessory circumstances, and gathering and combining analogies as it proceeds, arrives at length at a system of harmonious truth. This comprehensive energy is a quality to which acuteness is necessary, but which is not itself necessarily implied in acuteness; or rather it is a combination of qualities, for which we have not yet an exact name, but which forms a peculiar character of genius, and is, in truth, the very guiding spirit of all philosophic investigation.

That a long indulgence in the ingenuities of scepticism, though it may improve mere dialectic acuteness, has a tendency to deaden, if I may so term it, the intellectual perception of the objects on which it is wisdom to rest, and, by flinging the same sort of doubtful light over truth and error, to make error often appear as worthy of assent as truth, — at least if the error happens to be in any doctrine of the sceptic himself, — is, I think, what our knowledge of some of the strongest principles of the mind might naturally lead us to expect. That the evil, of which I speak, is truly to be found in the metaphysical speculations of Mr Hume, I may be wrong, indeed, in supposing; but, if any part of his abstract writings be marked with it, there is none, as I conceive, in which it is so conspicuous, as in those which relate to the subject that has been now under review. While he appears only as the combatant of error, in exposing the inadequacy of perception or mere reasoning to afford us directly any notion of the necessary connexion of events, it is impossible not to feel the force of the negative arguments which he urges, and equally impossible not to admire the acuteness and vigour of intellect which these display; but when, after these negative arguments, he presents to us opinions on the subject which he wishes us to receive as positive truth, a very slight consideration is all that seems necessary to show how strong the self-illusive influence must have been, that could make these opinions, unwarranted as they are by the evidence of observation or consciousness, appear to his own mind worthy of the credit which he expects to be given to them. It is fortunate for his intellectual character, that it is not as a dogmatist only he has given us opportunities of knowing him. The minor theories, involved in his doctrine of the origin of the notion of power, which we are about to consider, would certainly give a very unfavourable impression of his talents as a metaphysical inquirer, if his reputation as a metaphysician were to be founded wholly on this or other positive doctrines maintained by him, and not on the acuteness with which in many brilliant exercises of sceptical subtlety, he has exhibited what he wishes to be considered as errors in the systems of popular and scientific faith.

Nine

James Frederick Ferrier

1808-1864

James Frederick Ferrier was born on 16 June 1808 to a prominent Edinburgh family — his aunt was the novelist Susan Ferrier, and under the alias 'Christopher North' his uncle, Professor John Wilson, was one of 19th century Britain's leading men of letters.

Ferrier was educated at the High School of Edinburgh and Greenwich School outside London. In 1825 he enrolled at the University of Edinburgh where he studied for two years before becoming a Fellow Commoner at Magdalen College, Oxford from which he graduated in 1832. It was during his last year there that he met Sir William Hamilton.

Ferrier returned to Edinburgh, entered the 'Faculty of Advocates' and began work as a lawyer in 1833, but having little interest in a legal career, he continued his philosophical studies, and in 1837 published his first article in *Blackwood's Magazine*. This article — 'An Introduction to the Philosophy of Consciousness' — appeared in instalments over seven issues and established Ferrier as an important contributor to philosophical discussion in Scotland.

In 1841 Ferrier was appointed Professor of Civil History at the University of Edinburgh where he developed a close intellectual and personal relationship with Sir William Hamilton on whose recommendation he was appointed Professor of Moral Philosophy and Political Economy at the University of St Andrews. In 1854 he published his major work the *Institutes of Metaphysic*.

In 1853 Ferrier applied to Edinburgh University for the Chair of Moral Philosophy and then again in 1856, when Sir William Hamilton died, for the Chair of Logic and Metaphysics. Neither application was successful, partly because of the mixed reception the *Institutes* had received. The second competition was acrimonious and prompted Ferrier to publish a short work *Scottish Philosophy: the Old and the New*, in which he defended his philosophy as properly Scottish despite his express rejection of the School of Common Sense.

Ferrier spent his final years revising his lectures on Greek philosophy, which were published after his death. From 1857 onward Ferrier's health declined and he died in St Andrews on 11 June 1864. His collected works were published in three volumes in 1875.

Ferrier's essay on Reid and Common Sense, reprinted here, criticises Reid (and Stewart) with great ferocity, and argues for a return to the philosophy of Berkeley from which Reid had deliberately tried to depart. Ferrier's own work on 'The Philosophy of Consciousness' was influential for a time, but perhaps because of his florid, and occasionally intemperate style, is not much read today. Yet the distinction he draws between psychology and metaphysics in the study of the human mind, turned out to be prescient, since subsequent investigations into the human mind did indeed divide along these lines.

Biographical information: Phillip Ferreira, *Thoemmes Dictionary of C19 British Philosophers.*

READING XV
Reid and the Philosophy of Common Sense[1]

In entering on an examination of the system of Dr Reid, we must ask first of all, what is the great problem about which philosophers in all ages have busied themselves most, and which consequently must have engaged, and did engage, a large share of the attention of the champion of Common Sense? We must also state the *fact* which gives rise to the problem of philosophy.

The perception of a material universe, as it is the most prominent fact of cognition, so has it given rise to the problem which has been most agitated by philosophers. This question does not relate to the existence of the fact. The existence of the perception of matter is admitted on all hands. It refers to the nature, or origin, or constitution of the fact. Is the perception of matter simple and indivisible, or is it composite and divisible? Is it the ultimate, or is it only the penultimate, *datum* of cognition? Is it a relation constituted by the concurrence of a mental or subjective, and a material or objective element; or do we impose upon ourselves in regarding it as such? Is it a state or modification of the human mind? Is it an effect that can be distinguished from its cause? Is it an event consequent on the presence of real antecedent objects? These interrogations are somewhat varied in their form, but each of them embodies the whole point at issue, each of them contains the cardinal question of philosophy. The perception of matter is the admitted fact. The *character* of this fact,

---

[1] Extracted from *Philosophical Works of James Frederick Ferrier*, vol. III, Bristol: Thoemmes Press, 2001, pp. 407–42.

that is the point which speculation undertakes to canvass, and endeavours to decipher.

Another form in which the question may be put is this: We all believe in the existence of matter, but what *kind* of matter do we believe in the existence of? matter *per se*, or matter *cum perceptione* [with perception]? If the former, this implies that the given fact (the perception of matter) is compound and submits to analysis; if the latter, this implies that it is simple and defies partition.

Opposite answers to this question are returned by psychology and metaphysic. In the estimation of metaphysic, the perception of matter is the absolutely elementary in cognition, the *ne plus ultra* [nothing beyond which] of thought. Reason cannot get beyond, or behind it. It has no pedigree. It admits of no analysis. It is not a relation constituted by the coalescence of an objective and a subjective element. It is not a state or modification of the human mind. It is not an effect which can be distinguished from its cause. It is not brought about by the presence of antecedent realities. It is positively the FIRST, with no forerunner. The perception-of-matter is one mental word, of which the verbal words are mere syllables. We impose upon ourselves, and we also falsify the fact, if we take any other view of it than this. Thus speaks metaphysic, though perhaps not always with an unfaltering voice.

Psychology, or the science of the human mind, teaches a very different doctrine. According to this science, the perception of matter is a secondary and composite truth. It admits of being analysed into a subjective and an objective element, a mental modification called perception on the one hand, and matter *per se* on the other. It is an effect induced by real objects. It is not the first *datum* of intelligence. It has matter itself for its antecedent. Such, in very general terms, is the explanation of the perception of matter which psychology proposes.

Psychology and metaphysic are thus radically opposed to each other in their solutions of the highest problem of speculation. Stated concisely, the difference between them is this: — psychology regards the perception of matter as susceptible of analytic treatment, and travels, or endeavours to travel, beyond the given fact; metaphysic stops short in the given fact, and there makes a stand, declaring it to be an indissoluble unity. Psychology holds her analysis to be an analysis of things. Metaphysic holds the psychological analysis to an analysis of sounds, and nothing more. These observations exhibit, in their loftiest generalisation, the two counter doctrines on the subject of perception. We now propose to follow them into their details, for the purpose both of eliciting the truth and of arriving at a correct judgement in regard to the reformation which Dr Reid is supposed to have effected in this department of philosophy.

The psychological or analytic doctrine is the first which we shall discuss, on account of its connection with the investigations of Dr Reid, in regard to whom we may state, beforehand, our conclusion and its grounds, which are these: — that Reid broke down in his philosophy, both polemical and positive, because he assumed the psychological and not the metaphysical doctrine of perception as the basis of his arguments. He did not regard the perception of matter as absolutely primary and simple; but in common with all psychologists, he conceived that it admitted of being resolved into a mental condition and a material reality; and the consequence was, that he fell into the very errors which it was the professed business of his life to denounce and exterminate. How this catastrophe came about we shall endeavour shortly to explain.

Reid's leading design was to overthrow scepticism and idealism. In furtherance of this intention, he proposed to himself the accomplishment of two subsidiary ends, — the refutation of what is called the ideal or representative theory of perception, and the substitution of a doctrine of intuitive perception in its room. He takes, and he usually gets, credit for having accomplished both of these objects. But if it be true that the representative theory is but the inevitable development of the doctrine which treats the perception of matter analytically, and if it be true that Reid adopts this latter doctrine, it is obvious that his claims cannot be admitted without a very considerable deduction. That both of these things are true may be established, we think, beyond the possibility of a doubt.

In the first place, then, we have to show that the theory of a representative perception (which Reid is supposed to have overthrown) is identical with the doctrine which treats the perception of matter analytically; and, in the second, we have to show that Reid himself followed the analytic or psychological procedure in his treatment of this fact, and founded upon the analysis his own doctrine of perception.

First, The representative theory is that doctrine of perception which teaches that, in our intercourse with the external universe, we are not immediately cognisant of real objects themselves, but only of certain mental transcripts or images of them, which, in the language of the different philosophical schools, were termed ideas, representations, phantasms, or species. According to this doctrine we are cognisant of real things, not in and through themselves, but in and through these species or representations. The representations are the immediate or proximate, the real things are the mediate or remote, objects of the mind. The existence of the former is a matter of knowledge, the existence of the latter is merely a matter of belief.

To understand this theory, we must construe its nomenclature into the language of the present day. What, then, is the modern synonym for the 'ideas', 'representations', 'phantasms', and 'species', which the theory in question declares to be vicarious of real objects? There cannot be a doubt that the word *perception* is that synonym. So that the representative theory, when fairly interpreted, amounts simply to this, that the mind is immediately cognisant, not of real objects themselves, but *only of its own perceptions of real objects*. To accuse the representationist of maintaining a doctrine more repugnant to common sense than this, or in any way different from it, would be both erroneous and unjust. The golden rule of philosophical criticism is to give every system the benefit of the most favourable interpretation which it admits of.

This, then, is the true version of representationism, namely, that our perception of material things, and not material things *per se*, are the proximate objects of our consciousness when we hold intercourse with the external universe.

Now, this is a doctrine which inevitably emerges the instant that the analysis of the perception of matter is set on foot and admitted. When a philosopher divides, or imagines that he divides, the perception of matter into two things, perception *and* matter, holding the former to be a state of his own mind, and the latter to be no such state; he does, in that analysis, and without saying one other word, avow himself to be a thoroughgoing representationist. For his analysis declares that, in perception, the mind has an immediate or proximate, and a mediate or remote object. Its perception of matter is the proximate object, the object of its consciousness; matter itself, the material existence, is the remote object — the object of its belief. But such a doctrine is representationism, in the strictest sense of the word. It is the very essence and definition of the representative theory to recognise, in perception, a remote as well as a proximate object of the mind. Every system which does this is necessarily a representative system. The doctrine which treats the perception of matter analytically does this; therefore the analytic or psychological doctrine is identical with the representative theory. Both hold that the perceptive process involves two objects, an immediate and a mediate; and nothing more is required to establish their perfect identity. The analysis of the fact which we call the perception of matter, is unquestionably the groundwork and pervading principle of the theory of a representative perception, whatever form of expression this scheme may at any time have assumed.

Secondly, Did Dr Reid go to work analytically in his treatment of the perception of matter? Undoubtedly he did. He followed the ordinary psychological practice. He regarded the *datum* as divisible into perception and matter. The perception he held to be an act, if not a modification of our minds; the matter he regarded as something which existed out of the mind and irrespective of all perception. Right or wrong, he resolved, or conceived that he had resolved, the perception of matter into its constituent elements, these being a mental operation on the one hand and a material existence on the other. In short, however ambiguous many of Dr Reid's principles may be, there can be no doubt that he founded his doctrine of perception on an analysis of the given fact with which he had to deal. He says, indeed, but little about this analysis, so completely does he take it for granted. He accepted, as a thing of course, the notorious distinction between the perception of matter and matter itself; and, in doing so, he merely followed the example of all preceding psychologists.

These two points being established — *first*, that the theory of representationism necessarily arises out of an analysis of the perception of matter; and, *secondly*, that Reid analysed or accepted the analysis of this fact — it follows as a necessary consequence that Reid, so far from having overthrown the representative theory, was himself a representationist. His analysis gave him more than he bargained for. He wished to obtain only one, that is, only a proximate object in perception; but his analysis necessarily gave him two: it gave him a remote as well as a proximate object. The mental mode or operation which he calls the perception of matter, and which he distinguishes from matter itself, this, in his philosophy, is the proximate object of consciousness, and is precisely equivalent to the species, phantasms, and representations of the older psychology; the real existence, matter itself, which he distinguishes from the perception of it, this is the remote object of the mind, and is precisely equivalent to the mediate or represented object of the older psychology. He and the representationists, moreover, agree in holding that the latter is the object of belief rather than of knowledge.

The merits of Dr Reid, then, as a reformer of philosophy, amount in our opinion to this: he was among the first[2] to *say* and to *write* that the representative theory of perception was false and erroneous, and was the fountainhead of scepticism and idealism. But this admission of his merits must be accompanied by the qualification that he adopted, as the basis of his philosophy, a principle which rendered nugatory all his protestations. It is of no use to disclaim a conclusion if we accept the premises which inevitably lead to it. Dr Reid disclaimed the representative theory, but he embraced its premises, and thus he virtually ratified the conclusions of the very system which he clamorously denounced. In his language he is opposed to representationism, but in his doctrine he lends it the strongest support by accepting as the foundation of his philosophy an analysis of the perception of matter.

In regard to the *second* end which Dr Reid is supposed to have overtaken — the establishment of a doctrine of intuitive as opposed to a doctrine of representative perception — it is unnecessary to say much. If we have proved him to be a representationist, he cannot be held to be an

---

[2]   *Among the first.* He was not *the* first. Berkeley had preceded him in denouncing most unequivocally the whole theory of representationism. The reason why Berkeley does not get the credit of this is, because his performance is even more explicit and cogent than his promise. He made no phrase about refuting the theory, he simply refuted it. Reid *said* the business, but Berkeley *did* it. The two greatest and most unaccountable blunders in the whole history of philosophy are probably Reid's allegations that Berkeley was a representationist, and that he was an idealist; understanding by the word *idealist*, one who denies the existence of a real external universe. From every page of his writings, it is obvious that Berkeley was neither the one of these nor the other, even in the remotest degree.

intuitionist. Indeed, a doctrine of intuitive perception is a sheer impossibility upon his principles. A doctrine of intuition implies that the mind in perceiving matter has only one, namely, a proximate object. But the analysis of the perception of matter always yields, as its result, a remote as well as a proximate object. The proximate object is the perception, the remote object is the reality. And thus the analysis of the given fact necessarily renders abortive every endeavour to construct a doctrine of intuitive perception. The attempt *must* end in representationism. The only basis for a doctrine of intuitive perception which will never give way, is a resolute forbearance from all analysis of the fact. Do not tamper with it, and you are safe.

Such is the judgement which we are reluctantly compelled to pronounce on the philosophy of Dr Reid in reference to its two cardinal claims, the refutation of the ideal theory, and the establishment of a truer doctrine — a doctrine of intuitive perception. In neither of these undertakings do we think that he has succeeded, and we have exhibited the grounds of our opinion. We do not blame him for this: he simply missed his way at the outset. Representationism could not possibly be avoided, neither could intuitionism be possibly fallen in with, on the analytic road he took.

But we have not yet done with the consideration of the psychological or analytic doctrine of perception. We proceed to examine the entanglements in which reason gets involved when she accepts the perception of matter not in its natural and indissoluble unity, but as analysed by philosophers into a mental and a material factor. We have still an eye to Dr Reid. He came to the rescue of reason, how did it fare with him in the struggle?

The analysis so often referred to affords a starting point, as has been shown, to representationism: it is also the tap-root of scepticism and idealism. These four things hang together in an inevitable sequence. Scepticism and idealism dog representationism, and representationism dogs analysis of the perception of matter, just as obstinately as substance is dogged by shadow. More explicitly stated, the order in which they move is this: The analysis divides the perception of matter into perception and matter — two separate things. Upon this, representationism declares, that the perception is the proximate, and that the matter is the remote, object of the mind. Then scepticism declares, that the existence of the matter which has been separated from the perception is problematical, because it is not the direct object of consciousness, and is consequently hypothetical. And, last of all, idealism takes up the ball and declares, that this hypothetical matter is not only problematical, but that it is non-existent. These are the perplexities which rise up to embarrass reason whenever she is weak enough to accept from philosophers their analysis of the perception of matter. They are only the just punishment of her infatuated facility. But what has Reid done to extricate reason from her embarrassments?

We must remember that Reid commenced with analysis, and that consequently he embraced representationism, in its spirit, if not positively in its letter. But how did he evade the fangs of scepticism and idealism, to say nothing of destroying, these sleuth-hounds which on this road were sure to be down upon his track the moment they got wind of him? We put the question in a less figurative form: When scepticism and idealism doubted or denied the independent existence of matter, how did Reid vindicate it? He faced about and appealed boldly to our instinctive and irresistible *belief* in its independent existence.

The crisis of the strife centres in this appeal. In itself, the appeal is perfectly competent and legitimate. But it may be met, on the part of the sceptic and idealist, by two modes of tactic. The one tactic is weak, and gives an easy triumph to Dr Reid: the other is more formidable, and, in our opinion, lays him prostrate.

The First Sceptical Tactic. — In answer to Dr Reid's appeal, the sceptic or idealist may say, 'Doubtless we have a belief in the independent existence of matter; but this belief is not to be trusted. It is an insufficient guarantee for that which it avouches. It does not follow that a thing is true because we instinctively believe it to be true. It does not follow that matter exists because we cannot but believe it to exist. You must prove its existence by a better argument than mere belief'. This mode of meeting the appeal we hold to be pure trifling. We join issue with Dr Reid in maintaining that our nature is not rooted in delusion, and that the primitive convictions of common sense must be accepted as infallible. If the sceptic admits that we *have* a natural belief in the independent existence of matter, there is an end to him: Dr Reid's victory is secure. This first tactic is a feeble and mistaken manoeuvre.

The Second Sceptical Tactic. — This position is not so easily turned. The stronghold of the sceptic and idealist is this: they deny the primitive belief to which Dr Reid appeals to be *the fact*. It is not true, they say, that any man believes in the independent existence of matter. And this is perfectly obvious the moment that it is explained. Matter in its *independent* existence, matter *per se*, is matter disengaged in thought from all perception of it present or remembered. Now, does any man believe in the existence of such matter? Unquestionably not. No man by any possibility can. What the matter is which man really believes in shall be explained when we come to speak of the metaphysical solution of the problem, perhaps sooner. Meanwhile we remark that Dr Reid's appeal to the conviction of common sense in favour of the existence of matter *per se*, is rebutted, and in our opinion triumphantly, by the denial on the part of scepticism and idealism that any such belief exists. Scepticism and idealism not only deny the independent existence of matter, but they deny that any man believes in the independent existence of matter. And in this denial they are most indubitably right. For observe what such a belief requires as its condition. A man must disengage in thought, a tree, for instance, from the thought of all perception of it, and then he must believe in its existence thus disengaged. If he has not disengaged, in his mind, the tree from its perception (from its present perception, if the tree be before him; from its remembered perception, if it be not before him), he cannot believe in the existence of the tree disengaged from its perception; for the tree is *not* disengaged from its perception. But unless he believes in the existence of the tree disengaged from its perception, he does not believe in the independent existence of the tree, in the existence of the tree *per se*. Now, can the mind by any effort effect this disengagement? The thing is an absolute impossibility. The condition on which the belief hinges cannot be purified, and consequently the belief itself cannot be entertained.

People have, then, *no belief* in the independent existence of matter; that is, in the existence of matter entirely denuded of perception. This point being proved, what becomes of Dr Reid's appeal to *this belief* in support of matter's independent existence? It has not only no force, it has no meaning. This second tactic is invincible. Scepticism and idealism are perfectly in the right when they refuse to accept as the guarantee of independent matter belief which itself has no manner of existence. How can they be vanquished by an appeal to a nonentity?

A question may here be raised. If the belief in question be not the fact, what has hitherto prevented scepticism from putting a final extinguisher of Reid's appeal by *proving* that no such belief exists? A very sufficient reason has prevented scepticism from doing this, from explicitly extinguishing the appeal. There is a division of labour in speculation as well as in other pursuits. It is the sceptic's business simply to deny the existence of the belief: it is no part of his business to exhibit the grounds of his denial. *We* have explained these grounds; but were the sceptic to do this, he would be travelling out of his vocation. Observe how the case stands. The reason why matter *per se* is not and cannot be believed in, is because it is impossible for thought to disengage matter from perception, and consequently it is impossible for thought to believe in the disengaged existence of matter. The matter to be believed in is not disengaged from the perception, consequently it cannot be believed to be disengaged from the perception. But unless it be believed to be disengaged from the perception, it cannot be believed to exist *per se*. In short, as we have already said, the impossibility of complying with the *condition* of the belief is the ground on which the sceptic denies the *existence* of the belief. But the sceptic is himself disbarred from producing these grounds. Why? Because their exhibition would be tantamount to a rejection of the principle which he has *accepted* at the hands of the orthodox and dogmatic psychologist. That principle is the analysis so often spoken of — the separation, namely, of the perception of matter into perception and matter *per se*. The sceptic accepts this analysis. His business is simply to *accept*, not to discover or scrutinise principles. Having accepted the analysis, he then denies that any belief attaches to the existence of matter *per se*. In this he is quite right. But he cannot, consistently with his calling, exhibit the ground of his denial; for this ground is, as we have shown, the impossibility of performing the analysis, of effecting the requisite disengagement. But the sceptic has accepted the analysis, has admitted the disengagement. He therefore cannot now retract: and he has no wish to retract. His special mission, his only object, is to confound the principle which he has accepted by means of the reaction of its consequences. The inevitable consequence which ensues when the analysis of the perception of matter is admitted is the extinction of all belief in the existence of matter. The analysis gives us a kind of matter to believe in to which no belief corresponds. The sceptic is content with pronouncing this to be the fact without going into its reason. It is not his business to correct, by a direct exposure, the error of the principle which the dogmatist lays down, and which he accepts. The analysis is the psychologist's affair; let *him* look to it. Were the sceptic to make it his, he would emerge from the sceptical crisis, and pass into a new stage of speculation. He, indeed, subverts it indirectly by a *reductio ad absurdum*. But he does not *say* that he subverts it; he leaves the orthodox proposer of the principle to find that out.

Reid totally misconceived the nature of scepticism and idealism in their bearings on this problem. He regarded them as habits of thought, as dispositions of mind peculiar to certain individuals of vexatious character and unsound principles, instead of viewing them as catholic eras in the development of all genuine speculative thinking. In his eyes they were subjective crotchets limited to some, and not objective crises common to all who think. He made *personal* matters of them, a thing not to be endured. For instance, in dealing with Hume, he conceived that the scepticism which confronted him in the pages of that great genius was *Hume's* scepticism, and was not the scepticism of human nature at large — was not his own scepticism just as much as it was Hume's. *His* soul, so he thought, was free from the obnoxious flaw, merely because *his* anatomy, shallower than Hume's, refused to lay it bare. With such views it was impossible for Reid to eliminate scepticism and idealism from philosophy. These foes are the foes of each man's own house and heart, and nothing can be made of them if we attack them in the person of another. Ultimately and fairly to get rid of them, a man must first of all thoroughly digest them, and take them up into the vital circulation of his own reason. The only way of putting them back is by carrying them forward.

From having never properly secreted scepticism and idealism in his own mind, Reid fell into the commission of one of the gravest errors of which a philosopher can be guilty. He falsified the fact in regard to our primitive beliefs, a thing which the obnoxious systems against which he was fighting never did. He conceived that scepticism and idealism called in question a fact which was countenanced by a natural belief; accordingly, he confronted their denial with the allegation that the disputed fact, the existence of matter *per se*, was guaranteed by a primitive conviction of our nature. But this fact receives no support from any such source. There is no belief in the whole repository of the mind which can be fitted on to the existence of matter denuded of all perception. There-fore, in maintaining the contrary, Reid falsified the fact in regard to our primitive convictions, in regard to those principles of common sense which he professed to follow as his guide. This was a serious slip. The rash step which he here took plunged him into a much deeper error than that of the sceptic or idealist. They err in common with him in accepting as their starting-point the analysis of the perception of matter. He errs, by himself, in maintaining that there is a belief where no belief exists.

But do not scepticism and idealism doubt matter's existence *altogether*, or deny to it *any* kind of existence? Certainly they do; and in harmony with the principle from which they start they must do this. The *only* kind of matter which the analysis of the perception of matter yields, is matter *per se*. The existence of such matter is, as we have shown, altogether uncountenanced either by consciousness or belief. But there is no other kind of matter in the field. We must, therefore, either believe in the exis-tence of matter *per se*, or we must believe in the existence of *no* matter whatever. We do not, and we cannot, believe in the existence of matter *per se*; therefore we cannot believe in the existence of matter at all. This is not satisfactory, but it is closely consequential.

But why not, it may be said, why not cut the knot, and set the question at rest, by admitting at once that every man *does*, popularly speaking, believe in the existence of matter, and that he practically walks in the light of that belief during every moment of his life? This observation tempts us into a digression, and we shall yield to the temptation. The problem of perception admits of being treated in *three* several ways: *first*, we may ignore it altogether, we may refuse to entertain it at all; or, *secondly*, we may discuss it in the manner just proposed, we may lay it down as gospel that every man does believe in the existence of matter, and acts at all times upon this conviction, and we may expatiate dif-fusely over these smooth truths; or, *thirdly*, we may follow and contem-plate the subtle and often perplexed windings which reason takes in working her way through the problem — a problem which, though apparently clearer than the noonday sun, is really darker than the mys-teries of Erebus. In short, we may *speculate* the problem. In grappling with it we may trust ourselves to the mighty current of *thinking*, with all its whirling eddies, certain that, if our thinking be genuine objective thinking, which deals with nothing but *ascertained* facts, it will bring us at last into the haven of truth. We now propose to consider which of these modes of treating the problem is the best; we shall begin by making a few remarks upon the *second*, for it was this which brought us to a stand, and seduced us into the present digression.

It is, no doubt, perfectly true that we all believe in the existence of mat-ter, and that we all act up to this belief. The truth that 'each of us exists'; the truth that 'each of us is the same person to-day that he was yesterday'; the truth that 'a material universe exists, and that we believe in its existence'; all these are most important truths, most important things to know. It is difficult to see how we could get on without this knowledge. Yet they are not worth one straw in communication. And why not? Just for the same reason that atmospheric air, though absolutely indispensable to our existence, has no value whatever in exchange; this reason being that we can get, and have already got, both the air and the truths in unlimited abundance for nothing, and thanks to no man. It is not its *importance*, then, which confers upon truth its value in communication. The value of truth is measured by precisely the same standard which determines the value of wealth. This standard is in neither case the importance of the article; it is always its difficulty of attainment, its cost of production. Has *labour* been expended on its formation or acquisition: then the article, if a material commodity, has a value in exchange; if a truth, it has a value in communication. Has no labour been bestowed upon it, and has Nature herself furnished it to every human being in overflowing abundance: then the thing is altogether destitute of exchange-value, whether it be an article of matter or of mind; no man can, without impertinence, transmit or convey such a commodity to his neighbour. If this be the law on the subject (and we conceive that it must be so ruled) it settles the question as to the *second* mode of dealing with the problem of perception. It establishes the point that this method of treating the problem is not to be permitted.

The *first* and *third* modes of dealing with our problem remain to be considered. The first mode ignores the problem altogether; it refuses to have anything to do with it. Perhaps this mode is the best of the three. We will not say that it is not: it is at any rate preferable to the second. But once admit that philosophy is a legitimate occupation, and this mode must be set aside, for it is a negation of all philosophy. Everything depends upon this admission. But the admission is, we conceive, a point which has been already and long ago decided. Men must and will philosophise. That being the case the only alternative left is, that we should discuss the highest problem of philosophy in the terms of the *third* mode proposed. We have called this the speculative method, which means nothing more than that we should expend upon the investigation the uttermost toil and application of thought; and that we should estimate the truths which we arrive at, not by the scale of their importance, but by the scale of their difficulty of attainment, of their cost of production. *Labour,* we repeat it, is the standard which measures the value of truth as well as the value of wealth.

A still more cogent argument in favour of the strictly speculative treatment of the problem is this. The problem of perception may be said to be a *reversed* problem. What are the means in every other problem are in *this* problem the end; and what is the end in every other problem is in this problem the means. In every other problem the solution of the problem is the end desiderated: the means are the thinking requisite for its solution. But here the case is inverted. In *our* problem the desiderated solution is the means; the end is the development, or, we should rather say, the creation of speculative thought, a kind of thought different altogether from ordinary popular thinking. 'Oh! then', some one will perhaps exclaim, 'after all, the whole question about perception resolves it into a *mere gymnastic* of the mind'. Good sir, do you know what you are saying? Do *you* think that the mind itself is anything except a mere gymnastic of the mind? If you do, you are most deplorably mistaken. Most assuredly the mind only *is* what the mind *does*. The existence of thought is the exercise of thought. Now if this be true, there is the strongest possible reason for treating the problem after a purely speculative fashion. The problem and its desired solution, these are only the means which enable a new species of thinking (and that the very highest), viz., speculative thinking, to deploy into existence. This deployment is the end. But how can this end be attained if we check the speculative evolution in its first movements, by throwing ourselves into the arms of the *apparently* Common Sense convictions of Dr Reid? We use the word 'apparently', because, in reference to this problem, the apparently Common Sense convictions of Dr Reid are not the *really* Common Sense convictions of mankind. These latter can only be got at through the severest discipline of speculation.

Our final answer, then, to the question which led us into this digression is this: It is quite true that the material world exists; it is quite true that we believe in this existence, and always act in conformity with our faith. Whole books may be written in confirmation of these truths. They may be published and paraded in a manner which apparently settles the entire problem of perception. And yet this is not the right way to go to work. It settles nothing by what all men, women, and children have already settled. The truths thus formally substantiated were produced without an effort; every one has already got from Nature at least as much of them as he cares to have; and therefore, whatever their importance may be, they cannot, with any sort of propriety, be made the subjects of conveyance from man to man. We must either leave the problem altogether alone (a thing, however, which we should have thought of sooner), or we must adopt the speculative treatment. The argument, moreover, contained in the preceding paragraph, appears to render this treatment imperative; and accordingly we now return to it, after our somewhat lengthened digression.

We must take up the thread of our discourse at the point where we dropped it. The crisis to which the discussion had conducted us was this: that the existence of matter could not be believed in *at all*. The psychological analysis necessarily lands us in this conclusion: for the psychological analysis gives us, for matter, nothing but matter *per se*. But matter *per se* is what no man does or can believe in. We are reluctant to reiterate the proof; but it is this: to believe in the existence of matter *per se* is to believe in the existence of matter liberated from perception; but we cannot believe in the existence of matter liberated from perception, for no power of thinking will liberate matter from perception; therefore we cannot believe in the existence of matter *per se*. This argument admits of being exhibited in a still more forcible form. We commence with an illustration. If a man believes that a thing exists as one thing, he cannot believe that this same thing exists as another thing. For instance, if a man believes that a tree exists as a tree, he cannot believe that it exists as a house. Apply this to the subject in hand. If a man believes that matter exists as a thing *not* disengaged from perception, he cannot believe that it exists as a thing *disengaged* from perception. Now, there cannot be a doubt that the *only* kind of matter in which man believes is matter *not* disengaged from perception. He therefore cannot believe in matter *disengaged* from perception. His mind is already preoccupied by the belief that matter is *this one thing*, and, therefore, he cannot believe that it is *that other thing*. His faith is, in this instance, forestalled, just as much as his faith is forestalled from believing that a tree is a house, when he already believes that it is a tree.

There are two very good reasons, then, why we cannot believe in the existence of matter at all, if we accept as our starting-point the psychological analysis. This analysis gives us, for matter, matter *per se*. But matter *per se* cannot be believed in: 1st because the condition on which the belief depends cannot be compiled with; and 2dly, because the matter which we *already* believe in is something quite different from matter *per se*. In trying to believe in the existence of matter *per se*, we always find that we are believing in the existence of *something else*, namely, in the existence of matter *cum perceptione* [with perception]. But it is not to the psychological analysis that we are indebted for this matter, which is something else than matter *per se*. The psychological analysis does its best to annihilate it. It gives us nothing but matter *per se*, a thing which neither is nor can be believed in. We are thus prevented from believing in the existence of *any* kind of matter. In a word, the psychological analysis of the perception of matter necessarily coverts all those who embrace it into sceptics or idealists.

In this predicament what shall we do? Shall we abandon the analysis as a treacherous principle, or shall we, with Dr Reid, make one more stand in its defence? In order that the analysis may have fair play we shall give it another chance, by quoting Mr Stewart's exposition of Reid's doctrine, which must be regarded as a perfectly faithful representation. 'Dr Reid', says Mr Stewart, 'was the first person who had courage to lay completely aside all the common *hypothetical* language concerning perception, and to exhibit *the difficulty*, in all its magnitude, by a plain *statement of the fact*. To what, then, it may be asked, does this statement amount? Merely to this: that the mind is so formed that certain impressions produced on our organs of sense, by external objects, are *followed* by corresponding sensations, and that these sensations (which have no more resemblance to the qualities of matter, than the words of a lan-

guage have to the things they denote) are *followed* by a perception of the
existence and qualities of the bodies by which the impressions are made;
that all the steps of this process are equally incomprehensible' [*Elements
of the Philosophy of the Human Mind*, part I. ch.i.]. There are at least two
points which are well worthy of being attended to in this quotation.
First, Mr Stewart says that Reid 'exhibited the difficulty of the problem
of perception, in all its magnitude, by a plain statement of fact'. What
does that mean? It means this: that Reid stated, indeed, that fact cor-
rectly, namely, *that* external objects give rise to sensations and perceptions, but that still his statement did not penetrate to the heart of the
business, but, by his own admission, left the difficulty undiminished.
What difficulty? The difficulty as to *how* external objects give rise to sensations and perceptions. Reid did not undertake to settle that point — a
wise declinature, in the estimation of Mr Stewart. Now Mr Stewart,
understanding, as he did, the philosophy of causation, ought to have
known that every difficulty as to *how* one thing gives rise to another, is
purely a difficulty of the mind's creation, and not of nature's making,
and is, therefore, no difficulty at all. Let us explain this. A man says he
knows *that* fire explodes gunpowder; but he does not know *how* or by
what means it does this. Suppose, then, he finds out the means, he is still
just where he was; he must again ask how or by what means these discovered means explode the gunpowder; and so on *ad infinitum*. Now the
mind may quibble with itself for ever, and *make* what difficulties it
pleases in this way; but there is no *real* difficulty in the case. In considering any sequence, we always know the *how* or the means as soon as we
know the *that* or the fact. These means may be more proximate or more
remote means, but they are invariably given either proximately or
remotely along with and in the fact. As soon as we know *that* fire
explodes gunpowder, we know *how* fire explodes gunpowder; for fire is
itself the means which explodes gunpowder, the *how* by which it is
ignited. In the same way, *if* we knew that matter gave rise to perception,
there would be no difficulty as to *how* it did so. Matter would be itself the
means which gave rise to perception. We conceive, therefore, that Mr
Stewart did not consider what he was saying when he affirmed that
Reid's plain statement of facts exhibited *the difficulty* in all its magnitude.
If Reid's statement *be* a statement of fact, all difficulty vanishes, the question of perception is relieved from every species of perplexity. If it *be* the
fact that perception is consequent on the presence of matter, Reid must
be admitted to have explained, to the satisfaction of all mankind, *how*
perception is brought about. Matter is itself the means by which it is
brought about.

    Secondly, then, Is it the fact that matter gives rise to perception? That is
the question. Is it the fact that these two things stand to each other in the
relation of antecedent and consequent? Reid's 'plain statement of fact',
as reported by Mr Stewart, maintains that they do. Reid lays it down as a
fact, that perceptions *follow* sensations, that sensations *follow* certain

impressions made on our organs of sense by external objects, which stand first in the series. The sequence, then, is this: 1*st*, Real external objects; 2*d*, Impressions made on our organs of sense; 3*d*, Sensations; 4*th*, Perceptions. It will simplify the discussion if we leave out of account Nos. 2 and 3, limiting ourselves to the statement that real objects precede perceptions. This is declared to be a fact, of course an *observed* fact; for a fact can with no sort of propriety be called a fact, unless some person or other has *observed* it. Reid 'laid completely aside all the common *hypothetical* language concerning perception'. His plain statement (so says Mr Stewart) contains nothing but facts, facts established, of course, by observation. It is a fact of observation, then, according to Reid, that real objects precede perceptions; that perceptions follow when real objects are present. Now, when a man proclaims as fact such a sequence as this, what must he first of all have done? He must have observed the antecedent *before* it was followed by the consequent; he must have observed the cause out of combination with effect; otherwise his statement is a pure hypothesis or fiction. For instance, when a man says that a shower of rain (No.1) is followed by a refreshed vegetation (no.2), he must have observed both No.1 and No.2, and he must have observed them as two separate things. Had he never observed anything but No.2 (the refreshed vegetation), he might form what conjectures he pleased in regard to its antecedent, but he never could lay it down *as an observed fact*, that this antecedent was a shower of rain. In the same way, when a man affirms it to be a fact of observation (as Dr Reid does, according to Stewart), that material objects are *followed* by perceptions, it is absolutely necessary for the credit of his statement that he should have observed this to be the case; that he should have observed material objects before they were followed by perceptions; that he should have observed the antecedent separate from the consequent: otherwise his statement, instead of being complimented as a plain statement of fact, must be condemned as a tortuous statement of hypothesis. Unless he has observed No.1 and No.2 in sequence, he is not entitled to declare that this is an observed sequence. Now, did Reid, or did any man, ever observe matter anterior to his perception of it? Had Reid a faculty which enabled him to catch matter before it had passed into perception? Did he ever observe it, as Hudibras says, 'undressed'? Mr Stewart implies that he had such a faculty. But the notion is preposterous. No man can observe matter prior to his perception of it; for his observation of it presupposes his perception of it. Our observation of matter *begins* absolutely with the perception of it. Observation always gives the perception of matter as the *first* term in the series, and not matter itself. To pretend (as Reid and Stewart do) that observation can go behind perception, and lay hold of matter before it has given rise to perception, this is too ludicrous a doctrine to be even mentioned; and we should not have alluded to it, but for the countenance which it has received from the two great apostles of common sense.

This last bold attempt, then, on the part of Reid and Stewart (for Stewart adopts the doctrine which he reports) to prop their tottering analysis on direct observation and experience, must be pronounced a failure. Reid's 'plain statement of fact' is not a *true* statement of *observed* fact; it is a vicious statement of *conjectured* fact. Observation depones the existence of the perception of matter as the first *datum* with which it has to deal, but it depones to the existence of nothing anterior to this.

But will not abstract thinking bear out the analysis by yielding to us matter *per se* as a legitimate inference of reason? No; it will do nothing of the kind. To make good this inference, observe what abstract thinking must do. It must bring under the notice of the mind matter *per se* (No.1) as something which is *not* the perception of it (No.2); but whenever thought tries to bring No.1 under the notice of the mind, it is No.2 (or the perception of matter) which invariably comes. We may ring for No.1, but No.2 always answers the bell. We may labour to construe a tree *per se* to the mind, but what we always *do* construe to the mind is the perception of a tree. What we want is No.1, but what we always get is No.2. To unravel the thing explicitly, the manner in which we impose upon ourselves is this: as explanatory of the perceptive process, we construe to our minds *two number twos*, and one of these we *call* No.1. For example, we have the perception of a tree (no.2); we wish to think the tree itself (No.1) as that which gives rise to the perception. But this No.1 is merely No.2 over again. *It* is thought of as the perception of a tree, *i.e.*, as No. 2. We *call* it the tree itself, or No. 1; but we *think* it as the perception of the tree, or as No. 2. The first or explanatory term (the matter *per se*) is merely a repetition in thought (though called by a different name) of the second term, the term to be explained, viz., the perception of matter. Abstract thinking, then, equally with direct observation, refuses to lend any support to the analysis; for a thing cannot be said to be analysed when it is merely multiplied or repeated, which is all that abstract thinking does in regard to the perception of matter. The matter *per se*, which abstract thinking supposes that it separates from the perception of matter, is merely an iteration of the perception of matter.

Our conclusion therefore is, that the analysis of the perception of matter into the two things, perception and matter (the ordinary psychological principle), must on all accounts, be abandoned. It is both treacherous and impracticable.

Ten

Edward Caird

1835–1908

Edward Caird was born in Greenock, Scotland on 23 March 1835. He attended Greenock Academy, and matriculated at the University of Glasgow in 1850 to study for a degree in arts and divinity. His undergraduate career was interrupted by several bouts of ill-health. For a time he continued his divinity studies at the University of St Andrews before returning to Glasgow in 1857. In 1860 Caird entered Balliol College, Oxford as a Snell exhibitioner where he formed a lifelong friendship with T.H. Green. He graduated in 1863, gaining first class honours in classical moderations and *litterae humanories*. He held a Fellowship at Merton College, Oxford from 1864 until 1866 when he resigned in order to marry.

Caird's first article was an extended review of George Grote's *Plato and Other Companions of Socrates* (1865). In this and in his next published piece, 'The Roman Element in Civilisation' (1866) Caird made his debt to and enthusiasm for Hegel evident.

The growth of Caird's reputation was reflected in his appointment to the Chair of Moral Philosophy at the University of Glasgow in 1866 at the age of 31. Over the next twenty-seven years he was instrumental in raising Hegel's philosophical standing in Britain. His first book, *A Critical Account of the Philosophy of Kant with an Historical Introduction* (1877) attracted the attention not only of his friend T.H. Green, but of T.M. Lindsay, Henry Sidgwick and Arthur Balfour, and established Caird as a leading British Kant scholar. He used the subsequent exchanges, many of them in *Mind*, to reiterate and then develop his Hegelian reading and thus became a major contributor to the British idealist movement.

Caird was appointed Gifford Lecturer at the University of St Andrews for the sessions 1890–91 and 1891–2 and his lectures were subsequently published as *The Evolution of Religion* (1893). This work was widely acclaimed as a masterpiece and further enhanced his considerable reputation, which culminated in his being appointed Master of Balliol College, Oxford in 1893, following the death of Benjamin Jowett, the famous translator of Plato. In 1900–01 and again 1901–02 he returned to Glasgow to give a second set of Gifford Lectures, a revised and expanded version of which appeared as *The Evolution of Theology in the Greek Philosophers* (1904). He went on to write the Preface to the fifth edition of T.H. Green's *Prolegomena to Ethics* (1906), and his last major publication — *Lay Sermons and Addresses* (1907) — appeared shortly afterwards. He died in Oxford on 1 November 1908.

For his lecture to the British Academy (which along with the Royal Society, is Britain's most prestigious intellectual forum), Caird chose the topic of Idealism, the philosophical position with which his name was so closely associated. The lecture, reprinted here, offers a clear exposition of Idealism, and defends it cogently against the charge of being 'subjectivist', as well as identifying the shortcomings Caird detected in the school of common sense inspired by Reid.

Biographical information: Colin Tyler, *Thoemmes Dictionary of C19th British Philosophers*.

<hr />

READING XVI
Idealism and the Theory of Knowledge[1]

Since the publication of Kant's great work, almost all discussion of the theory of knowledge has turned upon the relation of the object to the subject or of the content of our experience to the formal character of our thinking. In some sense, therefore, we may call all modern theories of knowledge idealistic, and most of them have been so called by their authors. But this does not carry us very far: for the word idealism has been used with so many shades of meaning that it is loaded with misleading associations. It has even, it may be feared, led to confusion with each other of philosophies which have almost nothing in common. It becomes, therefore, a matter of some importance to disentangle the various senses in which the term has been employed, and the attempt to do so may perhaps furnish the best starting-point for a consideration of the real issues involved in the question.

Now with Plato, who first brought the word into philosophical use, an idea meant something that was primarily and emphatically objective. The idea of a thing was, as he constantly puts it, the thing itself. 'The good itself', 'the beautiful itself', 'the one itself', are the permanent objective realities to which all our conceptions of goodness, beauty and unity point, as distinguished from their phenomenal appearance; and the thought that they are present to our minds, or accessible to our consciousness, though never absent, is secondary and derivative. But with Locke an idea is primarily a state of mind, and Berkeley's doctrine that the *esse* of things is the *in percipi* has so deeply affected our philosophical language that in common usage the name idealism is most often applied to the theory which regards the modifications of our consciousness as

<hr />

[1]   Extracted from *Proceedings of the British Academy*, 1903–4, pp. 95–108.

the objects, or at least as the primary and immediate objects, of knowledge, and which treats the existence of the external world as an inference. This usage would not in itself be a matter for regret, but, as I have already suggested, it has not seldom led to a misconception of the meaning of philosophical writers who employ the word with something of its old Platonic significance.

Such a misconception is partly favoured by the way in which the so-called idealism of Germany has developed. Kant emphasized the relativity of objects to the unity of the self, but he still maintained the reservation that the objects so related are not in an ultimate sense real, apart from the subjectivity to which they are revealed. While, therefore, he contended that the world of experience cannot be regarded as independent of consciousness in general, and, indeed, of the consciousness of man, he still held to the distinction of the objects of experience from things in themselves. He thus, after all, seemed to seclude man in a world of his own consciousness, and to sever him entirely from reality. Hence when Kant was attacked as a Berkeleian, it gave him no little trouble to separate his own doctrine from that of Berkeley, and his attempts to work out his distinction are perhaps the obscurest parts of the *Critique of Pure Reason*. In fact, he was unable to achieve this result except by an argument which – if carried to all its consequences – would have been fatal to the distinction of phenomena from things in themselves, and would thus have transformed the most fundamental conceptions of the *Critique*. For the point of that argument is that we can be conscious of the subject only in distinction from, and in relation to, the object, and that, therefore, our consciousness of the external world is as *immediate* as our consciousness of the self, and our consciousness of the self as *mediate* as our consciousness of the external world. But if this argument be valid, the subjective point of view of Berkeley can once for all be set aside. To suppose that we are first conscious of our ideas, as our ideas, and then that secondly we proceed to infer from them the existence of objects, is to invert the order of our intellectual life, and to tear asunder its constituent elements. It is to invert its order: for, though the unity of the self may be implied in all consciousness of objects, yet it is to the object in the first instance that our attention is directed, and we observe the outward world and construe its meaning long before we turn the eye of reflection upon the inner life. And it is to tear the elements of it asunder: for the outer and the inner life are at every point in close correlation, and there is no experience of ours, theoretical or practical, in which we have not to do with both. The growth of our inner life is just the development of our knowledge of the outer world and of our interests in it, and the attempt to retire into ourselves and in a literal sense to make our mind a 'kingdom' to itself suicidal. It would be like the attempt of the abstract pleasure-seeker to get pleasure apart from all interest in anything but pleasure itself.

Berkeleianism, if we neglect the somewhat artificial expedients by means of which Berkeley tried to find his way back to an objective world or at least to an objective deity, may easily be pushed into the abyss of Solipsism. And, perhaps, there may still be some one who, taking the doctrine in this sense, would repeat the paradoxical assertion of Hume that Berkeley's argument 'cannot be refuted', though it 'carries no conviction'. In truth, it is so far from being incapable of refutation, that in its very statement it refutes itself, by setting up an '*ipse*' or self with no not-self as its correlate, and indeed, by assuming the possibility of the existence of a finite individual, who is conscious of himself in his individuality, and yet is not, *ipso facto*, aware of his relation to any greater whole in which he is a part. In like manner, in the similar but more developed doctrine of Leibniz the monads 'have no windows', or, perhaps we might say irreverently, no front-windows, through which they may come into real relations with objects; but the result is that they have to be conceived as under continual illumination by a God, who gives them the apparent experience of a world of which directly they could know nothing. They are isolated from reality in a phantom universe of their own, a sort of spiritual theatre set up in their own souls; but care is taken that the great drama of existence shall be re-enacted on this private stage. Berkeley, in the end, had accepted nearly the same modified form of Subjectivism, dismissing, what on this theory was superfluous, the reality of any world but a world of spirits and their conscious states. And in this shape, which is supposed to derive some support from Kant, the doctrine seems still to be accepted by some writers, as the genuine result of idealism, and it has been both attacked and defended on this basis. For, while there are those who find in such a doctrine a *reductio ad absurdum* of all idealism, there are others to whom, as to Berkeley, it seems a valuable safeguard against materialism, and a fundamental element in any spiritualistic theory of the world. Fearing the abyss of *Solipsism*, and reading in a one sided way the truth that all objects as such are relative to the subject, such writers would compromise with the enemy, and abandon to him all parts of the universe in which they cannot find thought and will, or at least some form of consciousness; and they would declare in this sense that 'all reality is spirit', that is, that reality consists solely of conscious beings and their states of consciousness. But I am afraid that the enemy will not be propitiated even by this sacrifice, and that the denial of the reality of the material world will inevitably lead to the denial of the reality of any world at all.

With such subjectivism the German idealism had no necessary connexion, at least after Fichte had removed the last fragment of it from his philosophy. The result of Kant's teaching, when it was freed from the contradictory notion of the 'thing in itself' – that Irish Bull in philosophy, as Heine calls it – was not to cast any, even the slightest, doubt on the reality of the external world, but only to show that a new element must be added to all that we know of it as an external world, namely, its relation to the subject. No doubt, this new element brings important modifications into our previous views of objectivity. For, on the one hand, it absolutely precludes the attempt to explain the spiritual by the material, and, indeed, compels us to conclude that there is no material world which is not also spiritual. And, on the other hand, as the correlation between the self and the not-self is not one sided, it brings with it also the conviction that there is no spiritual world which is not also material, or does not presuppose a material world. Thus the reality of that which is other than the self-conscious intelligence itself, and the one cannot be denied without the other.

But at this point a new difficulty has arisen. So soon as it is understood that the assertion that all objects are relative to the subject, involves the counter-assertion that the subject as such is relative to the object, we seem to be involved in an antinomy between two forms of consciousness, which can neither be reconciled nor separated. We seem, in fact, to be forced alternately to make the subject an adjective or property of the object, and the object an adjective or property of the subject; in other words, to set up two opposite theories, materialism and subjective idealism, each of which has its own independent value, and neither of which can be put aside in favour of the other. This balancing or dualistic view is substantially the theory adopted by Clifford and Huxley, and it has been fully worked out by Mr. Spencer. These writers, in short, use the double relativity of consciousness and self-consciousness, or of matter and mind, as the means of escaping both from the objections to materialism, and from the objections to subjective idealism: but what they set up in place of each of these theories is simply the assertion that, from a phenomenal point of view, they are both true, while from the point of view of reality, we cannot establish either of them. Thus there are two independent ways of looking at the world, each of which claims the whole field of existence for itself and is, therefore, absolutely opposed to the other. Each of them, indeed, has its usefulness for certain purposes of science, the one as a principle of physics, and the other as a principle of psychology, but neither can finally vindicate itself as the truth to the exclusion of the other. We are, therefore, in the presence of an immoveable difference which defies reconciliation; and the absolute reality which lies beyond these opposites, must for ever baffle our understanding, though, as Mr. Spencer holds, it is presupposed in the very nature of consciousness. Hence we may regard the world *either* as a connected system of motions in matter, *or* as a connected system of modes of consciousness, and from either of these hypotheses important scientific results may be derived: but we can neither decide for one of the alternatives to the exclusion of the other, nor can we rise to any higher point of view which would embrace them both. 'See then our predicament', says Mr Spencer, 'we can explain matter only in terms of mind: we can think of mind only in terms of matter. When we have pushed our explanation of the first to the farthest limit, we are referred back to the second for a final answer, and when we have got the final answer of the second, we are referred back to the first' [*Principles of Psychology*, i, p. 627, § 272].

There is a superficial plausibility in this view, but it is difficult to conceive one which is fundamentally more incoherent. It 'splits the world in two with a hatchet'. It breaks up consciousness into 'two consciousnesses', which are somehow united, though there is no logical way from the one to the other: and it fails altogether to explain the actual combination of the two in our daily experience. For, just because Mr. Spencer makes the difference of mind and matter absolute, he can admit the unity only in the form of an abstract 'One' in which all difference is lost. At the beginning of his *First Principles*, he lays down the logical doctrine, that thought is essentially the limitation of an infinite or unconditioned being, a being of which we have only a 'dim consciousness', as that which is presupposed in all definite apprehension either of the object or of the subject. But the unity thus presupposed is unknowable, and that which we know is confined to the phenomenal. Thus each of Mr. Spencer's two conceptions, his conception of the phenomenal world with its insoluble difference, and his conception of the unknowable being which alone is real, seems to require the other as its compliment. The abstraction of the unity leaves the duality of matter and mind without any connecting link, and the equally abstract duality of mind and matter cannot be reduced to unity except by the suppression of their distinctive characters. Hence the unity and the difference cannot be regarded as both real, and if, as with Mr. Spencer, the unity is treated as real, the duality must be regarded as merely phenomenal. All our science, therefore, deals merely with appearances, which we cannot bring into relation with reality. The impulse of reason to seek for unity cannot be set aside, but, under the conditions of Mr. Spencer's theory, it can be attained only by the sacrifice of knowledge itself. The result is instructive as pointing to the fate of all theories that set the 'one' against the 'many'. Abstract Monism and abstract Pluralism are not, strictly speaking, two philosophies but different aspects of the same philosophy. Polytheism always ends in setting up a fate beyond the gods.

The Spencerian philosophy, however, is valuable as a protest against its opposite, against any 'too easy monism'. It is a legitimate criticism both upon subjective idealism and upon materialism, though it only puts one one-sided theory against another, and maintains that both have equal rights. If we could not do better, it might be well to compromise upon the Spinozistic idea of the parallelism of the two unrelated attributes of extension and thought, or, upon Schelling's conception of the balanced equality of the real and ideal factors of the universe, even though the result, as with Mr. Spencer, were to leave us without any unity which was more than a name.

We are not however, shut up to such a desperate course; for the main result of modern philosophy and especially of modern idealism has been to put a concrete, in place of an abstract unity, or, in other words, to vindicate the essential correlation of the self and the not-self. Idealism in this sense has nothing to object to the strongest assertion of the reality of the distinctions and oppositions that enter into the theoretical and practical consciousness of man. But it maintains that there are no *absolute* differences or antagonisms in the intelligible world, no distinctions which do not imply relations, and, therefore also, an ultimate unity between the things distinguished: and, of course, it must refuse to admit that there is an unintelligible world, a world that cannot be brought in relation to the intelligence.

Here, however, we must stop to meet a possible misunderstanding. There are many at present who are justly jealous of an easy monism, and some, perhaps, who, less justly, carry their jealousy to the point of practically refusing to admit any ultimate unity at all. Hence, when it is stated to be an essential result of idealism that there is a unity beyond all difference and through all difference, they are apt to think that this involves the denial of the reality of the differences. Thus they seem to hold, as Spencer seems to hold, that we can distinguish without relating, or relate without admitting any unity within which the difference is embraced. And in this they get much support from the ordinary consciousness: for the 'plain man', as he is called, prior to reflection, is apt to alternate between unity and difference without bringing them together: he is ready, therefore, to take any distinction which he recognises as absolute: and, on the other hand, if any doubt is thrown on the absoluteness of such a distinction, he is inclined to infer that it ought to be dismissed as altogether unreal. No one who had got beyond this naïve state of consciousness, will allow himself to be impaled on either horn of its unreal dilemma. But, if we have once renounced such abstract ways of thinking, I do not see how we can stop short of the result that the one and the many, so far from being opposed, are factors of thought which cannot be separated without contradiction. An absolute difference would be no difference at all; for it would annihilate all relation between the things distinguished, and, in doing so, it would annihilate itself. This is a principle of logic often illustrated by the fate of dualistic systems of thought, which in seeking to emphasize the reciprocal exclusiveness of two opposite principles, have ended by depriving them both of the very character in virtue of which they were opposed. Thus Manichaeism, when it took evil as absolute, as a reality quite separate from good, inevitably made it lose its character as evil; for it thus turned evil into an independent substance, which in itself had no opposition, because no relation, to good. We can have opposition only within a unity, and, if we try to stretch it farther, we overreach our object, and end by making the opposition itself impossible or meaningless. Any one, therefore, who thinks that a refusal to admit pure abstract contradiction between two terms – say, between truth and falsehood, or good and evil – involves the denial of all validity or reality to the distinction in question, must be reminded that relative opposition is the only real or conceivable opposition, and that distinctions are in effect denied whenever they are made absolute. Thus those who carry any difference to the point of dualism do away with that very difference by over-emphasizing it, just as surely as those who disregard or abstract from difference in the interest of unity. The parts of the intelligible world mean nothing except in the whole, and the whole means nothing except as distributing itself to the parts, and constituting their spiritual bond.

If there is any truth in these views, the only reasonable controversy between philosophers must be, on the one hand, as to the nature of the all-embracing unity on which every intelligible experience must rest, and, on the other hand, as to the nature of the differences which it equally involves. To ask whether there *is* any such real unity, or whether it embraces real differences, is to attempt to leap off one's own shadow: it is to try to think, while attacking the only basis on which we can think. We cannot play the game of thought, if one might use such an expression, without taking our stand upon the idea that the world is a self-consistent and intelligible whole: though of course, this does not mean that any actual attempt to systematize our knowledge can be more than a step towards the attainment of the ideal of a perfect analysis and re-synthesis of the manifold content of experience. The problem of knowledge is to find out how the real unity of the world manifests itself through all its equally real differences, and we can show that any abstract view, such as those of Berkeley or Spencer, which would deprive us of any element in it, would make the progressive solution of it by science and philosophy impossible. But we cannot prove these presuppositions of all knowledge directly, or by making the system based upon them complete, if for no other reason, because with our increasing experience the problem itself is always enlarging. In this sense, the work of science, and still more the work of philosophy, must always be a work of faith, meaning by faith, not believing anything merely upon authority, but proceeding upon a principle the complete vindication or realization of which is for us impossible; for, obviously, nothing short of omniscience could grasp the world as a complete system. It is involved in the very idea of a developing consciousness such as ours, that while, as an intelligence, it presupposes the idea of the whole, and, both in thought and action, must continually strive to realize that idea, yet what it deals with is necessarily a partial and limited experience, and its actual attainments can never, either in theory or practice, be more than provisional. Aristotle has expressed both sides of this ideal in one of his most comprehensive sayings, when he declares that 'as, in practice, it is our highest aim, starting with what *seems* good to us individually, to make what is absolutely good our individual aim, so in theory, we have to start with what seems true to us individually, but the object we seek is to make what is really and naturally intelligible or true, true or intelligible for ourselves' [Met. 1029 b, 5 seq.]. In other words, we have to learn to look at the world, *in ordine ad universum* and not *in ordine ad individuum*, from its real centre and not from the centre of our own individual existence: and the task is not one which is forced upon us externally, but one which is laid upon us by the nature of the reason which is within us. Aristotle, therefore, holds that it is possible for us to make the universal point of view our own, as it is also possible for us to make the absolute good the end of our lives. But we have to add to what Aristotle says that his end is one which is ever *being* realized, and never is finally realized by us. It is a faith which is continually passing into knowledge, but never becomes complete knowledge.

If however in one sense we must call this idea a faith, we must remember that it is in no sense an arbitrary assumption: rather it is the essential faith of reason, the presupposition and basis of all that reason has achieved or can achieve. We may admit that, as Tennyson says, in this aspect of it our 'deepest faith' is also our 'ghastliest doubt' – the doubt whether the whole system of things to which we belong is not illusive and meaningless. But, apart from this inevitable shadow of our finitude, the real difficulties of knowledge and practice lie not in the idea or ideal of our intelligence, but rather in the application of it to the particulars of thought and life, in carrying out the effort to co-ordinate or affiliate the different appearances as elements of one reality, or, as Mr. Bradley would express it, to determine what is the 'degree of reality' that belongs to each of them, when brought in relation to all the rest, and to give it in our practical life the importance which really belongs to it. But to question whether the whole is an intelligible system, is as vain as to question whether any part of our experience, even the most transient and illusive of appearances, has a place in that system.

There is, indeed, a way of escaping from this view of reality as a systematic whole which has often been tried. This is to take our stand upon some particular principle or principles, or upon some particular fact or facts, as self-evidencing or immediately 'given' truth, on the fixed certitude of which we can build our further knowledge. Mr. Andrew Lang in his book upon Myth and Ritual, tells us of a theological child, who described the creation of the world in the following terms: 'God first made a little place to stand upon, and then he made the rest'. So philosophers have often sought for some special criterion of truth, for some basal principle, like the *Cogito ergo sum* of Descartes, or for some *datum* or *data* of sense, as a foundation on which they might build their system. But the search is a vain one. For, when we examine any such principle we discover that it is only one aspect of things, which has no claim to be taken as prior to the other aspects of them, and which proves the others only in the same sense in which it is proved by them; and also that in being brought in relation to those other aspects, it is subject to re-interpretation. And, in like manner, when we examine any supposed *datum* of sense, we find that it is merely one appearance, which helps us to explain other appearances only as it is explained by them, and that its

ultimate interpretation depends on the way in which it combines with
all our previous consciousness of things. All that is certain about any
such *datum*, in the first instance, is that it has an indubitable claim to be
recognized as an element in the intelligible world; but how much truth
there is in the first presentment of it we cannot tell, till we are able to
think it together with the other elements of our experience. In other
words, it must be interpreted so as to cohere with them, and they must
be interpreted so as to cohere with it. But whether this will lead to its
being explained, or to its being explained away, or, as is more likely,
partly to the one and partly to the other, we cannot tell *a priori*. We cannot, therefore, take our stand on any one *datum* or principle taken by
itself; for, taken by itself, it cannot be known for what it really is. We can
only take our stand on the unity of the whole system, in which everything that claims to be a fact or a truth must find a place. Thus the idea
that there are certain intuitions or perceptions which we can take for
granted as *prior* to, and above all criticism, and which remain, in all the
discourse of reason, as the fixed and immoveable basis of the whole edifice of science, involves a fundamental mistake. Indeed, the activities of
the intuitive and the discursive reason can never be separated without
making the former 'blind', and the latter 'empty'. We always presuppose the unity of the whole in every determination of the parts in distinction from, and in relation to each other: and no element of the whole can
be presented apart from the process whereby we distinguish and relate
it within that whole. We are thus, throughout all our intellectual life,
advancing from a confused, imperfectly differentiated, and therefore
imperfectly integrated, experience, towards an organic system of
knowledge, in which justice shall be done to all the differences and
oppositions of appearances, without sacrifice of their essential unity.
And it casts confusion upon the whole process, when we treat it as if it
were confined to the work of building upon fixed foundations, which
are given either in sensation or in thought, apart from any process at all.
On the contrary, it cannot be adequately represented except as an evolution, in which it is only the last product that shows distinctly the meaning of the germ out of which it sprang.

The view that has just been stated contains, I think, the essentials of
that conception of knowledge which has been maintained by the greatest representatives of modern idealism; and it is obvious that it has no
special kindred with the philosophy of Berkeley, and, from that point of
view, is no less realistic than it is idealistic. At the same time, it may be
acknowledged that in the process of working towards this result and,
especially, in seeking to reply to those who treated knowledge as something given to the mind from without, idealists have sometimes dwelt
too exclusively on the subjective aspect of knowledge. This was the case,
as we have seen, with Kant, and it is apt to be the case with those who go
back to Kant and take their start from him. We may add that it is apt to
seem to be the case with such writers, even when it is not really so. Thus

the views of T.H. Green are often misunderstood by those who do not recognize how much his language is coloured by opposition to authors like John Stuart Mill, whose philosophy was in the ascendant when Green began to write, but whose views are no longer prominent in the mind of this generation of philosophers as they were then. Hence difficulty is apt to be caused by Green's constant insistence on the constructive activity of the mind in knowledge, carried, as it necessarily is, to the point of denying that any element of truth can be given to the mind apart from such activity. Such a doctrine seems to many to involve a denial of the objectivity of knowledge, and it has even provoked in some a reaction against all idealism, and a tendency to fall back upon 'the given' in the sense of naïve realism, i.e. upon the idea that at least the basis of experience is presented to consciousness without any activity of its own. And even the most conclusive demonstrations that it is impossible to detect any such *pure datum* have failed of their effect, because of a lurking suspicion that the reality of the objects of consciousness was being undermined. When Disraeli on one occasion was questioned as to the political platform on which he stood for election to a seat in parliament, he answered that he 'stood upon his head'. But if that is a sufficient basis in politics, it can hardly be admitted to be so in the theory of knowledge. And when an idealist speaks of 'the judgement by which we sustain the world', however adequate may be his explanation of such language, it is apt to excite a suspicion that his theories, if they were completely carried out, would lead to the individual being regarded as his own universe and his own God. This suspicion, perhaps as much as any other reason, is what drives many to accept some *via media*, in which the subject and the object are represented as in some way acting and reacting on each other – some such view as is implied in the metaphor of 'impression by', or 'contact with' reality, and to substitute it for an organic conception of the relations between the mind and its object. Such a suspicion the idealist is bound to remove, if he expects his theories to be accepted; yet he must do so, of course, without compromising his fundamental conception of the relativity of the intelligible world to the intelligence.

Now, so far as this difficulty arises out of the Berkeleian theory that the mind has primarily to do only with its own ideas, it may be met by the considerations already suggested. As the consciousness of the self is correlative with the consciousness of the not-self, no conception of either can be satisfactory which does not recognize a principle of unity, which manifests itself in both, which underlies all their difference and opposition, and which must, therefore, be regarded as capable of reconciling them. When, therefore, we speak of the object as manifesting itself in, and to the subject, determining his perceptions, thoughts and desires, and when, on the other hand, we speak of the subject as constructing his world in knowledge, and making it in action the means of his own self-realization, we are using language that represents two aspects of the truth, which are apparently opposed, but each of which has a relative validity; and it is important that we should not allow either of these forms of expression to exclude the other. To say that the mind goes beyond itself to become conscious of the world, or to say that the object goes beyond itself to awake consciousness of itself in us, are two extreme ways of putting the fact of knowledge, which have opposite merits and opposite defects. And, in like manner, in regard to our practical life, to say that we are always determined by objects, or to say we are always determined by ourselves, is to utter half-truths. Neither of these statements is quite adequate: nor can we reach the whole truth merely by putting them together, and saying that we are partly determined from without and partly from within. For, if we accepted this reciprocal determination of subject and object as our final account of the matter, we should be left with a mechanical conception of action and reaction between two things which are external to each other, and we should be driven to deny that there is any unity which transcends the difference and manifests itself in it. Yet that, as I have attempted to show, is just the idea we have to admit, so soon as we realize that we can have no consciousness of the difference and relation of the two terms except on the basis of such a unity. We always presuppose the unity of consciousness in all our experience, inner and outer; but dualism seems natural to us because in our ordinary modes of thought we only *presuppose* it, and do not specially attend to it or reflect upon it. Our eyes are directed from the unity we tacitly assume to the differences we openly assert. Yet the whole problem of our lives, the problem of practice no less than the problem of the theory, is made insoluble if we begin by assuming the absoluteness of the difference between the self and the not-self, and only then ask how are we to mediate between them. If this were really the question, it could not be answered; but neither could it ever have arisen for us as a question at all. If, therefore, any one bases his theory on a presupposed dualism of subject and object, we may fairly ask how he comes to believe in it: and this is a question which he cannot answer at all without treating the difference as a relative one. But if it be so, the common notion that the Absolute, the ultimate reality, the Divine, or by whatever name we choose to name it, is a far-off something, a *Jenseits* or transcendental 'thing in itself', involves a fundamental mistake. And it is no less a mistake to suppose, with Mr. Spencer, that it is a mere indeterminate basis of consciousness, of which we can say nothing except that it is. It must be regarded as a principle of unity which is present in all things and beings, and from which they, in their utmost possible independence, cannot be separated. It must be conceived, in short, as that in which they 'live and move and have their being'. And in the case of consciousness and self-conscious beings such as we are, this unity must show itself as the underlying principle of all their conscious life. It is, therefore, no metaphor or overstatement of religious feeling, when we say that the consciousness of it is the presupposition both of the consciousness of objects and of the consciousness of self, if and only it be remembered that, just because it is *proton physei* (first by nature), it is *oustaton eimin* (the last for us), i.e. that it is the last thing which we make an object of our thought. On the other hand, though it be last in thought, yet it may be maintained that neither the consciousness of the objective world nor the consciousness of the inner life of the self can attain its highest and truest form until this presupposition is distinctly realized, as it is in religion, and also, we may add, until it is made the direct object of reflexion, as it is in philosophy. The greatest task of philosophy, indeed, is just to consider how the constant presence of this unity modifies the contents both of the subjective and of the objective consciousness. How far and how this task can be achieved, I cannot at present consider; but in any case it seems clear that neither the subject nor the object can be known for what it really is, until their reciprocal correlation is taken into account, and until this correlation is itself seen in the light of the unity which it presupposes.

Eleven

A.E. Taylor

1869–1945

Alfred Edward Taylor, was born at Oundle on 22 December 1869 and died in Edinburgh 31 October 1945. The elder son of a Wesleyan minister, Taylor was educated at Kingswood School, Bath, and at New College, Oxford, of which he was elected a scholar and, in 1931, an honorary fellow. He obtained first class in honour moderations (1889) and in *litterae humaniores* (1891). His academic career began with a prize fellowship at Merton College, Oxford from. From 1896 to 1903 he was an assistant lecturer in Greek and philosophy at the Owens College, Manchester (subsequently the University of Manchester). His next appointment was abroad, in Canada as the Frothingham Professor of Philosophy at McGill University, Montreal. In 1908 he returned to Britain and to Scotland where he spent the remaining 35 years of his distinguished career, first as Professor of Moral Philosophy at the University of St. Andrews (1908–24), and then moving to the Chair of Moral Philosophy at Edinburgh where his predecessors had included Adam Ferguson and Dugald Stewart. He retired in 1941, but continued to do the work of the chair until 1944.

Taylor was a man of remarkable learning. On Plato he was an authority of international repute. His early work was strongly influenced by the Oxford brand of Hegelian idealism, as evidenced in his *Elements of Metaphysics* (1903) which ran to many editions. He gradually moved away from this form of idealism to a more theistic metaphysics, and was the author of the article on 'Theism' in the Hastings *Encyclopaedia of Religion and Ethics*. This reflected his deep interest in the problems of religion and led him to the study of mediaeval philosophy. But apart from his studies of Plato, his most important contribution, as befitted the famous Chairs he occupied, was to moral philosophy. He wrote and lectured on a variety of moral philosophical themes, culminating in *The Faith of a Moralist*, the two series of Gifford Lectures that he gave at St Andrews after his move to Edinburgh.

In line with a longstanding Scottish practice, in both St Andrews and Edinburgh, as holder of the Chair he lectured to the general class in moral philosophy and conveyed to several generations of students a powerful sense of standing in a great tradition of reflection on the problems of conduct, which he was concerned to expound and develop. This tradition included the perpetual need to respond to Humean scepticism, and to do so from the point of view of metaphysical theism. 'David Hume and the Miraculous', reprinted here, was the Leslie Stephen Lecture at the University of Cambridge in 1927. It is a devastating analysis of Hume's famous essay (See Reading V), in which Taylor uncovers deeper underlying metaphysical differences between theists and non-theists. It is not the scale of confusion and error that Taylor detects in Hume's argument so much as a certain unseriousness in Hume's approach to the question, that led him to conclude, famously, 'I have to own to a haunting uncertainty whether Hume was really a great philosopher, or only a very clever man'.

Taylor was elected a Fellow of the British Academy in 1911 and to similar learned academies in Italy and Germany. He died at Edinburgh in 1945.

Biographical information: *Dictionary of National Biographies*, 1940–45.

READING XVII
David Hume and the Miraculous[1]

When the University of Cambridge did me the high honour of inviting me to deliver this lecture, I could not but feel that the invitation, in some sort, determined for me the subject of my discourse. The character of the field of letters in which Sir Leslie Stephen achieved such well-deserved renown made it plain that my theme must be the life or doctrine of a British philosopher, by preference a philosopher of that eighteenth century which Sir Leslie Stephen himself had done so much to illustrate by his writings. To the occupant of a Chair of Moral Philosophy in the University of Edinburgh the philosopher could not well be any one but David Hume, the most famous, even if not the greatest, of all Scottish metaphysical thinkers and, with the single exception of Walter Scott, the most distinguished man of letters whose life has been closely connected with the city of Edinburgh. The philosophical thought of Hume, as a whole, is no topic for the discourse of an hour, but that space of time may be profitably, and I trust not unentertainingly, spent on a consideration of the side-issue raised by the once notorious tenth section of the *Enquiry Concerning Human Understanding* which deals with *Miracles*. Historically, this essay is interesting by reason of the scandal it created, and was perhaps intended by its author to create. To it, and not to the *Dialogues concerning Natural Religion*, which were not published during Hume's life, our philosopher owed the ill-repute he enjoyed alike with the orthodox Presbyterians of Aberdeen and the High Anglican

----

[1]   Extracted from *David Hume and the Miraculous*, Cambridge, 1927, pp. 1–54

Churchmen of Oxford, the set of Johnson and Wesley; to it, in the main, he owes the admiration of modern 'anticlericals', who have regarded him as a hero of militant 'free-thought'. The entertaining feature of the situation, to the reflective mind, is that this reputation, for good or ill, is quite undeserved. It is as certain as anything in biography can be that Hume was, in point of fact, no anticlerical zealot, but an amiable and easy-going man of the world whose chosen social circle consisted largely of the 'moderates' among the Edinburgh Presbyterians. The members of that circle, to be sure, were not men of the faith which removes mountains and conquers the world. But they valued established beliefs as a bulwark of comfort, peace and social order, and would have been the last persons to sanction a violent and wanton attack on any set of doctrines which serve to keep the 'vulgar' in their place and to guarantee the 'thinking' minority against disturbers of their ease and leisure. They may fairly be presumed to have understood that Hume's assault on the 'bigotry, ignorance, cunning and roguery' of that considerable 'part of mankind' who profess belief in the miraculous meant very much less than it looked, on the face of it, to mean. They would be confirmed in the suspicion, if they entertained it, by observing that, for the purposes of the *Enquiry*, the whole section is completely superfluous, while the known character of Hume makes it impossible to account for its presence as the irrelevancy of the fanatic who has got, for the time being, upon his dangerous topic. The irrelevance is, indeed, so manifest that it seems best explained by the suggestion of Hume's learned editor, Mr Selby-Bigge, who supposes that the philosopher's motive in the assault was a simple craving for notoriety at any cost. The 'learned world', as we know, 'said nothing to the paradoxes' of Hume's *Treatise*; he was determined that it should say something to them in their amended version, and none too scrupulous about the methods by which publicity was to be ensured. Hence the combined violence and irrelevance of a section which was at least certain to get the *Enquiry* talked about, as it very effectually did. A similar explanation can, as I hope to show, be given of the apparently strange logic of Hume's argument. On the face of it, there would seem to be something amiss with reasoning which proceeds from the principle that 'a wise man proportions his belief to the evidence' to the conclusion that in a vast, if none too well defined, field, the 'wise man' will simply refuse to consider 'the evidence' at all. We cannot be surprised that Hume's admirer, Huxley, should have been much more perturbed by reasoning of this kind than his unfriendly critic Green, whose objection to the argument, indeed, does not go further than to urge that it does not come with the best of grace from the mouth of our professed sceptic. If we look more closely, I believe we shall see that the reasoning, interpreted in the light of Hume's professed general doctrine, certainly proves something, but something very different from what Hume had suggested by his boast of having discovered an argument which 'will, with the wise and learned, be an everlasting check to all kinds of superstitious delusion'. What has really been proved, as Hume himself says at the end of the whole discussion, would certainly not destroy the faith of the average Presbyterian of the eighteenth century, though it should leave a thinking Presbyterian dissatisfied; as Hume does not say, it should also leave the serious believer in science at least equally concerned. The 'academic' or 'sceptical' philosopher of Hume's own type is, in fact, left in the position of an amused spectator of the conflict between two irrationalities. We miss half of Hume's irony unless we understand that it is meant to hit not only 'dangerous friends or disguised enemies to the Christian religion' but also 'dangerous friends or disguised enemies' to Newtonian science. I trust I need not say that I do not myself regard amused detached contemplation of either Christianity or natural science as a right attitude in a rational man. But it is an attitude very characteristic of the century of so-called 'good sense', and none the less likely to be the secret attitude of David Hume, that it is hard to say which would have been more enraged by it, if he had understood it, John Wesley or T. H. Huxley.

It is desirable, before we go any further, to set out the steps of the argument we are to consider as briefly and boldly as we can. If we try to do so, it will be found, I think, to fall into eleven successive propositions, which I will state in order, with a minimum of exegetical comment. We begin (1) with the proposition, taken from Archbishop Tillotson, that the evidential value of the testimony of others, so long as it is considered as the testimony of others and nothing more, is always inferior to that of our own senses, a thesis I should not be too ready to concede myself without a great deal of qualification, since in many cases I should put vastly more confidence in the report of a trained observer than I should in my own eyes.

(2) We are next told that this general principle is now to be applied to 'accounts of miracles and prodigies found in all history, sacred and profane'. 'Miracle' is here apparently equated with 'prodigy', and neither word receives any definition. In the course of the argument, we shall find two other incidental definitions of 'miracle' introduced. Unfortunately, the definitions are not coincident, and to adopt either seriously obscures the nature of the reasoning. For the present, so far as can be seen from the context, 'miracle' and 'prodigy' both mean any very unusual and unexpected event, anything which, to use a definition I once heard given by a divine, makes one say 'O!'

(3) We now take it into account that some events are found in experience to be 'constantly conjoined'; other conjunctions are more variable. Here we must, of course, remember that it is part of Hume's general metaphysical doctrine that there is no 'necessary connection' between events. All events are separate, and there is nothing in the character of any event which demands that it should be continued in one way rather than in another. All our information is that certain types of event have

been found, we do not and cannot know why, to be continued in certain ways and not in others.

(4) A wise man, then, will always 'proportion' his belief in any statement about a succession of events related to have taken place 'to the evidence'. This is interpreted to mean that he will *count* the number of 'instances' in which a conjunction of the kind in question has occurred, and the number of instances in which one member of the conjoined pair of events has occurred without being continued by the other. It is on this counting that the wise man will base his judgment of the *probability* of the alleged narrative.

(5) Further, all inference is founded solely on 'our experience of the constant and regular conjunction' of events and on nothing else. Among the events covered by this principle are the true and false statements made to us by others. Hence the principle applies, among other things, to our inferences about the trustworthiness or untrustworthiness of human testimony.

(6) Hence, when we are offered testimony to alleged facts which 'partake of the extraordinary and the marvellous', there is a 'conflict of opposite experiences'. We have, in fact, to balance our knowledge that the unusual and unexpected sometimes happens against our knowledge that informants sometimes, from various causes, speak falsely, whether intentionally or not. This is why it was reasonable in 'the Indian prince' to be incredulous when he was first told of the freezing of water in our northern winter, though it would have been unreasonable to persist in his incredulity if he had had numerous independent reports to the same effect from informants with no motive for deception. The general result, so far, then, is that the strangeness of an alleged sequence of events diminishes the probability of its reality, except when the testimony for the sequence is so strong that it would be still stranger that all the witnesses should be mistaken or untruthful.

(7) There is one case in which the value of testimony is not merely diminished by the 'conflict of experiences', but actually reduced to zero. This is the case when the event testified to is a 'miracle', that is to say, a *violation* of the 'laws of nature', or, what comes to the same thing, of 'the common course of nature'. This would be the case with testimony to the resuscitation of a dead man, since such a conjunction between death and subsequent resuscitation has 'never been observed'. There is 'uniform experience against it'. Here we observe that the reasoning is affected by the introduction of a disturbing element, a new definition of 'miracle'. We have been concerned with the general question of the worth of testimony to the unusual and unexpected *in genere*, and it has been assumed that we know nothing of 'laws' of 'patterns' in nature which prescribe one continuation of a course of events rather than any other. The only difference permissible according to our fifth proposition is that between a familiar and an unfamiliar continuation, and the only conclusion to which we are really entitled is that it is *natural* to be incredulous when

we are told of the unfamiliar, as the Indian prince was mistakenly incredulous about the freezing of water. The shift from the unfamiliar to the 'contrary to uniform experience' is confusing and unjustified, but indispensable to the further development of the argument, and directly causes the inconsequence on which Hume's critics have remarked. It is quietly forgotten that, on the premises, there cannot be said to be 'uniform experience' against the resuscitation of the dead man or any other sequence of events. At best I have only a uniformity within the range of *my own* experience to urge; a narrator who professes to have seen the resuscitation is actually appealing to his own experience as the foundation of his story. Thus, unless I am to assume that my own personal experiences are the standard of the credible — and if I do assume this, there is an end of all correction of expectations — it is a *petitio principii* [begging the question] to say that there is 'uniform experience' against any event to which any man claims to be able to testify, and there is no basis for any distinction between the 'miraculous' and that which is merely unfamiliar, and therefore startling, to a particular person. The paradox that the principle that 'belief should always be proportioned to evidence' justifies, in a certain class of cases, rejection of testimony without examination, is only established by the illegitimate device of changing a fundamental definition in the course of the argument. A footnote which introduces a further *distinguo* seems to show that Hume is a little uneasy about this procedure. It admits that the testimony may, after all, really justify belief in a fact which *seems* 'miraculous', *i.e.* a fact to which my experience affords no analogy, though it does not justify belief in the 'miraculous' character of the fact. This leads to a third definition of a 'miracle' as 'a transgression of the laws of nature *by a particular volition of the Deity or by the interposition of an invisible agent*'. Apparently, then, in spite of what has been said, Hume would admit that there may be adequate testimony to the resuscitation of a dead man. There might be evidence which would require us to admit the fact, though none which would establish the point that the fact was due to a 'particular volition of the Deity'. (The reference to the 'invisible agent' appears to be a needless rhetorical amplification.) This third definition of 'miracle', sprung on us in a footnote, seems to be the most unfortunate feature of the argument. It obviously disposes at once of all which had apparently been secured by the appeal to the inviolability of 'laws of nature', since it permits us to accept as facts the sequences of events which that appeal was intended to rule out, provided only that we do not profess to have proved by testimony that the facts have 'a particular volition of the Deity' as their cause. In this version of the matter, there is no story of legend or folk-lore which a sufficient number of testimonies might not require us to accept as a genuine account of facts, provided only that we eliminate all reference to 'the Deity' or 'invisible agents'. It is not clear how a principle compatible with this position is to be of any use to 'the wise and learned' as an 'everlasting check to all kinds of superstitious delusion'; yet it is clear that this, and not the much more radical procedure of dismissing a whole class of alleged events without scrutiny of the testimony for them, is the only consequence really compatible with the principles on which Hume's polemic professedly rests. The upshot, after all, is no more than the statement, which might be made about all testimony to anything, that no testimony can establish a fact unless the falsity of the testimony would be more unlikely than the unreality of the alleged fact. This is virtually admitted when Hume proceeds to formulate his eighth proposition.

(8) In no actual case of a reported 'miracle' do we find the testimony to be of this strength. This is, of course, itself an allegation about a fact, and we observe that before we are entitled to make it, we must tacitly surrender what appeared to have been secured by the appeal to 'inviolable laws'. If the weakness of the testimony is to be a relevant consideration in determining the credibility of the supposed event, we must examine the testimony before we can pronounce it to be weak. The proposed dismissal of testimony without examination has thus led us to nothing, and ought to be eliminated from the reasoning as a superfluous complication. How completely the ambiguity of the word 'miracle' has vitiated the argument is shown when Hume goes on, in this connection, to urge it as a grave objection to stories of alleged marvels in the career of Mohammed that Plutarch, Livy and Tacitus record marvels as occurring in their own age at Rome. This is meant to suggest the objection that the marvels, if they occur, must be regarded as 'evidences' in favour of a religion, but evidences in favour of incompatible religions may be considered as destructive of one another. Plainly, this consideration, whatever it may be worth, has no bearing on the value of the historical testimony, considered simply as testimony to the actual occurrence of an unusual fact. It concerns not the fact, but the 'theological' interpretation of the fact. Thus it appears to be an authenticated fact that the first volley of the firing party told off to execute the *Bāb* severed the cord by which the victim was secured without doing him any injury. Hume's reasoning would require us to discount the excellent testimony to the fact, on the plea that similar stories related in the *Acts* of Christian martyrs may be regarded as so many *testimonies* against the occurrence of the fact in the case of the *Bāb*.

(9) We now reach what is meant to be the conclusion from all the considerations so far put before us. No testimony to a 'miracle' has ever amounted to a probability, much less to a proof, and even if the testimony, in any case, did amount to proof, it would be opposed by another proof derived from the 'very nature of the fact which it would endeavour to establish'. Here, as it seems to me, confusion of thought reaches a maximum. To know that it is a fact that no such testimony *has* ever amounted to a probability, we must, of course, have examined the amount and character of the testimony, and thus have made it a duty to do the very thing Hume originally proposed to show superfluous. It is at

least difficult to understand the suggestion that there could be a *proof* of any proposition if there were also a *proof* of a second and incompatible proposition, unless the remark is meant as a mere rhetorical amplification of the statement that proof of the 'miraculous' is not forthcoming. The final appeal to 'the very nature of the fact', which proof of the 'miraculous' would 'endeavour to establish', takes us back again to the position which has just been incidentally abandoned, that there is a whole class of cases in which testimony may properly be dismissed *without* examination, and this, if justified, makes the very weakness of the testimony, the point on which Hume is specially insisting, irrelevant.

(10) We next have a variously qualified retraction of its attempted return to the abandoned position. The occurrence of 'violations of the usual course of nature' may actually be *proved* by testimony, but they cannot be so proved as to make them 'the foundation of a system of religion'. Since we have never been told exactly what is meant by a 'religion', this admission is not very enlightening, but it is illustrated by a singular example. There might be testimony which would not merely make it probable, but actually prove that the whole earth was covered by a mysterious darkness for the first week of January 1600. If the testimony were abundant and of good quality, we should have to accept this as a fact, and look for an explanation, though our present knowledge of science suggests none. But no testimony whatever could give to us any ground to believe that Queen Elizabeth died on January 1st of that year, was buried, reappeared again and resumed the government in the following month. And 'if this miracle should be ascribed to any new system of religion', we might dismiss the testimony without examination. I confess I cannot see on what ground Hume makes any distinction between the two cases he has, with notable bad taste, been pleased to imagine. If it is true that experience is our only criterion, the two imagined sequences seem exactly alike in being wholly startling and unfamiliar, and I should have thought that the same kind and amount of testimony might serve indifferently to accredit either. There is as much or as little precedent for one as for the other. And, again, it is hard to understand why testimony to either, seeing that on Hume's own theory it would have some initial value, however slight, should lose all that value merely because the belief in the event has led *ex post facto* to the appearance of a 'new system of religion'. Presumably, the thought in Hume's mind is that the partisans of a 'system of religion' already in existence, especially of one fighting its way to victory over its rivals, are likely to be unduly disposed to believe in, or even to invent, stories of marvels which recommend it, and that this diminishes the evidential value of their testimony. This, no doubt, is a truth, though not a specially novel one. But he appears to be using this obvious reflection in a surely illegitimate way to destroy the whole value of testimony, even outside testimony, to marvellous events which have preceded and caused the 'new system of religion'. Where the 'system' has actually been called into being by antecedent belief in

the occurrence of a 'miracle', manifestly the fact that the belief has had this historical effect cannot in any way diminish the probability of the truth of the antecedent belief, except in so far as we might have reason to suspect the adherents of the 'new system' of successful suppression of evidence which would tell against the truth of their story. This would be a relevant consideration, but one which could only be taken into account on the assumption that we scrutinise testimonies and do not dismiss them unexamined.

(11) We come at last to the surprising and famous *volte-face* with which Hume ends his essay. There is nothing in what we have heard in spite of obvious allusions in the worst of taste, which plays into the hands of opponents of 'our most holy religion'. For that is founded altogether in faith, not on reason. The Scripture history is full of incidents which are infinitely improbable. The testimony for them, judged by the principles which have been laid down for our guidance, amounts to nothing at all, and we might therefore suppose that the benefit promised at the beginning of the essay to the 'wise' would prove to be the abolition of Christianity. But Hume reminds himself at the close that since, on his own showing, 'the Christian religion... cannot be believed by any reasonable person' without a miracle, any one who does believe 'is conscious of a continued miracle in his own person, which subverts all the principles of his understanding', and the arguments against 'miracles' must obviously fail when addressed to a person who has the actual present experience of one in himself. The lameness of the conclusion, when it is compared with the vaunting of Hume's *exordium*, has naturally given rise to the current view that it is a mere piece of mockery — a transparent substitute for the true ending, like the *finale* of a Euripidean tragedy on Dr Verall's interpretation of the poet. That there is mockery in the language is undeniable. The question I propose to raise is whether, after all, the conclusion, satisfactory or not, is not that which follows from the reasoning on Hume's principles, and the violent contrast between *exordium* and peroration itself a part of the mockery.

It we are to find any coherence in Hume's argument, we must, in the first place, eliminate an ambiguity which can hardly be accounted for except by the writer's determination to make a sensation, the ambiguity of the term 'miracle' itself. A 'miracle' may mean either of two very different things; it may mean simply an unusual and arresting event, an event 'out of common course', or it may mean an event, not necessarily particularly unusual, which is held to disclose, as most events do not, the *direct* activity of God as author and controller of events; a miracle may be either a mere 'wonder' or it may be a 'sign', and, as every one knows, in the language of theology no event is called a 'miracle' unless it combines both characters. But the second is, from the theologian's point of view, the more important. St Thomas [Summa contra Gentiles III; 101], for example reckons among minor 'miracles' such events as the relief of a 'fever' by the offering of a prayer, a process which he must have believed to be illustrated by daily occurrences, and Dante is following the same doctrine when he appeals to the story of the opportune cackling of the Capitoline geese as evidence that 'miracles' prove the divine selection of the Roman people for universal empire. Manifestly it is clear that there are two quite distinct, though connected, questions which need to be carefully distinguished: (1) What sort and amount of evidence is needed to justify belief in the reality of an unusual occurrence? (2) Whether such occurrences, if there is evidence for them, can rightly be employed as proof of the control of events by a divine purpose. It is one question whether there can be adequate evidence of the occurrence of events 'out of the common course', another what the evidential worth of such events as testimony to the doctrines of a 'religion' may be. The first question belongs to inductive logic, the second to theology, and nothing but confusion can come of the attempt to treat the two questions as one. It is also clear on the face of it that Hume's essay begins as a discussion of the first question, and that the introduction of the second is a piece of irrelevance. The conclusion which was to deliver the 'wise' from 'superstition' once and for all should have been that events sufficiently out of the daily routine are so inherently improbable that any counter-probability suggested by the amount of testimony in their favour may be dismissed as infinitesimal. This, if it could be established, would make the raising of the theological issue superfluous. Or, at most all that it would be relevant to urge would be the subsidiary consideration that the theological convictions of witnesses of the alleged events are likely to be a source of antecedent bias. Even this reflection should, in strict logic, be dispensed with, if it can be independently established that *no* amount of testimony, biased or not, has any weight, if only the event testified to is sufficiently strange. Now if Hume had confined himself to this contention, his argument would have gained in force and coherence: there would have been none of the perplexities introduced by the repeated change of the initial definition of a 'miracle', nor would the whole reasoning have been imperilled, as it is, by the damaging concession that a departure from 'uniform law' may after all be accounted as a fact, if the testimony is abundant and good enough, or by the arbitrary decision that testimony might be sufficient to prove the occurrence of a world-wide darkness of a week's duration and yet not require any examination it if were offered in favour of a 'resurrection'. We do less than justice to Hume's acuteness if we imagine that he was not alive to the havoc made in his argument by this confusion of the issues, and it is only reasonable to suppose that the irrelevance is due to a purpose. Without the sensational attack on the theologians, the main argument would probably have attracted no particular attention from any one; the *Enquiry* would have been as little talked about as the *Treatise*, and Hume was, above everything, determined that he would be talked about.

What remains to be considered, then, is the question of what Hume's main argument amounts to when all the irrelevance has been removed, and it is taken simply as an argument about the value of testimony to the strange and unprecedented. Even when taken in this way, at first sight the argument is bound to seem curiously wrong-headed. We are apparently told that assent should always be based on a careful weighing of the direct and indirect evidence on both sides of a question, and this is, then, strangely enough made the ground for asserting that, if only an alleged occurrence is unusual enough, we need not weigh the evidence produced for it. We may confidently dismiss our witnesses unheard. If this were really Hume's meaning, it is clear that his conclusion and his premises would be oddly at variance, and it is not surprising that a disciple like Huxley, who was anxious to maintain the conclusion, but to maintain it with some appearance of logic, should have restated the case in a way which abandons Hume's main contention. With Huxley, the main weight of the conclusion is made to rest on the assertion that in actual fact the testimony which has been produced to the occurrence of 'miracles' has always been dubious or inadequate. Whether this is the fact or not, it is at least an appeal to what is itself an ascertainable fact, and can only be made after that very scrutiny of the testimony in the particular case from which Hume promises to deliver 'the wise'. If we are careful, however, to remember certain fundamental positions of Hume's general philosophy, we shall see that, before we can get at the real meaning of his argument, we have to translate its terms into the language of Humian scepticism, and that when we do so, the reasoning proceeds to a conclusion which is valid enough, though quite unsensational.

We have to bear in mind, to begin with, Hume's peculiar doctrine about the nature of assent or belief, a doctrine proclaimed loudly enough both in the *Treatise* and in the *Enquiry*. A belief, we must remember, is explicitly asserted to be simply 'a lively idea' associated with a 'present impression'; it is only in respect of its superior 'liveliness' that a belief differs from a fancy, or assenting to a proposition from merely framing it. 'I believe this', we are told in so many words, means only 'I feel at this moment a strong propension to consider things in this light', and it is because belief means no more than this, that Hume professes to believe his own metaphysic, though, as he ingenuously says, he forgets about it and virtually denies it whenever he mixes in the social life of his fellows. While he is meditating alone in his study, though at no other time, he feels a strong propension to consider things in the fashion of the *Treatise*, and this, of itself, *is* believing, for the time, in the *Treatise* and its doctrines. It is another of Hume's convictions that, though beliefs have causes, they never have sufficient justifying reasons, and that in the sequence of events, there are 'customary conjunctions', but never discernible 'connections'. There is no pattern in the course of events in virtue of which any event should require one continuation into the future rather than another. Each even has its own special character and all events are loose and separated. There is no discoverable reason why any one event should not be 'conjoined' with any other whatsoever as its sequel. What events are followed by what we discover only by experience, and experience is a purely passive awareness of sequence. It follows that, when we hear from Hume of 'uniform experience' and of 'laws of nature', uniform experience can mean no more than a type of sequence which has been regular so far as our own recollection and that of the other persons with whom we are in communication, goes. (Indeed, it is plain that it is only by the courtesy of an opponent that Hume is entitled to bring in the reference to the experience of any one but myself. A second person who makes a statement to me about *his* experience may always be mistaken or untruthful, and, in the end, it will be my own personal acquaintance with the sequence of events by which I have to judge whether or not he is a credible witness.) Similarly, an 'inviolable law of nature', when we translate the words into their equivalent in Humean metaphysics, means no more than a type of sequence which, so far as my own recollections, eked out by those of any other persons in whom I rightly or wrongly put credence, go, has been uniform. Next we have to remember that the same consideration must be applied in interpreting the statement that our knowledge of the sequences in nature depends on 'customary experience'. This does not mean, and in the *Treatise* Hume is at pains to make the point clear, that there is any discoverable reason why there should be a fixed routine in the course of events, and a routine which each of us can discover from the small fragment of the sequence open to his personal observation. There is no logical ground for expecting that the sequence of events will conform to any rule; any one event might perfectly well be succeeded by any other. All that is meant is that it is an inexplicable, non-rational tendency of the human mind to *expect* that the usual will happen and that the unusual will not. Repetition gives rise to a subjective 'association of ideas' and therefore to expectation; in fact, the probability of an event, as is explained in the *Treatise*, means neither more nor less than the degree of 'vivacity' with which some one imagines, and therefore anticipates, it. 'Customary sequence' is thus only a cause, not a justifying ground, for our anticipations. To put the point quite simply, all our judgments are judgments, true or false, about actual fact; there are no judgments of value, neither a logical *ought* nor a moral *ought*. Just as 'this is right' means only 'the disinterested spectator, as a fact, contemplates this with pleasure', so 'this is probable', 'this is certain', means only that 'actual observers expect this with a less or greater degree of confidence'. This universal reduction of all propositions to statements about actual occurrences is the most characteristic and important peculiarity of Hume's whole philosophy. The ideal before his mind is the same which inspires the chief work of Avenarius, the elimination from all assertions of every element which is not 'pure experience', a simple record of the event without interpretation or valuation. The problem he has not faced is that directly suggested by the *Critique of Pure Experience*, the question whether intelligence, as distinguished from mere insignificant reaction to stimulus, would not vanish completely from a community in which the ideal had been realised.

Let us, then, re-state Hume's main argument in the terms of his own philosophy. It will be seen, I think, that it amounts to this. It is a fact, and a fact of which no explanation can be given, that repetition gives rise to 'associations of ideas', and that the strength of these associations depends on the frequency of the repetition. The more often I have seen A followed by B, and the less often I have seen A occur without being followed by B, the harder I find it to believe that A will occur or has ever occurred, without being followed by B. Similarly, if I have never seen A followed by C, I shall not imagine C, and consequently shall not expect C, to occur as a continuation of A. This is the ultimate causal explanation of habits of thought and expectation. They are, in fact, prejudices without logical value, as the *Treatise* declares in deliberately provocative language, but the strength of the prejudice may be, as a fact of my mental make-up, invincible. This, and no more, is all that Hume is entitled, on his own principles, to mean when he talks of the inconceivability of the violation of a uniform law of nature. Properly speaking, there are no laws of nature to be violated, but there are habits of expectation which any one of us, as a fact, finds himself unable to break through. Since, again, we discover, also as a fact for which we can give no reason, that it is 'customary repetition' which appears to be the foundation of these habits, it is also the fact that we expect a certain sequence with the greater confidence the more familiar its type is to us, and that, if an alleged sequence of events is sufficiently startling and contrary to our expectations, we feel a stronger propensity to consider the statements of witnesses as mistakes or lies — things of which we have some experience — than to accept them as true. We find it easier to imagine vividly that our witness is deceived, or is deceiving us, than to imagine the events he describes. The conclusion to which we are led is thus, like the premises from which we started, a simple proposition of fact. Men find the unusual hard to imagine in proportion to its unusualness, and there is a point, for any one of us, when the difficulty amounts to a psychological impossibility. When this point is reached, the unimaginable event is a 'miracle'. Thus the conclusion to which the argument is leading us is really the assertion of fact that a 'miracle' is not believed in by anyone, being simply any event so unexpected that we find it easier to imagine the falsity of the testimony than to imagine the occurrence of the event.

Now, if Hume had ended his essay at this point, it could not have brought him notoriety, and it could have not proved anything which could well be disputed. The pious and the impious, the orthodox and unorthodox alike, might well have agreed that there are some things which any man does find incredible. The trouble is that men differ so much from one another in the matter of what, in particular, each finds incredible. What we want to know, if we are to write or read history, is not what a given man finds credible or incredible, but what we *ought* as rational beings to pronounce credible or incredible, and the philosopher of 'pure experience' can give us no guidance here. Hume, for example, indicates that in his opinion a resurrection from the dead is flatly incredible, no matter what the apparent testimony for it may be, whereas a week of world-wide darkness is credible, if there is enough testimony for it, though both events seem equally to baffle our powers of rational explanation. Any one of us who does not feel the special 'propensions' of Hume on this point, may obviously ask him to justify his position, if he can, by showing that there is some difference in principle between the two cases. What is more, any man who finds any event whatever not wholly unimaginable may pertinently ask Hume why that particular event should be placed in the category of those which may be disposed of as unreal without examination of testimony. It is this obvious reflection which both justifies and demands the apparently inconsistent concession to the Christian believer with which Hume has seen fit to end his essay. The tone of *persiflage* is manifest throughout the paragraphs, but the whole is not *persiflage*; there is a real concession which is absolutely demanded by Hume's own radical 'positivism'.

The main result really reached had been that, in point of fact, men find it hard to believe the marvellous, and if the marvel is sufficiently astounding, they refuse to believe. In plain language, this ought to mean that no one ever does believe in the reality of a sequence of events quite unlike the routine of his customary experience. But this conclusion would be manifestly false in fact. For Hume could not deny that, to take the most familiar example, there were many sincere orthodox Christians in his own society and that they did, as a fact, believe in the reality of certain events to which their customary experience afforded no analogy. It might be argued, though not very reasonably by an avowed irrationalist, that the orthodox have no right to hold their convictions; but the fact that they did hold them, and hold them with assurance, was beyond dispute, and it has to be shown that this fact is itself consistent with Hume's own principles. Otherwise the principles would themselves be completely discredited as leading, by logical necessity, to a conclusion false in fact. This explains the serious motive for the apparently paradoxical concessions which Hume proceeds to make. There would be a real paradox, if it were part of Hume's case that 'customary experience', and it only, provides a rational justification for our beliefs about the course of events. But his position is that none of these beliefs have any rational justification; belief, as the *Treatise* says, is more of the nature of sensation than of the nature of reason. The only problem that can be raised about our beliefs is that of their cause, and Hume has insisted strongly on the point that all we can say about the cause of belief is that, as a fact, it is commonly produced by 'customary experience'. We could not say that it cannot be produced in any other way, for to say so would be to go beyond the limits of the factual. And the existence of a single genuine believer in the unusual is empirical proof that, as a matter of fact, 'customary experience', though the commonest, is not the only cause of belief. Now Hume has been careful to protest against any assumption that there is a rational connection of any kind between customary repetition and belief. That the repetition of a certain sequence of events should make us expect its recurrence with the greater confidence, the oftener the repetition has been noted, is, according to him, a fact of human nature which we can observe, but for which we can allege no justifying reason. (It is on a par with the gambler's belief in the continuation of a run of luck, a belief neither more nor less rational than the opposing belief, also found among gamblers, that the 'luck must change'.) It is this as only what might be expected — if in a world where there are only 'conjunctions' we can talk of what may be expected — that 'custom' should be only the customary, not the invariable, cause of belief. And, since there is no discoverable connection between repetition and belief, you cannot tell the man who confidently believes in the reality of the unparalleled that his belief is unreasonable. He finds in himself, as Hume takes care to put it, 'a determination to believe what is contrary to custom and experience'. But, on Hume's own showing, to believe what is contrary to custom is neither more nor less reasonable than to believe what is conformable to custom. It is less usual, and we have no right to say anything more. This is, in fact, what Hume does say, in more provocative language, when he speaks of the Christian believer as having a standing 'miracle' within himself, which makes him proof against all reasoning against the miraculous. The strict meaning of the statement is simply that in this case the believer's 'propension to see things in a certain light' has causes which are not those of other men's belief, nor of his own beliefs about the majority of things. Stated thus baldly, Hume's conclusion would be at once proper to a consistently 'sceptical' philosophy and quite acceptable to the vast majority of the orthodox. In fact, what would be shocking to any man who was deeply religious as well as orthodox would be the suggestion that the motives of credibility in matters of religion are of the same order as those involved in believing or disbelieving a newspaper report of travel or exploration. Why the statement that this is not so should have been couched in language which was certain to create scandal can hardly be explained except by Hume's resolution to attract notice at all costs.

There is another side to the matter which demands a word or two. From the position of his own sceptical philosophy, Hume is not entitled to regard the belief of the man who 'has the miracle in himself' as inherently more or less unreasonable than his own. But there can be no doubt in what light Hume was himself 'strongly inclined' to view all such matters, and we can quite understand that he would contemplate the orthodox, whose, 'propensions' are so unlike his own, with a detached amusement. To his eminently secular mind they would no better than entertaining oddities. But there is another party whom Hume must have found equally entertaining for precisely the same reason, the militant rationalist who assails orthodoxy in the name of science. Rational science goes outside the limits of a philosophy of pure experience in much the same way as dogmatic theology. The greater part of Hume's *Treatise* had been devoted to an attempt to demolish the foundation-stones of a rational science of nature. Necessary connection, the permanence of substance, the extra-mental reality of the physical world, are all dismissed as superstitions. To use more modern language, no 'constants' are left in nature, unless we can give the name of a 'natural constant' to our own inexplicable and unjustified prejudice in favour of the usual and familiar. From this point of view, the man of science, who builds on the 'uniformity of nature', and the divine, who appeals to the immutable attributes of his God, are alike constructing dogmatic theories on a basis of 'extra-belief'. Spinoza, the typical assertor of natural necessity, and the theologians may both be beaten equally effectually with the same stick, since both go beyond the limits of fact in precisely the same fashion, by 'feigning' that there is real 'connection' where they should have been content to record mere 'conjunction'. It follows that 'our most holy religion' does not stand alone in being founded on a 'faith' which has no foundation in reason. The same faith is also the foundation of our most admirable science. The only difference which could be pleaded as giving an advantage to science is that the predictions of the scientific man, up to the present, have largely been found to be verified by the course of events; the predictions of the theologian, which concern an unseen order, are naturally incapable of this verification. On closer scrutiny the apparent advantage is found to vanish. For we have no means of knowing that the theologian's predictions, too, *may* not get their verification; the predictions of science are never verified more than approximately, and we do not know that the course of events may not change its character at any moment in a way which would deprive them of even approximate verification. That they have proved trustworthy up to the present is no more than a curious and inexplicable 'happy coincidence'.

Hume's light-hearted irony has, then, a double edge. As he says, in effect the Christian believer is staking his all on a mere promise which, for all we can prove, may remain eternally unfulfilled. As he does not say in the context, but in effect urges all through his polemic against rationalist dogmatism, the convinced believer in science is equally staking everything on a promise of the same kind to which the course of events may give the lie at any moment. The believer in God and the believer in an order of nature both have the same consciousness of a 'miracle' within their own breasts. That either should excommunicate the other for their common guilt of 'extra-belief' is the feature of the situation which the 'academical' philosopher finds entertaining. The 'naturalist' who derides his neighbour's 'groundless' anticipations of the joys of Paradise forgets that, on Hume's showing, his own anticipation that the sun will rise tomorrow is equally groundless. If only the half of this condemnation of all anticipations of the course of things as alike unintelligent is actually expressed in the essay, the reason must be that notoriety was to be got by an attack on the Church; an attack on the Royal Society would pass unregarded.

As a contribution to logic, Hume's essay is thus an attack not so much on the credibility of 'miracles' as on the validity of induction. His point, if one works it out, is that all inference from the present occasion to anything beyond itself presupposes some metaphysical theory of the structure of the world as a whole, whereas the world revealed to us by 'experience' has *no* structure; it is a mere series of loose and separate incidents. Now this is half the truth. Even if it were the case, as Dr Broad has so brilliantly shown that it is not, that scientific induction can be reduced, as Hume tries to reduce it, to a mere application of the theory of Probability, the difficulty would still remain. For — to appeal again to a principle which has been made specially clear by the work of Cambridge philosophers — there is no such thing as *the* probability of a given event, there are only probabilities relative to a given set of premises, and such a set of premises inevitably includes some metaphysical assumption about the structure of the world as a whole. Hume himself makes one such wholly indemonstrable assumption of the utmost importance when he rests his whole philosophical edifice on the proposition, admitted by himself to be incompatible with other equally indispensable postulates, that 'all our perceptions are distinct existences, and the mind never perceives any connection between its ideas', in other words, that all events are loose and separate. This assumption, once made, ought to dispose not merely of all dogmatism, theological or scientific, as Hume intended it should, but of every attempt to regard any one event as more or less probable than any other. In principle it excludes all inference from the particular occasion to anything beyond itself, and therefore leads direct to the denial of the very possibility of science even when the pretensions of science have been reduced to the most modest proportions. If the doctrine is to be carried out regardless of consequence, even the most abstract pure logic and mathematics cannot escape condemnation. For if there is really no means of transcending the particularity of the particular occasion, even my statement that two and three make five can be no more than a record of the event that I have, on this occasion, counted with this result; I can have no guarantee that the result will be the same the next time I perform the counting. All I am entitled to say is that at present I feel a 'propension' to consider the matter in that light. It would be of no avail to introduce a distinction between particular data of sense and 'universals' which pervade the data, in the hope of preserving, at any rate, scientific knowledge of the inter-relations of 'universals', for, if all events are loose and separate, there can be no warrant for assertions about 'pervasive' elements in them. The attempt at analysis itself already implicitly transcends the supposed disconnection of events. Dr Whitehead thus seems to me wholly in the right of it when he insists on the point that the 'induction' indispensable to science is not to be regarded as a process of generalisation but as one in which we 'divine' some characteristics of a particular future from the known characteristics of a particular past, except for the slight oversight by which he has spoken of the conclusion inferred to as though it must be 'future'. No one, I take it, knows better than Dr Whitehead that the inference may equally well be from one particular past occasion to another equally past. But, of course, the very admission that it is a legitimate procedure to divine any of the characteristics of one occasion from what we know of another occasion demands the surrender of the assumption that 'occasions' are simply loose and separate, or in other words, that 'experience' is mere awareness of a series of disconnected 'events' which are only externally 'conjoined'. I cannot dwell long on the point, but I would only urge that in principle this must mean that a scientific view of nature must be much more like that of Leibniz than like that of Hume. So far from being merely 'conjoined' as earlier and later, events must have a pattern in virtue of which each brings with it traces of all that has gone before and is big with all that is to come. And to admit so much is to admit that, in the end, the course of events as a whole has a supreme pattern which appears, with the needful modifications, as the dominant factor in determining the patterns of its parts. What the dominant pattern is, in its detail, we naturally cannot say, since we never see more than fragments of it. But we can, on the supposition that such a pattern is really there, make 'divinations' which are more or less true to the main scheme, and these divinations, without which inference could not advance a single step, are the commonly unconscious metaphysical presuppositions which guide us in our judgments of probabilities. They furnish premises without which we should have no logical justification for pronouncing any one anticipation of experience more or less probable than any other. Were it true that 'connection' is, as Hume supposed, not 'divined' but simply 'feigned', induction would not even be what Mr Bertrand Russell once called it, a method of making 'plausible' guesses. It would be guessing without any method, and there would be no sense in calling one guess any more plausible than any other.

The very existence of a dispute between the divine and the man of secular science about the reality of 'miracles' is only possible because, unlike Hume, the parties are both, at bottom, rationalists in their conscious or unconscious metaphysics. In a purely non-rational world, any one occurrence is just as much or as little of a 'wonder' as any other. You may say, with Hume, that it is only from customary experience that we can derive the expectation that an event will have a given continuation, or, with the most supranaturalistic of Mohammedans, that the only reason why anything happens is that 'Allah almighty disposes it so'; the formulae are different, but their sense is identical. The distinction between the 'ordinary' or 'normal' and the 'astounding' or 'miraculous' (in the etymological sense) can only be made on the basis of a metaphysic

which recognises a real connection of events by a coherent and all pervasive pattern. Only where this is a common metaphysical dogma does it
become justifiable to raise the question whether better testimony is
required to establish the unusual and surprising.

If by a miracle we mean simply an unusual occurrence, it may then
become a mere problem in the estimation of opposing probabilities to
determine whether the reality of such an occurrence is credible. From
this point of view there could be no question of dismissing testimony
unexamined as intrinsically worthless, but it would be possible to accept
the general principle that the antecedent unlikeliness of the facts testified to makes it reasonable to demand exceptionally abundant and
weighty testimony. The one criticism one would feel inclined to pass
upon Hume's version of this principle would be that he forgets that the
probabilities with which we have to reckon in matters of history are
mostly not of the kind which admit of exact mathematical expression. A
wise man is regularly determined in his decision to credit human testimony by 'imponderables' to which no calculus can assign probability
coefficients.

The real issue, in the case of 'miracles' appealed to as of significance
for religion, is not the bare antecedent probability of unusual events. The
unusual event gets its significance as a 'miracle', in the religious sense of
the word, from the conviction that it is an event in which the character of
a divine purpose underlying the whole course of events becomes exceptionally transparent; it is a 'sign' of the mercy, the justice, the power of
God. It follows at once that our whole attitude towards the credibility of
miracles is profoundly affected by our ultimate metaphysical position.
The problem cannot even be discussed with any profit between two parties of whom one is a Theist and the other an atheist or a pure agnostic.
For they will differ profoundly about the nature of the pattern which
binds nature into a connected system. On any rationalistic hypothesis,
startling and singular events must be reasonably expected to occur from
time to time, and there can, so far as I can see, be no means of saying in
advance how startling the surprises which the course of events contains
may prove to be to us, who are familiar, after all, with so small a fragment of the whole. But, in an atheistic or neutral metaphysical scheme,
there would be no reason to expect the surprises to wear any special
character, or to be distributed in any special way over space and time.
We should expect them to make their appearance as simple 'freaks'. If
our philosophical world-scheme is definitely theistic, the case is altered
completely. For we shall then conceive of the pattern of events as a
whole not merely as providing a connection between them, but as providing a connection which is intelligent in the sense that, like the structure of a symphony, or a well-lived life, it exhibits the realisation of an
end of absolute value. We should, thus, antecedently look for the 'singu-
larities' in nature and history to exhibit a special kind of concentration,
exactly as the surprises in the construction of a great piece of music or the

conduct of a life of wise originality exhibit the same concentration. The intelligence of the great musician or the great statesman shows itself neither in unbroken adherence to an iron routine nor in wild eccentricity. It reveals itself in the way in which conformity to routine, where there is nothing to be gained by departure, is combined with bold and original departure from routine because the situation makes the demand for it. A Theist, conceiving of the pattern of events in the light of such analogies, will thus reasonably regard it as to be expected that surprises of a certain kind and in certain historic connections, surprises which contribute, so to say, to a plan, 'worthy of God', should occur in history and that others should not, exactly as one would expect some kinds of musical surprises in a newly discovered symphony professing to be by Beethoven, but would emphatically not expect others. Thus the difference in ultimate metaphysical outlook between a Theist and non-theistic philosopher would make a difference between the two sets of initial premises relatively to which each estimates the probability of certain events. It is not in the least unreasonable, for example, in a convinced Theist to be satisfied with evidence for the resurrection of Jesus Christ which would not satisfy him of the resurrection of his next-door neighbour, since he may well ascribe to the resurrection of Christ a unique spiritual value for the whole history of the human race which he could not ascribe to the resurrection of his neighbour. We should be misconceiving the whole issue if we did not bear in mind that what is affirmed by the Christian creed is not simply the resurrection of some man, but the resurrection of just this one man and no other.

This is what I meant when I said, a little while back, that the motives of credibility to which the religious man, who is also a thinking man, appeals are of a kind quite other than those which Hume takes into consideration. The determining factor in leading him to believe in certain 'miracles', assuming for the moment that he professes a religion which includes this belief, is his underlying conviction that the plan of the world is dominated by certain absolute values, and that these events are the most striking and transparent examples of the dominance of just these values. They are like the comparatively few critical moments in which we find a revelation of the inmost character of a friend and from which we then proceed to interpret the whole of his more ordinary behaviour. It follows, of course, that the whole question of the reality of 'miracles', in any but the bare etymological senses of the word, is secondary to the much graver question of the legitimacy of a theistic interpretation of life. The alleged occurrence of miracles cannot itself be rationally made a premise for the argument for Theism. Two Theists of different creeds, provided they agree in attributing a certain character to God, may discuss the question whether the 'miracles' of one of the different creeds are or are not worthy of the character of God. It would be idle to ask any man to accept Theism in any form on the evidence of any kind of 'miracle', since, unless he already admits what you are seeking to prove, the most irrefragable evidence that the facts to which you appeal are genuine facts would establish no more than the hardly disputable conclusion that strange things do sometimes happen. It is thus not surprising that, as Francis Bacon remarks, miracles have been wrought to convince idolaters, but none to convince atheists.

The point I want to make, then, is this. The problem of Hume's essay, as Hume himself states it, is vitiated by illegitimate simplification. When we are dealing with testimony to a startling event which claims also to have the value of a 'sign' from the unseen, we have two questions, not one only, on our hands. There is, of course, the preliminary question, which arises whenever we have to decide for or against accepting testimony, the question of the quality of the testimony, the intelligence and *bona fides* of the witnesses, the nature of the agreements and disagreements between their reports, the presumption that these reports are independent, and the like. When we have satisfied ourselves, if we succeed in doing so, that our evidence is unexceptional in all these respects, there still remain two real questions, not to be disposed of by these antecedent considerations: (1) Is it more likely that the most unexceptional witnesses should fail us in this case or that the event to which they testify is a fact, and (2) if it is a fact, is it merely a puzzling fact, or has it the value of a 'sign'? Our answer to *both* questions, I hold, is legitimately influenced by our metaphysic. If our metaphysic is definitely theistic, it will be rational to regard such 'signs' as likely to mark the course of history; if it is anti-theistic or neutral, the same expectations will not be, for us, rational. Whether it is rational to be prepared to acknowledge 'miracle' as a feature of the historical process is thus a question which depends on a prior question: Is it irrational to be Theists in our metaphysics? As I have said, it would involve an obvious circle in our reasoning if we alleged the occurrence of miraculous events as the ground for adopting a theistic metaphysic. If a theistic interpretation of the course of events is to be justified, the justification must be based on the *cursus ordinarius* of nature. Our metaphysic, if it is to be more than an idle play of fancy, must be a response of thought to the full concrete reality of the world in which our life is set. And I think it follows that we cannot expect to arrive at a metaphysic of any great worth so long as we confine our contemplation to the domain of formal logic, or epistemology, or even of experimental science. We and our fellows are ourselves a part of the world to be interpreted, and we have no right to assume at the outset that we may not even be its most important part. The material for interpretation is supplied not only by the natural sciences of the laboratory, the observatory, and the field, but by the whole history of man with his ideals, his achievements, his failures, his self-condemnations, his hopes and his fears. For the tissue of life is inextricably woven of all these strands, though we are tempted, in an age of unavoidable specialism, to forget the fact when we retire to our studies or our laboratories and concentrate our attention on the artificial and poverty-stricken extract from the wealth of the real world which we call our special 'subject'. Like the Ephesians of the time of Heraclitus, we retire each into a poor little private world of our own, and forget the 'common', and this, as that great man said, is to live like men half asleep. Indeed, it is so to be logicians, or chemists, or historians or ethnologists that we forget to be men. The fault is not wholly our own, and it cannot well be escaped by our generation, though we may be permitted to imagine with innocent envy the possible happier lot of our successors, if some great social and economic change should simplify this intellectual problem by leading to the destruction of the masses of accumulated misapplied 'erudition' which are our nightmare. But it is our fault if we make no attempt to escape complete subdual to that in which — for our sins — we have to work. The final verdict on the question whether theism is not a legitimate, or, it may be, a necessary feature of a metaphysic which can 'give account' of the real world in all its real fullness could be expected neither from an age of specialists like our own, nor from an age of gentlemanly loiterers, like the literary coteries of the eighteenth century. For a voice which might speak with compelling authority we have to look to a society which has an intensely rich and full life of its own and yet is not mastered by it but masters it, 'sees it steadily and sees it whole'.

For my own part, I think I know what the verdict of such a society would be. I cannot, of course, expect that all my hearers should be of my mind. What kind of response one makes to life will, no doubt, for better or worse, depend on the sort of man one is for good or bad. ... But we can all make it our purpose that our philosophy, if we have one, shall be no mere affair of surface opinions, but the genuine expression of a whole personality. Because I can never feel that Hume's own philosophy was that, I have to own to a haunting uncertainty whether Hume was really a great philosopher, or only a 'very clever man'.

Twelve

C.A. Campbell

1897–1974

Charles Arthur Campbell was Professor of Logic and Rhetoric at the University of Glasgow from 1938-1961. Born in 1897, he was educated at Glasgow Academy before proceeding to Glasgow University from which he graduated MA in 1914.

In accordance with a very long established tradition, Campbell went from Glasgow to take a second undergraduate degree at Balliol College Oxford, but in 1915 he was called to served in the First World War as a 2nd Lieutenant in the 10th Border Regiment. After service in Egypt, he was invalided out in 1917 and resumed his studies in Oxford. In 1924, he returned to Glasgow, where he had been appointed an Assistant to the Professor of Moral Philosophy, and a year later became a Lecturer. In 1932 he was appointed Professor of Philosophy at the University College of North Wales in Bangor, where he remained for six years before returning once more to Glasgow to take up the established Chair of Logic and Rhetoric. Here he formed a close philosophical relationship with his opposite number in the Chair of Moral Philosophy, W G Maclagan.

For the most part, Campbell's philosophical work appeared in essays — in *Mind*, *Philosophy* and the *Proceedings of the Aristotelian Society*, but during his occupancy of the Chair he gave two series of Gifford Lectures at the University of St Andrews. A revised version of these was published as a book in the prestigious and influential Muirhead Library of Philosophy under the title *On Selfhood and Godhood*.

Campbell's Inaugural Lecture as Professor of Logic and Rhetoric 'In Defence of Free Will' (reprinted in a slightly shortened version here) is a fine example of his careful articulation and defence of unfashionable positions. And though he does not use the expression 'common sense' at any point, he endorses its philosophical method with the claim that 'we are entitled to put our trust in a belief which is so deeply embedded in our experience as practical beings as to be ineradicable from it'.

Campbell became Emeritus Professor on his retirement in 1961 and died in March 1974.

Biographical information: *Who's Who*, 1897 – 1996.

READING XVIII
In Defence of Free Will[1]

In casting about for a suitable topic upon which to address you today, I have naturally borne in mind that an inaugural lecture of this sort should be devoted to some theme of much more than a merely esoteric import: to some theme, for preference, sufficiently central in character to have challenged the attention of all who possess a speculative interest in the nature of the universe and man's place within it. That is a principal reason why I have chosen today to speak on free will. Mighty issues turn, and turn directly, on the solution of the free will problem. It is in no way surprising that for centuries past it has exercised a fascination for thinkers both within and without the ranks of the professional philosophers that is probably not paralleled in the case of any of the other great problems of metaphysics.

There are, however, other considerations also which have governed my choice of subject. More particularly, I have been influenced by a conviction that the present state of philosophical opinion on free will is, for certain definitely assignable reasons, profoundly unsatisfactory. In my judgment, a thoroughly perverse attitude to the whole problem has been created by the almost universal acquiescence in the view that free will in what is often called the 'vulgar' sense is too obviously nonsensical a notion to deserve serious discussion. Free will in a more 'refined' sense — which is apt to mean free will purged of all elements that may cause embarrassment to a Deterministic psychology or a Deterministic metaphysics — is, it is understood, a conception which may be defended by the philosopher without loss of caste. But in its 'vulgar' sense, as maintained, for example, by the plain man, who clings to a belief in genuinely open possibilities, it is (we are told) a wild and even obnoxious delusion, long ago discredited for sober thinkers.

Now, as it happens, I myself firmly believe that free will, in something extremely like the 'vulgar' sense, is a fact. And I am anxious today to do what I can, within the limits of a single lecture, to justify that belief. I propose therefore to develop a statement of the Libertarian's position which will try to make clear why he finds himself obliged to hold what he does hold, and to follow this up with a critical examination of the grounds most in vogue among philosophers for impugning this position. Considerations of time will, I fear, compel a somewhat close economy in my treatment of objections. But I shall hope to say enough to instigate a doubt in some minds concerning that validity of certain very fashionable objections whose authority is often taken to be virtually final. And if no other good purpose is served, it will at least be of advantage if I can offer, in my positive statement, a target for the missiles of the critics more truly representative of Libertarianism than the targets at which

[1] Extracted from *In Defence of Free Will: With Other Philosophical Essays*, London: Allen & Unwin, 1967, pp. 35-55

they sometimes direct their fire — targets, I may add, upon which even the clumsiest of marksmen could hardly fail to register bull's-eyes.

Let us begin by noting that the problem of free will gets its urgency for the ordinary educated man by reason of its close connection with the conception of moral responsibility. When we regard a man as morally responsible for an act, we regard him as a legitimate object of moral praise or blame in respect of it. But it seems plain that a man cannot be a legitimate object of moral praise or blame for an act unless in willing the act he is in some important sense a 'free' agent. Evidently free will in some sense, therefore, is a pre-condition of moral responsibility. Without doubt it is the realization that any threat to freedom is thus a threat to moral responsibility — with all that that implies — combined with the knowledge that there are a variety of considerations, philosophic, scientific, and theological, tending to place freedom in jeopardy, that gives to the problem of free will its perennial and universal appeal. And it is therefore in close connection with the question of the conditions of moral responsibility that any discussion of the problem must proceed, if it is not to be academic in the worst sense of the term.

We raise the question at once, therefore, what are the conditions, in respect of freedom, which must attach to an act in order to make it a morally responsible act? It seems to me that the fundamental conditions are two. I shall state them with all possible brevity, for we have a long road to travel.

The first condition is the universally recognised one that the act must be *self*-caused, *self*-determined. But it is important to accept this condition in its full rigour. The agent must be not merely *a* cause but the *sole* cause of that for which he is deemed morally responsible. If entities other than the self have also a causal influence upon an act, then that act is not one for which we can say without qualification that the *self* is morally responsible. If in respect of it we hold the self responsible at all, it can only be for some feature of the act — assuming the possibility of disengaging such a feature — of which the self *is* the sole cause. I do not see how this conclusion can be evaded. But it has awkward implications which have led not a few people to abandon the notion of individual moral responsibility altogether.

This first condition, however, is quite clearly not sufficient. It is possible to conceive an act of which the agent is the sole cause, but which is at the same time an act *necessitated* by the agent's nature. Some philosophers have contended, for example, that the act of Divine creation is an act which issues necessarily from the Divine nature. In the case of such an act, where the agent could not do otherwise than he did, we must all agree, I think, that it would be inept to say that he *ought* to have done otherwise and is thus morally blameworthy, or *ought not* to have done otherwise and is thus morally praiseworthy. It is perfectly true that we do sometimes hold a person morally responsible for an act, even when we believe that he, being what he now is, virtually could not do otherwise.

But underlying that judgment is always the assumption that the person has *come* to be what he now is in virtue of past acts of will in which he *was* confronted by real alternatives, by genuinely open possibilities: and, strictly speaking, it is in respect of these *past* acts of his that we praise or blame the agent *now*. For ultimate analysis, the agent's power of alternative action would seem to be an inexpungable condition of his liability to moral praise or blame, i.e. of his moral responsibility.

We may lay down, therefore, that an act is a 'free' act in the sense required for moral responsibility only if the agent (*a*) is the sole cause of the act; and (*b*) could exert his causality in alternative ways. And it may be pointed out in passing that the acceptance of condition (*b*) implies the recognition of the inadequacy for moral freedom of mere 'self-determination'. The doctrine called 'Self-determinism' is often contrasted by its advocates with mere Determinism on the one hand and Indeterminism on the other, and pronounced to be the one true gospel. I must insist, however, that if 'Self-determinism' rejects condition (*b*), it cannot claim to be a doctrine of free will in the sense required to vindicate moral responsibility. The doctrine which demands, and asserts, the fulfilment of both conditions is the doctrine we call 'Libertarianism'. And it would in my opinion minister greatly to clarify it if it were more widely recognized that for any doctrine which is not a species of Libertarianism to pose as a doctrine of 'free will', is mere masquerade.

And now, the conditions of free will being defined in these general terms, we have to ask whether human beings are in fact capable of performing free acts; and if so, where precisely such acts are to be found. In order to prepare the way for an answer, it is desirable, I think, that we should get clear at once about the significance of a certain very familiar, but none the less formidable, criticism of free will which the Self-determinist as well as the Libertarian has to meet. This is the criticism which bases itself upon the facts of heredity on the one hand and of environment on the other. I may briefly summarize the criticism as follows.

Every historic self has an hereditary nature consisting of a group of inborn propensities, in range more or less common to the race, but specific to the individual in their respective strengths. With this equipment the self just *happens* to be born. Strictly speaking, it antedates the existence of the self proper, i.e. the existence of the self-conscious subject, and it is itself the effect of a series of causes leading back to indefinitely remote antiquity. It follows, therefore, that any of the self's choices that manifests the influence of his hereditary nature is not a choice of which *he*, the actual historic self, is the sole cause. The choice is determined, at least in part, by factors external to the self. The same thing holds good of 'environment'. Every self is born and bred in a particular physical and social environment, not of his own choosing, which plays upon him in innumerable ways, encouraging this propensity, discouraging that, and so on. Clearly any of the self's choices that manifests the influence of environmental factors is likewise a choice which is determined, at least in part, by factors external to the self. But if we thus grant, as seems inevitable, that heredity and environment are external influences, where shall we find a choice in the whole history of a self that is not subject to external influence? Surely we must admit that every particular act of choice bears marks of the agent's hereditary nature and environmental nurture; in which case a free act, in the sense of an act determined solely by the self, must be dismissed as a mere chimera.

To this line of criticism the Self-determinist — T.H. Green is a typical example — has a stock reply. He urges that these factors, heredity and environment, are not, in so far as their operation in willing (and therefore in conduct proper) is concerned, 'external' to the self at all. For the act of willing, when we analyse it, reveals itself to be in its nature such that no end can be willed save in so far as it is conceived by the self as a good for the self. A 'native propensity' cannot function *as such* in willing. It can function only in so far as the self conceives its object as a good for the self. It follows that the self in willing is essentially *self*-determining; not moved from the outside, but moved always by its own conception of its own good. Inherited nature and environmental circumstance do play their part; but not as factors external to the self. They can function only in so far as their suggestions are, as it were, incorporated by the self in its conception of its own good. Consequently — so we are told — the threat to self-determination from the side of inheritance and environment disappears on an adequate analysis of the act of willing.

I am afraid, however, that this argument, though it contains important truth, cannot bear the heavy weight that is here imposed upon it. Let us grant that inheritance and environment can operate in willing only in the medium of the self's conception of its own good. But then let us ask, how is the self's conception of its own good constituted? Self-consciousness is required, of course: but mere self-conscious reflection *in vacuo* [in a vacuum] will not furnish the self with any conception of a personal good whatsoever. Obviously to answer the question in regard to any agent we are obliged to make reference to certain sheer external facts; viz., to the quality and strength of that person's inherited propensities, and to the nature of the influences that are brought to bear upon him from the side of environment. It seems certain, then, that the self's conception of its own good is influenced directly by its particular inheritance and environment. But to admit this surely involves the admission that external determination enters into choices. It may be true that the self's choices are always determined by its conception of its own good. But if what it conceives to be its own good is always dependent, at least partly, upon inheritance and environment, as external facts, then it is idle to deny that the self's choices are externally influenced likewise.

Indeed I cannot but regard the attempt to save self-determination by denying the externality of the influence of heredity and environment as a quite desperate expedient. It is significant that nobody really believes it in practice. The externality of these influences is taken for granted in our reflective practical judgments upon persons. On those occasions when we are in real earnest about giving a critical and considered estimate of a man's moral calibre — as, e.g., in any serious biographical study — we impose upon ourselves as a matter of course the duty of enquiring with scrupulous care into his hereditary propensities and environmental circumstances, with a view to discovering how far his conduct is influenced by these factors. And having traced these influences, we certainly do not regard the results as having no bearing on the question of the man's moral responsibility for his conduct. On the contrary, the very purpose of the enquiry is to enable us, by due appreciation of the *external* influences that affect his conduct, to gain as accurate a view as possible of that which can justly be attributed to the man's own *self*-determination. The allowances that we all of us do in practice make for hereditary and environmental influences in passing judgment on our fellows would be meaningless if we did not suppose these influences to be in a real sense 'external' to the self.

Now the recognition of this externality is, of course, just as serious a matter for the Libertarian as for the Self-determinist. For the Libertarian, as we saw, accepts condition (*a*) no less wholeheartedly than the Self-determinist does: i.e. that an act is free only if it is determined by the self and nothing but the self. But though we have not been *directly* advancing our course by these recent considerations, we have been doing so indirectly, by narrowing and sharpening the issue. We know that condition (*a*) is not fulfilled by any act in respect of which inheritance or environment exerts a causal influence. For that type of influence has been shown to be in a real sense external to the self. The free act of which we are in search has therefore got to be one into which influences of this kind do not enter at all.

Moreover, one encouraging portent has emerged in the course of our brief discussion. For we noticed that our reflective practical judgments on persons, while fully recognizing the externality of the influence of heredity and environment, do nevertheless presuppose throughout that there is *something* in conduct which is genuinely self-determined; something which the agent contributes solely on his own initiative, unaffected by external influences; something for which, accordingly, he may justly be held morally responsible. That conviction may, of course, be a false one. But the fact of its widespread existence can hardly be without significance for our problem.

Let us proceed, then, by following up this clue. Let us ask, why do human beings so obstinately persist in believing that there is an indissoluble core of purely *self*-originated activity which even heredity and environment are powerless to affect? There can be little doubt, I think, of the answer in general terms. They do so, at bottom, because they feel certain of the existence of such activity from their immediate practical experience of themselves. Nor can there be in the end much doubt, I think, in what function of the self that activity is to be located. There seems to me to be one, and only one, function of the self with respect to which the agent can even pretend to have an assurance of that absolute self-origination which is here at issue. But to render precise the nature of that function is obviously of quite paramount importance: and we can do so, I think, only by way of a somewhat thorough analysis — which I now propose to attempt — of the experiential situation in which it occurs, viz., the situation of 'moral temptation'.

It is characteristic of that situation that in it I am aware of an end A which I believe to be morally right, and also of an end B, incompatible with A, towards which, in virtue of that system of conative dispositions which constitutes my 'character' as so far formed, I entertain a strong desire. There may be, and perhaps must be, desiring elements in my nature which are directed to A also. But what gives to the situation its specific character as one of moral temptation is that the urge of our desiring nature towards the right end, A, is felt to be *relatively* weak. We are sure that if our desiring nature is permitted to issue directly in action, it is end B that we shall choose. That is what is meant by saying, as William James does, that end B is 'in the line of least resistance' relatively to our conative dispositions. The expression is, of course, a metaphorical one, but it serves to describe, graphically enough, a situation of which we all have frequent experience, viz., where we recognise a specific end as that towards which the 'set' of our desiring nature most strongly inclines us, and which we shall indubitably choose if no inhibiting factor intervenes.

But inhibiting factors, we should most of us say, *may* intervene: and that in two totally different ways which it is vital to distinguish clearly. The inhibiting factor may be of the nature of another desire (or aversion), which operates by changing the balance of the desiring situation. Though at one stage I desire B, which I believe to be wrong, more strongly than I desire A, which I believe to be right, it may happen that before action is taken I become aware of certain hitherto undiscerned consequences of A which I strongly desire, and the result may be that now not *B* but *A* presents itself to me as the end in the line of least resistance. Moral temptation is here overcome by the simple process of ceasing to be a moral temptation.

That is one way, and probably by far the commoner way, in which an inhibiting factor intervenes. But it is certainly not regarded by the self who is confronted by moral temptation as the *only* way. In such situations we all believe, rightly or wrongly, that even although B *continues* to be in the line of least resistance, even although, in other words, the situation remains one with the characteristic marks of moral temptation, we *can* nevertheless align ourselves with A. We can do so, we believe, because we have the power to introduce a new energy, to make what we call an 'effort of will', whereby we are able to act contrary to the felt balance of mere desire, and to achieve the higher end despite the fact that it continues to be in the line of greater resistance relatively to our desiring nature. The self in practice believes that it has this power; and believes, moreover, that the decision rests solely with its self, here and now, whether this power be exerted or not.

Now the objective validity or otherwise of this belief is not at the moment in question. I am here merely pointing to its existence as a psychological fact. No amount of introspective analysis, so far as I can see, even tends to disprove that we do as a matter of fact believe, in situations of moral temptation, that it rests with our self absolutely to decide whether we exert the effort of will which will enable us to rise to duty, or whether we shall allow our desiring nature to take its course.

I have now to point out, further, how this act of moral decision, at least in the significance which it has for the agent himself, fulfils in full the two conditions which we found it necessary to lay down at the beginning for the kind of 'free' act which moral responsibility presupposes.

For obviously it is, in the first place, an act which the agent believes he could perform in alternative ways. He believes that it is genuinely open to him to put forth effort — in varying degrees, if the situation admits of that — or withhold it altogether. And when he *has* decided — in whatever way — he remains convinced that these alternative courses were really open to him.

It is perhaps a little less obvious, but, I think, equally certain, that the agent believes the second condition to be fulfilled likewise, i.e. that the act of decision is determined *solely* by his self. It appears less obvious, because we all realize that formed character has a great deal to do with the choices that we make; and formed character is, without a doubt, partly dependent on the external factors of heredity and environment. But it is crucial here that we should not misunderstand the precise nature of the influence which formed character brings to bear upon the choices that constitute conduct. No one denies that it determines, at least largely, what things we desire, and again how greatly we desire them. It may thus fairly be said to determine the felt balance of desires in the situation of moral temptation. But all that that amounts to is that formed character prescribes the nature of the situation *within* which the act of moral decision takes place. It does not in the least follow that it has any influence whatsoever in determining that act of decision itself — the decision as to whether we shall exert effort or take the easy course of following the bent of our desiring nature: take, that is to say, the course which, in virtue of the determining influence of our character as so far formed, we feel to be in the line of least resistance.

When one appreciates this, one is perhaps better prepared to recognize the fact that the agent himself in the situation of moral temptation does not, and indeed could not, regard his formed character as having any influence whatever upon his act of decision as such. For the very nature of that decision, as it presents itself to him, is as to whether he will or will not permit his formed character to dictate his action. In other words, the agent distinguishes sharply between the self which makes the decision, and the self which, as formed character, determines not the

decision but the situation within which the decision takes place. Rightly
or wrongly, the agent believes that through his act of decision he can
oppose and transcend his own formed character in the interest of duty.
We are therefore obliged to say, I think, that the agent *cannot* regard his
formed character as in any sense a determinant of the act of decision as
such. The act is felt to be a genuinely creative act, originated by the self *ad
hoc*, and by the self alone.

Here then, if my analysis is correct, in the function of moral decision in
situations of moral temptation, we have an act of the self which at least
appears to the agent to satisfy both of the conditions of freedom which we
laid down at the beginning. The vital question now is, is this ' appearance' true or false? Is the act of decision really what it appears to the
agent to be, determined solely by the self, and capable of alternative
forms of expression? If it is, then we have here a free act which serves as
an adequate basis for moral responsibility. We shall be entitled to regard
the agent as morally praiseworthy or morally blameworthy according as
he decides to put forth effort or to let his desiring nature have its way.
We shall be entitled, in short, to judge the agent as he most certainly
judges himself in the situation of moral temptation. If, on the other hand,
there is good reason to believe that the agent is the victim of illusion in
supposing his act of decision to bear this character, then in my opinion
the whole conception of moral responsibility must be jettisoned altogether. For it seems to me certain that there is no other function of the self
that even looks as though it satisfied the required conditions of the free
act.

Now in considering the claim to truth of this belief of our practical
consciousness, we should begin by noting that the onus of proof rests
upon the critic who rejects this belief. Until cogent evidence to the contrary is adduced, we are entitled to put our trust in a belief which is so
deeply embedded in our experience as practical beings as to be, I venture to say, ineradicable from it. Anyone who doubts whether it is
ineradicable may be invited to think himself imaginatively into a situation of moral temptation as we have above described it, and then to ask
himself whether in that situation he finds it possible to *disbelieve* that his
act of decision has the characteristics in question. I have no misgivings
about the answer. It is possible to disbelieve only when we are thinking
abstractly about the situation; not when we are living through it, either
actually or in imagination. This fact certainly establishes a strong prima
facie presumption in favour of the Libertarian position. Nevertheless I
agree that we shall have to weigh carefully several criticisms of high
authority before we can feel justified in asserting free will as an ultimate
and unqualified truth.

Fortunately for our purpose, however, there are some lines of criticism which, although extremely influential in the recent past, may at the
present time be legitimately ignored. We are not today confronted, for
example, by any widely accepted system of metaphysic with implica-

tions directly hostile to free will. Only a decade or two ago one could hardly hope to gain a sympathetic hearing for a view which assigned an ultimate initiative to finite selves, unless one were prepared first to show reason for rejecting the dominant metaphysical doctrine that all things in the universe are the expression of a single Mind or Spirit. But the challenge so lately offered by monistic Idealism has in the present age little more significance than the challenge once offered by monistic Materialism.

Much the same thing holds good of the challenge from the side of physical science. Libertarianism is certainly inconsistent with a rigidly determinist theory of the physical world. It is idle to pretend that there can be open possibilities for psychical decision, while at the same time holding that the physical events in which such decisions manifest themselves are determined in accordance with irrevocable law. But whereas until a few years ago the weight of scientific authority was thrown overwhelmingly on the side of a universal determinism of physical phenomena, the situation has, as everybody knows, profoundly altered during the present century more specifically since the advent of Planck's Quantum Theory and Heisenberg's Principle of Uncertainty. Very few scientists today would seek to impugn free will on the ground of any supposed implications of the aims or achievements of physical science. I am not myself, I should perhaps add in passing, disposed to rest any part of the case against a universal physical determinism upon these recent dramatic developments of physical science. In my view there never were in the established results of physical science cogent reasons for believing that the apparently universal determinism of inorganic processes holds good also of the processes of the human body. The only inference I here wish to draw from the trend of present-day science is that it removes from any *contemporary* urgency the problem of meeting one particular type of objection to free will. And it is with the contemporary situation that I am in this paper anxious to deal.

I may turn at once, therefore, to lines of argument which do still enjoy a wide currency among anti-Libertarians. And I shall begin with one which, though it is a simple matter to show its irrelevance to the Libertarian doctrine as I have stated it, is so extremely popular that it cannot safely be ignored.

The charge made is that the Libertarian view is incompatible with the *predictability* of human conduct. For we do make rough predictions of people's conduct, on the basis of what we know of their character, every day of our lives, and there can be no doubt that the practice, within certain limits, is amply justified by results. Indeed if it were not so, social life would be reduced to sheer chaos. The close relationship between character and conduct which prediction postulates really seems to be about as certain as anything can be. But the Libertarian view, it is urged, by ascribing to the self a mysterious power of decision uncontrolled by character, and capable of issuing in acts inconsistent with character,

denies that continuity between character and conduct upon which prediction depends. If Libertarianism is true, prediction is impossible. But
prediction *is* possible, therefore Libertarianism is untrue.

My answer is that the Libertarian view is perfectly compatible with
prediction within certain limits, and that there is no empirical evidence
at all that prediction is in fact possible beyond these limits. The following considerations will, I think, make the point abundantly clear.

1) There is no question, on our view, of a free will that can will just
   anything at all. The range of possible choices is limited by the
   agent's character in every case; for nothing can be an object of
   possible choice which is not suggested by either the agent's
   desires or his moral ideals, and these depend on 'character' for us
   just as much as for our opponents. We have, indeed explicitly
   recognised at an earlier stage that character determines the situation within which the moral decision takes place, although not
   the act of moral decision itself. This consideration obviously furnishes a broad basis for at least approximate predictions.

2) There is *one* experiential situation, and *one only*, on our view, in
   which there is any possibility of the act of will not being in accordance with character; viz. the situation in which the course which
   formed character prescribes is a course in conflict with the
   agent's moral ideal: in other words, the situation of moral temptation. Now this is a situation of comparative rarity. Yet with
   respect to all other situations in life we are in full agreement with
   those who hold that conduct is the response of the agent's formed
   character to the given situation. Why should it not be so? There
   could be no reason, on our view any more than on another, for the
   agent even to consider deviating from the course which his
   formed character prescribes and he most strongly desires, *unless*
   that course is believed by him to be incompatible with what is
   right.

3) Even within that one situation which is relevant to free will, our
   view can still recognise a certain basis for prediction. In that situation our character as so far formed prescribes a course opposed
   to duty, and an effort of will is required if we are to deviate from
   that course. But of course we are all aware that a greater effort of
   will is required in proportion to the degree in which we have to
   transcend our formed character in order to will the right. Such
   action is, as we say, 'harder'. But if action is 'harder' in proportion as it involves deviation from formed character, it seems reasonable to suppose that, on the whole, action will be of rarer
   occurrence in that same proportion: though perhaps we may not
   say that at any level of deviation it becomes flatly impossible. It
   follows that even with respect to situations of moral temptation
   we may usefully employ our knowledge of the agent's character
   as a clue to prediction. It will be a clue of limited, but of by no
   means negligible, value. It will warrant us in predicting, e.g., of a

person who has become enslaved to alcohol, that he is unlikely, even if fully aware of the moral evil of such slavery, to be successful immediately and completely in throwing off its shackles. Predictions of this kind we all make often enough in practice. And there seems no reason at all why a Libertarian doctrine should wish to question their validity.

Now when these three considerations are borne in mind, it becomes quite clear that the doctrine we are defending is compatible with a very substantial measure of predictability indeed. And I submit that there is not a jot of empirical evidence that any larger measure than this obtains in fact.

Let us pass on then to consider a much more interesting and, I think, more plausible criticism. It is constantly objected against the Libertarian doctrine that it is fundamentally unintelligible. Libertarianism holds that the act of moral decision is the *self's* act, and yet insists at the same time that it is not influenced by any of those determinate features in the self's nature which go to constitute its 'character'. But, it is asked, do not these two propositions contradict one another? Surely a *self*-determination which is determination by something other than the self's *character* is a contradiction in terms? What meaning is there in the conception of a 'self' in abstraction from its 'character'? If you really wish to maintain, it is urged, that the act of decision is not determined by the self's character, you ought to admit frankly that it is not determined by a *self* at all. But in that case, of course, you will not be advocating a freedom which lends any kind of support to moral responsibility; indeed very much the reverse.

Now this criticism, and all of its kind, seem to me to be the product of a simple, but extraordinarily pervasive, error: the error of confining one's self to the categories of the external observer in dealing with the actions of human agents. Let me explain.

It is perfectly true that the standpoint of the external observer, which we are obliged to adopt in dealing with physical processes, does not furnish us with even a glimmering of a notion of what can be meant by an entity which acts causally and yet not through any of the determinate features of its character. So far as we confine ourselves to external observation I agree that this notion must seem to us pure nonsense. But then we are *not* obliged to confine ourselves to external observation in dealing with the human agent. Here, though here alone, we have the inestimable advantage of being able to apprehend operations from the *inside*, from the standpoint of *living experience*. But if we do adopt this internal standpoint — surely a proper standpoint, and one which we should be only too glad to adopt if we could in the case of other entities — the situation is entirely changed. We find that we not merely can, but constantly do, attach meaning to a causation which is the self's causation but is yet not exercised by the self's character. We have seen as much already in our analysis of the situation of moral temptation. When confronted by such a situation, we saw, we are certain that it lies with our *self* to decide whether we shall let our character as so far formed dictate our action or whether we shall by effort oppose its dictates and rise to duty. We are certain, in other words, that the act is *not* determined by our *character*, while we remain equally certain that the act *is* determined by our *self*.

Or look, for a further illustration (since the point we have to make here is of the very first importance for the whole free will controversy), to the experience of effortful willing itself, where the act of decision has found expression in the will to rise to duty. In such an experience we are certain that it is our self which makes the effort. But we are equally certain that the effort does not flow from that system of conative dispositions which we call our formed character; for the very function that the effort has for us is to enable us to act against the 'line of least resistance', i.e. to act in a way *contrary* to that which our formed character inclines us.

I conclude, therefore, that those who find the Libertarian doctrine of the self's causality in moral decision inherently unintelligible find it so simply because they restrict themselves, quite arbitrarily, to an inadequate standpoint: a standpoint from which, indeed, a genuinely creative activity, if it existed, never *could* be apprehended.

It will be understood, of course, that it is no part of my purpose to deny that the act of moral decision is in *one* sense 'unintelligible'. If by the 'intelligibility' of an act we mean that it is capable, at least in principle, of being inferred as a consequence of a given ground, then naturally my view is that the act in question is '*un*intelligible'. But that, presumably, is not the meaning of 'intelligibility' in the critics mind when he says that the Libertarian holds an 'unintelligible' doctrine. If it were all he meant, he would merely be pointing out that Libertarianism is not compatible with Determinism! And that tautologous pronouncement would hardly deserve the title of 'criticism'. Yet, strangely enough, not all of the critics seem to be quite clear on this matter. The Libertarian often has the experience of being challenged by the critic to tell him *why*, on his view, the agent now decides to put forth moral effort and now decides not to, with the obviously intended implication that if the Libertarian cannot say 'why' he should give up his theory. Such critics apparently fail to see that if the Libertarian *could* say why he would already have given up his theory! Obviously to demand 'intelligibility' in this sense is simply to prejudge the whole issue in favour of Determinism. The sense in which the critic is entitled to demand intelligibility of our doctrine is simply this; he may demand that the kind of action which our doctrine imputes to human selves should not be, for ultimate analysis, meaningless. And in that sense, as I have already argued, our doctrine is perfectly intelligible.

Let us suppose, then, that the Determinist, confronted by the plain evidence of our practical self-consciousness, now recognizes his obligation to give up the position that the Libertarian doctrine is without qualification 'meaningless', and concedes that from that standpoint of our practical self-consciousness at any rate it is 'meaningful'. And let us ask what will be his next move. So far as I can see, his most likely move now will be to attack the value of that 'internal' standpoint, contrasting it unfavourably, in respect of its claim to truth, with the rational, objective, standpoint of 'pure philosophy'. 'I admit', he may tell us, 'that there is begotten in the self, in the practical experience you refer to, a belief in a self-causality which is yet not a causality exercised through the self's character. But surely this must weigh but lightly in the balance against the proposition, which appeals to our reason with axiomatic certainty, that an act cannot be caused by a self if it has no ground in the determinate nature of that self. If the choice lies between either disbelieving that rational proposition, or in dismissing the evidence of practical self-consciousness as illusion, it is the latter alternative which in my opinion any sane philosophy is bound to adopt'.

But a very little reflection suffices to show that this position is in reality no improvement at all on that from which the critic has just fallen back. For it is evident that the proposition alleged to be axiomatic is axiomatic, at most, only to a reason which knows nothing of acts or events save as they present themselves to an external observer. It obviously is *not* axiomatic to a reason whose field of apprehension is broadened to include the data furnished by the direct experience of acting. In short, the proposition is axiomatic, at most, only to reason functioning *abstractly*; which most certainly cannot be identified with reason functioning *philosophically*.

What is required of the critic, of course, if he is to make good his case, is a reasoned justification of his cavalier attitude towards the testimony of practical self-consciousness. That is the primary desideratum. And the lack of it in the bulk of Determinist literature is in my opinion something of a scandal. Without it, the criticism we have just been examining is sheer dogmatism. It is, indeed, dogmatism of a peculiarly perverse kind. For the situation is, in effect, as follows. From our practical self-consciousness we gain a notion of a genuinely creative act — which might be defined as an act which nothing determines save the agent's doing it. Of such a character is the act of moral decision as we experience it. But the critic says 'No! This sort of thing cannot be. A person cannot without affront to reason be conceived to be author of an act which bears, *ex hypothesi* [as the case supposes], no intelligible relation to his character. A mere intuition of practical self-consciousness is the solitary prop of this fantastic notion, and surely that is quite incapable of bearing the weight that you would thrust upon it'. Now observe the perversity! The critic says, excluding the evidence of practical self-consciousness, the notion makes nonsense. In other words, excluding the only evidence there ever *could* be for such a notion, the notion makes nonsense! For, of course, if there should be such a thing as creative activity, there is absolutely no other way save an intuition of practical self-consciousness in which we could become aware of it. Only from the inside, from the standpoint of the agent's living experience, can 'activity' possibly be apprehended. So that what the critic is really doing is to condemn a notion as nonsensical on the ground that the only evidence for it is the only evidence there ever could be for it...

There is much more that I should have liked to say: much more, in my opinion, that badly requires to be said. I should have liked, perhaps above all, to have been able to give more space to an analysis of the experience we call 'effort of will', and to have attempted to expose the fallacies which seem to me to underlie all attempts to explain away that experience by resolving it into something other than itself. That, however, is a matter with which I have partially dealt on a previous occasion, and to which I propose to return under conditions more appropriate to the full-length treatment which can alone be of much service on a difficult psychological theme of this kind. Meantime I can only hope that the little I have been able to say may do something towards regaining for free will in the 'vulgar' sense a place in serious philosophical discussion: that it may do something — to use language of an appropriate vulgarity — towards putting Libertarianism 'on the map' once more. It is not, in my opinion, 'on the map' at all at present. It cannot be, when critics are so often content to make slogans and shibboleths do the work of analysis and argument; when a few satirical references to the 'mysterious fiat' of a 'pure ego' are regarded in so many quarters as a sufficient rejoinder to the Libertarian's claims. Prejudicial phrases like these have certainly a good deal of power. They are evocative of an acutely hostile emotional atmosphere. But, unless accompanied by the most careful analysis, they seem to me to stand for bad habits rather than for good reasons. And it would be no disservice to philosophy if they were extruded from the literature of the free will problem altogether.

Thirteen

John Macmurray

1891–1976

John Macmurray was born at Maxwellton in the Scottish borders in 1891. He moved (with his family) to Aberdeen at around the age of ten and attended Aberdeen Grammar School and Robert Gordon's College before proceeding to Glasgow University, from which he graduated both M.A and LLB. After completing his Honours Classics work at Glasgow in September 1913, he follow in the long tradition of Snell Exhibitioners, exceptional Glasgow graduates awarded scholarships to Balliol College, Oxford. There he studied history and philosophy, but his tutor, the philosopher A.D. Lindsay, helped strengthen his interest in philosophy by bringing him to see it as a preparation for life and service.

During the First World War Macmurray served with the British army in France, and was awarded a Military Cross in 1918. Early in 1917 he wrote his first known published piece of writing – 'Trench Religion' – a short reflection on a soldier's image of God in the midst of the carnage at the front. In 1919 this appeared in a book entitled *The Army and Religion*, and the same year he returned to Balliol where his academic career properly began with his appointment to the John Locke Scholarship, graduating M.A. with distinction in *litterae humaniores*.

His first academic post was a lectureship in philosophy at Manchester University, but before long he accepted an invitation to become Professor of Philosophy at Witwatersrand University in Johannesburg. His time in South Africa lasted only eighteen months before he returned to Oxford and to Balliol as Jowett Lecturer and Classical Tutor, a position he held from 1922 to 1928. In 1928 he moved again, this time to become Grote Professor of Mind and Logic at University College London. There he remained until 1944 when he finally returned to Scotland as Professor of Moral Philosophy at the University of Edinburgh in succession to A E Taylor, who had also preceded him at Manchester. He retired from the Chair of Moral Philosophy at Edinburgh in 1957. Having for most of his life been a somewhat hesitant Christian, in retirement he became a member of the Society of Friends. He died in 1976.

Macmurray's most substantial philosophical work arose from the Gifford Lectures he gave at the University of Glasgow in 1953–4. These were subsequently published in two volumes — *The Self as Agent* (1957) and *Persons in Relation* (1961). In the introduction (reprinted here) he identifies a crisis in philosophy — 'The tradition is broken, and cannot be re-established' — but he rejects both the leading philosophies of his day, existentialism and logical empiricism. He thus remained largely an outsider in world of professional British philosophy, and this includes philosophy in the Scottish universities. But elements of the kind of philosophy he learnt at Glasgow persisted throughout his career, first the belief that philosophy should address itself to a wider cultural context than simply that of professional colleagues, and secondly the conviction that philosophy must 'start from common experience at its most universal'. At a minimum, then, his conception of philosophy can be said to have a strong affinity with the Scottish intellectual tradition.

Biographical information: Jack Costello, 'The Life and Thought of John Macmurray', in *John Macmurray: Critical Perspectives*, ed. David Fergusson and Nigel Dower.

READING XIX

The Crisis of the Personal[1]

The Form of the Personal' was the subject which I chose for the two series of Gifford Lectures which were delivered in the University of Glasgow in the Spring of 1953 and of 1954. For this choice I had two main reasons; the first, that it is, in my judgment, the emergent problem for contemporary philosophy; the second, that it directs attention to that aspect of our common experience from which religion springs, and is in this respect appropriate to the purpose of the Gifford foundation. For it is characteristic of religion that it behaves towards its object in ways that are suitable to personal intercourse; and the conception of a deity is the conception of a personal ground of all that we experience. If then human reason, unaided by revelation, can contribute anything to theology, it is through a philosophical analysis of the personal that we should expect this to be brought to light.

I must treat this theme as a philosopher, for that is my only competence. But here I am embarrassed by the widespread doubt whether a natural theology is at all possible; whether indeed such a branch of knowledge properly exists. If it can be made possible, then it must be a part of philosophy; yet among philosophers today the most prevalent view would seem to be that there can be no natural theology, but at most a philosophy of religion. If we disregard philosophies which are grounded in a dogmatic theology on the one hand or in a dogmatic atheism on the other, it would be fair to say that for the most part the debate

---

[1]   Extracted from *The Self as Agent*, London: Faber and Faber Ltd., 1957, pp. 17–38

about the status of theological belief turns upon the validity or illusoriness of specifically religious experience. But this would appear to rule out, by implication, the possibility of any natural theology. For by this term is meant, as I understand it, a theology which is based upon our common human experience of the world, and which requires no help from special experiences of a peculiarly religious kind. It must be discoverable by reason alone, without the need to have recourse to faith.

This philosophical tendency to discount the possibility of a natural theology is confirmed by the most vigorous and challenging of contemporary developments in theology itself. The Theology of Crisis has stressed the complete otherness of God to a point where the notion that reason could even suggest the divine becomes evidently irrational, and the idea of a natural theology itself unnatural. So, in our time, philosophers and theologians tend to unite, it would seem, in agreement that religion must rest upon its own evidence, and that any knowledge we may have of the divine must be revealed to us in 'religious' experiences whose validity is evidenced by an inner conviction of their authenticity in those to whom they are granted.

When both philosophy and theology tend in this matter to recognize an impassable gulf between faith and reason, it would seem that the philosopher, who must stand by reason, should conclude to atheism. He cannot admit, as premises of his argument, any special experiences, religious or other, whose validity is at all questionable. He must start from common experience at its most universal and its most ordinary; and his procedure must be by rational analysis and rational inference. At no point can he admit as evidence any experience which is radically heterogeneous with this commonplace starting-point, and which could point to no evidence in common experience to bear witness for it. Such a disparity between normal and religious experience would convict of unreality the abnormality of the latter. If there is no point at which faith and reason can meet, then it is unreasonable to accept the deliverances of faith, and atheism is the reasonable conclusion.

It is undeniable that the historic development of modern philosophy has moved in this direction. In its beginnings it is unquestionably theist, and confident of its capacity to demonstrate the existence of God. Even Hobbes and Machiavelli profess a religious belief which we should consider hardly compatible with their modes of thought. This early confidence has gradually faded; and in the end has been replaced by the conviction that any attempt to sustain religion by philosophical reasoning is to be suspected of special pleading. The long argument which Descartes initiated has moved decisively in the direction of atheism.

It may be said that this is only history, and that it merely reflects the progressive decline of the authority of religion in our civilization during the modern period. There is truth in this. Yet the history of our philosophy is our social history at its most serious, its most reflective and its most logical. May not the failure of reason to sustain the argument for religion be in turn part of the explanation of the decline of faith? I do not wish to argue these issues now. I shall content myself, at this stage, with expressing my belief that the more closely modern philosophy keeps to its programme, and the more purely objective its procedure becomes, the more inevitable is the atheism of its conclusion. Within the limits of its assumptions no other result is permissible.

Yet I cannot accept the conclusion, in spite of its logical necessity; and that I am not alone in this seems to be shown by the reluctance of so many competent philosophers explicitly to draw it. When I forget the course of the argument, I find the conclusion unreasonable, and indeed *prima facie* incredible. I do not mean that atheism is *prima facie* irrational. But the view that there is no path from common experience to a belief in God; that religion rests upon some special extraordinary type of experience apart from which it could not arise — this seems to me hardly credible. For if it were true we should expect to find (should we not?) that religion developed late in the history of culture, and sporadically, under the influence of unusual conditions of life. Interest in religion, one would imagine, would be confined to special types of men, with abnormal and possibly somewhat deranged sensibilities; and we should expect also to find no connexion between religion and more usual forms of reflective activity. Yet the opposite of all this is the case. Religion is the original, and the one universal expression of our human capacity to reflect; as primitive and as general as speech. It is atheists and agnostics who have been exceptional and abnormal. They have indeed constituted a very small minority at all times, although their numbers have tended to increase in epochs of social dissolution. So far, too, from being heterogeneous with other aspects of culture, and resting upon abnormal experience which contrasts with our common awareness of the world, religion is the source from which the various aspects of human culture have been derived; and the belief in a radical disparity between philosophy and theology is an exceptional and recent phenomenon.

These considerations do nothing, of course, to prove the validity of religious belief; but they do make it unlikely that our common, primary experience provides no evidence tending to support it. If then modern philosophy fails to find any, may it not be because it works within limits which exclude the evidence from its consideration; or that it rests upon assumptions, so familiar perhaps that they have lapsed from consciousness, which require scrutiny and modification? This is the view, at least, to which my own reflection has led me, and which determines the method which I shall pursue in the discussion of my theme. Quite apart from all specifically theological questions, I believe that the emergent problem of contemporary philosophy necessitates a revision of traditional assumptions; and that when this revision has been made the direction of the argument will be so altered that it will tend thereafter to a theistic conclusion.

Since I am of this mind, I propose to put aside any discussion of religion until it arises in the natural development of the argument, and to proceed, in a purely philosophical manner, upon an inquiry which arises, within the normal field of modern philosophy, from the analysis and interpretation of common human experience. I shall invite attention to what I take to be the emergent problem of contemporary philosophy, and initiate the criticism of current assumptions which it requires. If this leads, as I believe it does, to modifications of outlook which require a theistic conclusion I shall have fulfilled the intentions of the founder of the Gifford lectureship, though indirectly, yet in the best way that is open to me.

I have referred to the form of the personal as the emergent problem of contemporary philosophy, and this requires both to be explained and to be justified. For it is far from being the case that this is the problem with which philosophy is particularly concerning itself at present. What is meant is rather that the historical situation in which we find ourselves presents us with a philosophical problem for solution, and that this problem concerns the form of the personal. The decisive questions of serious philosophy are never determined at random. They have their origins in a historical necessity, not in the chance interests of a particular thinker. Philosophy aims at a complete rationality. But the rationality of our conclusions does not depend alone upon the correctness of our thinking. It depends even more upon the propriety of the questions with which we concern ourselves. The primary and the critical task is the discovery of the problem. If we ask the wrong question the logical correctness of our answer is of little consequence.

There is of necessity an interplay, in all human activities, between theory and practice. It is characteristic of Man that he solves his practical problems by taking thought; and all his theoretical activities have their origins, at least, in his practical requirements. That they also find their meaning and their significance in the practical field will command less general assent; yet it is, in my belief, the truth of the matter, and one of the major theses to be maintained here. Activities of ours which are purely theoretical, if this means that they have no reference to our practical life, must be purely imaginary — exercises of fantasy which are not even illusory unless we relate them to the practical world by a misplaced belief. The truth or falsity of the theoretical is to be found solely in its reference to the practical.

This may be what is intended by the assertion current in some philosophical circles that the meaning of a proposition is the method of its verification. If so, I can have no quarrel with this doctrine. I should like to be sure, however, that it is recognised that the method of verification with which the physical sciences have made us familiar is not the only way in which the theoretical can refer to the practical. There are other modes of verification; indeed, if there were not, the scientific mode would itself be invalid and indeed impossible. But this is not the moment to enter into these issues in detail. We must limit ourselves to what seems reasonable at a first inspection. For every inquiry must start from what is the case *prima facie*. We know how large a part of our thinking is concerned with the solution of practical issues. In such cases it is obvious to everyone that the reference is to practical behaviour, and that conclusions which have no bearing upon the solution of our practical problems are without significance. The theoretical question is posed by the practical situation; for that very reason the significance and the verification of the theoretical conclusion lie in the practical field. Indeed the theoretical result, if it is meaningful at all, is the solution of a *practical* problem. If then, as seems indubitable, all theoretical problems have their ultimate, if not their immediate, origin in our practical experience it seems reasonable to expect that all must find their ultimate meaning in a reference to the practical. It may indeed turn out otherwise. There may be generated, by the investigation of practical experience, a set of theoretical activities which have their meaning in themselves and require no practical reference to sustain or to validate them. But it would be a methodological error to assume this from the start.

This does not mean, however, that the reference of theoretical to practical activities is always direct or obvious. Nor does it mean that in our reflection we can or should always be aware of the practical reference. It does not justify a pragmatic theory of truth nor suggest that we should not seek knowledge for its own sake. The disinterested pursuit of the truth may be, and, I am convinced, is a fact, a condition of the practical efficacy of reflection. The inner life of the spirit is not merely technological: it is not condemned to a servitude to practical ends which are set for it without its knowledge or consent. The essential reference of theoretical to practical activities does not involve the control of theory by practice. It consists even more significantly in the control of practice by theory; in the determination, through reflection, of the ends of action. All that is contended for is this, that there is a necessary relation between our theory and our practice; that the activities of reflection can never be totally unrelated to practical life; that it is always legitimate to ask, of any theory which claims to be true, what practical difference it would make if we believed it. It may often be difficult to answer this question; but if the correct answer were that it would make no difference at all, then the theory would be a mere exercise of fantasy, neither true nor false, but meaningless.

I have laboured a truism because I am thinking primarily of philosophy. For here, if anywhere, it might seem to be true that we are involved in a theoretical activity which has no practical reference. This I am concerned to deny. In philosophy, indeed, the reference to practice is indirect and remote throughout much of its range. Here too it is especially important that the question of the ultimate reference to practice should not obsess the thinker, or control the processes of his reflection. But it is also in philosophy that the ultimate reference of theory to practice is most decisive and far-reaching. It is not for nothing that some have held that a philosophy is a way of life; or that common tradition conceives the philosopher as a man of a balanced temper, who meets fortune or disaster with equanimity. Our western philosophy began with the breakdown of a way of life in ancient Greece, which posed the question 'What should we do?' If it has found itself driven to dwell almost exclusively with the sister question 'How can we know?' it remains true that this question is incomplete in itself; and that the complete question, in the end, is 'How can we know what we should do?'

Now action is inherently particular; and therefore questions of the form 'What shall I do?' have a historic reference. They cannot be answered without regard to the circumstances in which we have to act. Since philosophy, like all modes of reflection, involves, however indirectly, a practical reference, it is not exempt from the changes of circumstance. However eternal may be the problems to which it seeks a solution, philosophy has a history, and this is essential, not accidental to it. This reference to history has a double aspect. There is a historical process within philosophy which preserves a continuity of development from one age to its successor, and which calls for historical study and understanding. But also philosophy is itself one element in the social process, and is linked in numerous and essential ways to the other aspects of historical development. One can never fully understand, and may easily misunderstand a past philosophy, if one does not also understand in some measure the practical history of the era of its origin.

Instead of saying that a philosophy is a way of life, it would be better to say that any way of life implies a philosophy. For if it is a way of life at all it must be a relatively satisfactory adjustment to Reality, exhibiting a systematic structure, and, to a considerable degree, a consistency of direction. Any effort to give reflective expression to such a way of life must formulate a system of beliefs about the nature of the world and a system of priorities in valuation. The expression of a social tradition provides, therefore, if not a philosophy, at least the raw material for one. To achieve such a formulation would in itself provide a task of immense magnitude and difficulty if it had to begin from scratch, as it were. But the individual philosopher finds the tradition which he shares already formulated, if not analytically systematized. And since the formulation is never fully satisfactory, reflection will find, and will tend to concentrate attention upon the inconsistencies and incoherences which are involved and which reflect, in their fashion, the strains and stresses arising from a practical inadequacy. The philosophical effort to achieve consistency implies then, even if it does not intend, a modification of the way of life itself which would eliminate what is practically unsatisfactory in its working. We see here the practical ground of the two conditions that any valid philosophy must satisfy — a theoretical consistency and a comprehensive adequacy. The need for consistency is obvious. The demand for adequacy arises from this, that the effort to overcome any practical maladjustment in a way of life may, by its success, generate even more serious difficulties in other departments.

That there is such an interrelation, indirect enough and largely uncon- scious, between philosophical theory and social processes of a more empirical kind, is evident from any study of the history of philosophy which looks for it. The philosophy of any historical period reflects the life of the period even more evidently that does its art. One aspect of this to which I would draw attention is particularly obvious. The breakdown of a social tradition involves a break in the continuity of philosophical development, and the more revolutionary is the social crisis, the more thorough is the break in the philosophical tradition. One might instance the change in ancient philosophy which marks the fall of the city-state and the rise of the empires; or in modern philosophy in the transition from the mediaeval world. In such revolutionary periods philosophy responds to the practical transformation of the way of life by a radical transformation of its central problem. A new starting-point is discov- ered and a new era of reflection begins. So long as a way of life remains viable, the philosopher works within a framework of thought which in its general structure and in its general concepts remains stable. His prob- lems are problems of relative detail, and he finds them set for him by dif- ficulties in the theoretical field itself. Their relation to the practical problems of his society is indirect and need not be noticed. But with a break in tradition this is no longer the case. His criticism no longer touches this or that inconsistency or inadequacy in a continuing tradi- tion, but the basis of tradition itself. He must find a new starting-point; and his success depends on the discovery of the emergent problem for philosophy in his own time.

Perhaps I have said enough to suggest a *prima facie* case for the view that there is a necessary relation between philosophy and social practice. My immediate purpose falls short of this. It is to explain what is meant by saying that the form of the personal is the emergent problem for con- temporary philosophy. That we are living through a period of revolu- tionary change is already a commonplace. We are all aware of this, though we may differ in our estimate of the depth and the extent of the transformation that has already occurred or that is inevitable as we go forward. To me it seems certain that the scale of change must dwarf the transformation of medieval into modern Europe. For that historic revo- lution fell within the development of Western Christendom, and rested upon a deeper continuity of Graeco-Roman tradition; while ours arises from the incompatibility of age-old ways of life in a world already largely forced into unity at the economic and technological levels. The European tradition, not to speak of its national variations, is now only one factor in a conflict of traditions which must achieve a practical com- patibility if civilization is to maintain itself.

But these are large speculations upon which we shall not enter. We need only recognize the break with traditions which is apparent in all fields in our own society — in religion and morals, in politics and economics, and in the arts. In such circumstances we should expect to find a break in the continuity of philosophical development, a radical criticism of traditional philosophy and a search for new ways and new beginnings. And this we do find. We need only think of such developments as phenomenology, logical empiricism or existentialism to realize that new modes of philosophy are being created and spreading rapidly, which stand in strong contrast with the main stream of traditional thought. The first of these is confessedly an effort to start afresh where Descartes started, but employing a catharsis of the mind to remove prejudice and achieve an innocence of immediate vision for whatever can be an object for thought. Logical empiricism, armed with a high-powered analytic technology, is concerned to make an end of all metaphysics, and to include under metaphysics most of what has traditionally been considered the substance of philosophical doctrine. Its main interest in the past is to show how it was constantly led, not into error, but into meaningless debate by failure to perform the only proper task of philosophy, the logical analysis of language. Existentialism, on the other hand, has so altered the focus of attention, and so largely turned its back upon the established methods of procedure that many have doubted its claim to be a philosophical discipline at all.

These two contemporary forms of philosophy, logical empiricism and existentialism, represent, it would seem, opposite reactions to the breakdown of the tradition. They are united in the extremity of their difference, not merely by their negative attitude to the philosophical past, but if I mistake not, by a common conviction from which both arise. I may express this roughly by saying that both rest upon the decision that the traditional method of philosophy is incapable of solving its traditional problems. But whereas the logical empiricists discard the problems in order to maintain the method, the existentialists relinquish the method in wrestling with the problems. So the latter achieve a minimum of form; the former a minimum of substance. The logical empiricists are content to elaborate the subtleties of formal analysis — and often with the beauty of genius; so far as the substantial problems go, they use their formalism to erect notices on every path which say 'No road this way!'. For all the roads that do not lead to the impassable bogs of metaphysics belong to the special sciences. The existentialists, determined to grapple with the real problems — and their sensitivities to the darkness of human despair lead them to discover the emergent problem of our time — find no formal analysis that is adequate to the task. They are constrained to quit the beaten track; to wallow in metaphor and suggestion; to look to the drama and the novel to provide an expression, albeit an aesthetic expression, for their discoveries.

Where is the way forward? Do we go along with one of these contemporary schools of thought? Or should we count them as aberrations engendered by the stress and sickness of our age, and hold to the beaten

paths of traditional thought? My own answer to this decisive question is
as follows. We *cannot* keep to the old ways. The tradition is broken, and
cannot be re-established. It is true, as the new movements imply, that the
traditional methods cannot answer the traditional questions. Form and
matter, in philosophy, have parted company. Then what of the new
modes? Phenomenological analysis is a useful device. We can be grateful for it, and use it when we find it helpful. But if it is taken as more than
this; if it means that we go back to Descartes and the modern starting-point and do properly what we have so far done poorly, we must
answer that there is no going back. History does not repeat itself. Yet
when I turn to choose between the other two schools, I find I can accept
neither. To the logical empiricists I find I must say this: 'Philosophy, like
any branch of serious reflective inquiry, is created and defined by its
problems; and its problems are not accidental, but necessary; grounded
in the nature of human experience. If I find that my method of attempting to answer them is unsuccessful, if it fails even to discover a meaning
in them, then I must conclude that there is something wrong with the
method, and seek a better one. To discard the problems in order to retain
the method; to seek for problems which the method *could* solve, would
be neither serious nor reasonable'. To the existentialists I should say this:
'Philosophy, as you would agree, is an intellectual discipline. It is therefore necessarily formal and must work through concepts which seek for
clarity and exact definition both in themselves and in their systematic
interrelation. It is right to hold firmly to the substantial problems, however metaphysical and elusive, which form the centre of gravity of the
philosophic enterprise. It is an important contribution to the progress of
the enterprise to trace them to their origins in the strains and stresses of
the personal life. But if this results in the dissolution of the formal struc-
tures of traditional philosophy, what is required is the search for a new
form which shall be not less but more logical and intellectual than the
inadequate forms that have to be discarded'. We may sum up this estimate of these two emergent philosophical tendencies in a sentence, even
though, like all such judgments, it must need qualification in detail.
Existentialism has discovered, with sensitiveness of feeling, that the
philosophical problem of the present lies in a crisis of the personal: logical empiricism recognises it as a crisis of logical form and method. Both
are correct, and both are one-sided. The cultural crisis of the present is
indeed a crisis of the personal. But the problem it presents to philosophy
is a formal one. It is to discover or to construct the intellectual form of the
personal.

I need hardly labour to convince you that the cultural crisis of our time
is a crisis of the personal. This is too general a conclusion of those who
look deeper into the troubles of our society than the superficial level of
organizational strain, whether economic or political. I need only refer to
two aspects of the situation, both very familiar, in order to make clear
what I mean by a crisis of the personal. One of these is the tendency

towards an apotheosis of the state; the other the decline of religion. The two are intimately connected; since both express a growing tendency to look for salvation to political rather than to religious authority. The increasing appeal to authority itself reflects a growing inability or unwillingness to assume personal responsibility. The apotheosis of political authority involves the subordination of the personal aspect of human life to its functional aspect. The major social revolutions of our time all wear this livery, whether they are fascist or communist in type. The justification offered by the democracies for resistance to the death against both is the same, that they rest upon a philosophy which sacrifices the personal values, and so the personal freedom of men to the exigencies of political and economic expediency. At this level, the crisis of the personal is the crisis of liberalism, which was an effort, however ambiguous, to subordinate the functional organization of society to the personal life of its members. Yet nothing could be more revealing of the depth of the crisis we are facing than one fact. Communism rests upon a criticism of liberal democracy. Liberalism, it maintains, contradicts itself. While it stands, in theory, for human freedom, in practice it is a defence of human exploitation. Communism set out to resolve this contradiction by abolishing exploitation and realizing freedom in social practice. The declared intention was to achieve a form of society in which the government of men would give place to the administration of things. Yet its own practice, we see, defeats its intention, and leads to an apotheosis of the State and to an organised and efficient exploitation of its citizens. In communist practice the personal is subordinated to the functional to a point at which the defence of the personal becomes itself a criminal activity.

The decline of religious influence and of religious practice in our civilization bears the same significance. Such a decline betrays, and in turn intensifies, a growing insensitiveness to the personal aspects of life, and a growing indifference to personal values. Christianity, in particular, is the exponent and the guardian of the personal, and the function of organised Christianity in our history has been to foster and maintain the personal life and to bear continuous witness, in symbol and doctrine, to the ultimacy of personal values. If the influence is removed or ceases to be effective, the awareness of personal issues will tend to be lost, in the pressure of functional preoccupations, by all except those who are by nature specially sensitive to them. The sense of personal dignity as well as of personal unworthiness will atrophy, with the decline in habits of self-examination. Ideals of sanctity or holiness will begin to seem incomprehensible or even comical. Success will tend to become the criterion of rightness, and there will spread through society a temper which is extraverted, pragmatic and merely objective, for which all problems are soluble by better organization. In such conditions the religious impulses of men will attach themselves to the persons who wield political power, and will invest them with a personal authority over the life of the community and of its members. The state is then compelled to perform the functions of a church (for which by its nature it is radically unfitted) and its efforts to do so will produce, the more rapidly the more whole-hearted they are, a crisis of the personal. If we remember that history has brought us to a point where we must think of human society as a whole, and not limit our outlook to the confines of our own nation, there must be few who will fail to recognise, whether they welcome it or recoil from it, that we are involved in such a crisis.

It may be asked, however, whether this has any relevance for philosophy. To answer this doubt requires a reference to the broad outline of the history of modern philosophy. For brevity's sake, and because my purpose is to explain and clarify my own choice of subject, I may perhaps be permitted to speak somewhat dogmatically. Modern philosophy is characteristically *egocentric*. I mean no more than this: that firstly, it takes the Self as its staring-point, and not God, or the world or the community; and that, secondly, the Self is an individual in isolation, an ego or 'I', never a 'thou'. This is shown by the fact that there can arise the question, 'How does the Self know that other selves exist?' Further, the Self so premised is a thinker in search of knowledge. It is conceived as the Subject; the correlate in experience of the object presented for cognition. Philosophy then, as distinct from Science, is concerned with the formal characters of the processes, activities or constructions in and through which the object is theoretically determined. And since the Self is an element, in some sense, of the world presented for knowing, it must be determined through the same forms as every other object.

Now the outstanding feature of the modern development of knowledge as been the creation of the positive sciences, and this has meant that there has been a determining relation between philosophy and science throughout. The relation has not been one-sided, but reciprocal. It has been the task of philosophy to create the conceptual forms and systems of categories which provide the logical structure, and so determine the general attitude of mind favourable to the production and to the reception of scientific knowledge. This was not, on the whole, intentional, except where the philosophical work was carried out by scientists in pursuit of their own objectives; and many philosophers have also been scientists. For the most part the philosophers were concerned to determine general forms of knowledge with a metaphysical or quasi-metaphysical purpose in mind. In particular, they were concerned to determine the formal structure of the Self and its experience, both individual and social, both theoretical and practical, in their character as objects for philosophical knowledge.

The result of this interrelation of science and philosophy is that modern philosophy has completed two distinct phases, which correspond respectively to the creation of the physical and of the biological sciences. The first is usually reckoned as running from Descartes to Hume; the second from Kant to the present day. It would be more accurate to see the beginning of the second phase in Rousseau, and its continuation in the German idealist movement from Lessing to Hegel, with Kant standing ambiguously between the stretching out a hand to both. The key-concept of the first phase is 'substance'; its form and method are mathematical. Substance, then, is that which is determined by thought as a mathematical system. Pure mathematics provides the ideal form of all valid knowledge, and whatever cannot be determined in this form is unknowable. Since such indeterminables must in some sense be presented to the self, they must be referred not to the object, but to the subject, and must find their origin in a creative spontaneity of the mind. The process of thought distinguishes between what is objective and what is subjective in experience. The objective is valid: the subjective unreal, illusory or imaginary.

The crux of the matter comes, for philosophy, in the attempt to determine, in this form, the Self and its activities, and centrally, its activities as thinker. The mathematical form proves adequate for the scientific determination of the material world. But the attempt to conceive the self as substance and to determine it through the mathematical form meets difficulties which prove insuperable, and lead to scepticism. For it becomes clear that the activities of the self in providing the form through which the object is determined themselves involve a constructive spontaneity of the mind — an *a priori* synthesis — for which no objective basis can be assigned; and the substantial self appears to be itself the product of such a subjective construction.

This first phase of modern philosophy arises through a primary attention to the form through which the material world — the world of substantial objects — can be rationally determined. Its problem was the form of the material. It broke down in its effort to universalise this form to cover the whole field of knowledge, and, in particular, in the attempt to conceive the Self on the analogy of the material world. The inadequacy of this analogy lies in the element of spontaneous construction, of self-determining and self-directed development which is present in the activity of the Self, but which is excluded from the conception of the material. The second phase, seeking a more adequate form, turned its attention from the material to the living. For it is in the phenomena of life, and particularly in the processes of growth, that this spontaneity of inner self-determination and directed development seems, at least, to be characteristically manifest. Its key-concept is not substance, but organism, and its problem is the form of the organic. In contrast to the mathematical form, which is a combination of identical units, the organism is conceived as a harmonious balancing of differences, and in its pure form, a tension of opposites; and since the time factor — as growth, development or becoming — is of the essence of life, the full form of the organic is represented as a dynamic equilibrium of functions maintained through a progressive differentiation of elements within the whole.

This proved to provide an adequate conceptual form for the development of the biological sciences. It is indeed the formal expression of the notion of organic evolution. But as a philosophical conception it is necessarily universal, and is thought as the form of the whole Real. In particular it must be the form of thought, and serve for the conception of the Self and its activities. The Self is no longer a substance, but an organism, and since the Self is still essentially the subject of experience the process of knowledge must appear as a self-determining development in which an original undifferentiated unity differentiates itself progressively while maintaining a functional coherence of its elements. The logical form of thought is no longer mathematical but dialectical; not analytic but synthetic; a progressive synthesis of opposites.

It may be objected that this applies only to the development of Hegelian idealism, and can hardly be said to characterise the philosophy of the last century. There is some truth in this; but it does not touch the major issue, which is not tied to an acceptance, as it stands, of the Hegelian dialectic. It is the dominance of the biological analogy in philosophy which is decisive, and this clearly will cover all organic and evolutionary types of philosophy down to those of Alexander and Whitehead, not to speak of dialectical materialism. But more than this is required to answer the doubt, and I shall offer one or two further suggestions.

The first of these is that the rise of biology did not mean the suppression of physics; correspondingly, the rise of the organic philosophies did not mean the disappearance of the mathematical. The new type of thought developed from the beginning in tension with and under criticism from the older type; but, the older type in its persistence was under the necessity of considering and dealing with the aspects of experience upon which the newer philosophy was concentrating attention, under penalty of ceasing to be contemporary. The second suggestion concerns the development of biology itself. The chemists began to apply the methods of physical science, with their associated system of concepts, in the organic field, and were increasingly successful. The evolutionary hypothesis, though useful and indeed essential up to a point, began to appear as a framework within which the biochemists could build a true *science* of the organic; or even as a scaffolding which would ultimately be dispensed with. In the debate between vitalists and biochemists which followed, it was the biochemists who were victorious. Their success was made possible by, and in turn stimulated, a development of mathematical theory which in the long run amounted to a transformation. The new instruments of mathematical analysis proved capable of representing and elucidating functional and developmental processes and relations.

The corresponding process in philosophy may be briefly summarized. Realism developed as an internal criticism of the organic philosophy, with an empirical temper. The criticism has a double edge. It denies the adequacy of the organic form and its dialectical logic in the philosophical field, as formal analysis of the Self as thinker. This is the realist criticism of the idealist theory of knowledge. It denies also its necessity and its usefulness as an instrument for the empirical analysis of organic process. Until the contemporary break with tradition was established, philosophical realism remained conditioned by and tied to the organic concept, as an antithesis is tied to its thesis. The two aspects of the philosophy are complementary as well as antithetical. If this is concealed from a superficial view it is because of a realist concentration on the positive task of showing that a transformed formal logic based upon the transformation of mathematical theory can provide an instrument of analysis adequate for all scientific purposes. But there is no victory for either party and no synthesis. The development is rather a commentary on the Kantian conclusion that though the teleological idea may have an indispensable heuristic function, all scientific inquiry is necessarily mathematical. But success in this formal task is not self-interpreting. Whitehead and Russell collaborated in *Principia Mathematica*; but while the latter interprets their joint achievement as a refutation of the organic idea, the former interprets it as leading to a realistic philosophy of organism. However firmly realists may reject Hegelianism and its offshoots, and go back behind Kant to link up with the earlier mathematical period, the result is not to reinstate the concept of substance on its throne.

What brings the period to an end is not then the refutation of idealism by the realists, but a relapse into scepticism and the re-emergence of a new problem. As happens so often in the history of thought, anticipations of this process are to be found. The Danish eccentric, Kierkegaard, discovered that the Hegelian philosophy was ludicrously incapable of solving — even, indeed, of formulating — the problem of 'the existing individual'. If we apply the Hegelian logic to the data of personal reality, we produce, he showed, 'a dialectic without a synthesis'; for the process of the personal life generates a tension of opposites which can be resolved, not by reconciliation but only by a choice between them, and for this choice no rational ground can be discovered. He concluded that we must abandon philosophy for religion, reason for faith. His older contemporary, Auguste Comte, had more in common with him than would at first appear. Both are profoundly under the influence of the organic philosophy; and both are concerned to apply it to the understanding of personal reality. But whereas Kierkegaard emphasises its individual aspect, Comte is interested in human society. In this, like Karl Marx, he remains closer to Hegel, and to the general philosophical tradition, so that his criticism lacks the depth and the absoluteness of Kierkegaard's. It does not touch the form, but only the content of the organic philosophy. So Comte abandoned metaphysics, that is to say, philosophy as a speculative knowledge of human reality, in favour of science, and therefore of empirical sociology. In the result, he became the founder at once of modern sociology and of modern positivism. Had he been more aware of his own debt to the organic philosophy which he rejected, he would have realised that the *form* of his science of society was of philosophical origin, and his relation to contemporary logical positivism would have been more obvious. He would stand to that aspect of contemporary philosophy as Kierkegaard does to contemporary existentialism; and the relation, in both cases, is highly ambiguous. Kierkegaard would never have admitted that 'existential thinking' could be philosophical; for him it was a form of art. 'I am a poet', he maintained, 'that is my category'.

There is no reason to suppose that this phase of scepticism is any more final than others that philosophy has overcome in the past. For Comte, as for Kierkegaard, we must remember, philosophy is identified with a particular *type* of philosophy; that type which constructs itself on the form of the organic. If they discover that philosophy is incapable of formulating , either in its individual or its social aspect, the nature of personal experience, this need not mean that philosophy is invalid, but only that an organic conception of the personal is inadequate to the facts. Since philosophy must include the personal in its field of inquiry, this can only mean that we must abandon the organic form as inadequate for the philosophical purpose, and initiate a search for the form of the personal.

If we are correct in suggesting that there is, in the modern period, a close relation between the development of science and of philosophy, this is the conclusion which we shall naturally expect. If science moves from an established physics to the foundation of scientific biology, we find that philosophy moves from a mathematical to an organic form. We should expect, then, that the emergence of a scientific psychology would be paralleled by a transition from an organic to a personal philosophy. The form of the personal will be the emergent problem. Such a new phase of philosophy would rest on the assertion that the Self is neither a substance nor an organism, but a person. Its immediate task would be to discover the logical form through which the unity of the personal can be coherently conceived.

The transition from an organic to a personal conception of unity, however, cannot be so simple as that from a physical to an organic conception. The transformation involved is much more fundamental. The difficulties are of the same type as those which beset the effort to establish psychology on a sure scientific basis. There are two major difficulties. Firstly, so long as psychology is conceived as a science of mind, consciousness or the subjective, it fails. To establish itself it must think of itself as a science of human *behaviour*. Similarly in the philosophical transition, we can no longer conceive the Self as the subject in experience, and so as the knower. The Self must be conceived, not theoretically as subject, but practically, as agent. Secondly, human behaviour is comprehensible only in terms of a dynamic social reference; the isolated, purely individual self is a fiction. In philosophy this means, as we shall see, that the unity of the personal cannot be thought as the form of an individual self, but only through the mutuality of personal relationship. In face of both difficulties a radical modification of our philosophical tradition is demanded. The first requires us to substitute for the Self as subject, which is the starting-point of modern philosophy, the Self as agent; and to make this substitution is to reject the traditional distinction between the subjective and the objective. The second compels us to abandon traditional individualism or egocentricity of our philosophy. We must introduce the second person as the necessary correlative of the first, and do our thinking not from the standpoint of the 'I' alone, but of the 'you and I'.